Stadia

The authors, Geraint John and Rod Sheard at Arsenal Football Club, London.

Professor Geraint John Dip Arch (UCL) RIBA CISRM MILAM FRSA works with HOK + LOBB Sports, Leisure & Entertainment Architecture. He is Visiting Professor of Architecture: Sports Building Design at the University of Luton: this chair is unique in Britain, possibly in the world. He is an active member of the International Union of Architects and a Director of their Programme: Sport and Leisure. Geraint also sits on the Sports Ground Initiative Committee, and is the co-ordinator of RIBA's Client Focus Groups on Participation and Spectator Facilities. Until 1996 Geraint was the Chief Architect and Head of the Technical Unit for Sport at the Sports Council.

Geraint is the co-author of books on Sports Building Design and has written extensively for professional journals. He has spoken at numerous conferences worldwide. Environmentally Sustainable Development has always been of great interest to him and he has helped with environmental aspects of the FA's bid for the 2006 World Cup and has been advising the Environmental Commission of the International Olympic Committee. He sits on the Environmental Committee of the London bid for the 2012 Olympics.

Rod Sheard Dip Arch QUT RIBA ARAIA FRSA is Senior Vice-president and a main board member in HOK + LOBB, the world's largest architectural practice and the world's leading sports design firm.

Rod has a great enthusiasm for the future of sport, leisure and entertainment design, and has a clear vision for the next century which will herald a new breed of facilities which will be more user friendly, better serviced and more exciting than any which have been built before.

Stadia

*A Design and
Development Guide*

Third edition

Geraint John
Rod Sheard

Architectural Press

OXFORD AMSTERDAM BOSTON LONDON NEW YORK PARIS
SAN DIEGO SAN FRANCISCO SINGAPORE SYDNEY TOKYO

Architectural Press
An imprint of Elsevier Science
Linacre House, Jordan Hill, Oxford OX2 8DP
200 Wheeler Road, Burlington MA 01803

First published 1994
Second edition 1997
Reprinted 1998
Third edition 2000
Reprinted 2001, 2003

British Library Cataloguing in Publication Data
John Geraint
    Stadia: a design and development guide. – 3rd ed.
    1.   Stadiums – Design and construction
    I.   Title   II. Sheard, Rod
    725.8′27

ISBN 0 7506 4534 2

Library of Congress Cataloguing in Publication Data
John, Geraint.
    Stadia: a design and development guide/Geraint John, Rod Sheard.
      p. cm.
    Includes bibliographical references and index.
    ISBN 0 7506–4534 2
    1.   Stadiums–Design and construction.   2.   Stadiums–Management.
    I.   Sheard, Rod.   II. Title

    GV413. J64
    725′.8043–dc21   99–050059

For information on all Architectural Press publications
visit our website at www.architecturalpress.com

Typeset by Keyword
Printed and bound in Great Britain by The Bath Press, Bath

Contents

Contents

Foreword by Juan Antonio Samaranch

I have been asked to write a foreword for this book, STADIA, and I shall do so with my best will and with the conviction that the subject it deals with – the construction of new stadia – is of great importance at the present time.

Several centuries ago, the outstanding buildings were of a religious nature, such as the cathedrals we can still admire today.

In the 20th century, especially over the last fifty years, the most important buildings have tended to be these new cathedrals that are the major stadia. I think of those in Munich, Tokyo, Mexico, Barcelona and many others as great works of architectural art admired by everyone. I sincerely believe that stadia and sports facilities will continue to be built at a growing rate with the intention of providing not only the best conditions for athletes, but also every comfort for spectators, without ever forgetting the necessary safety measures.

I would like to congratulate the authors of this magnificent book, Geraint John and Rod Sheard, on the work they have produced, as they have done a great service to the present and future of that great phenomenon, sport.

Juan Antonio Samaranch
Marquis of Samaranch

Foreword by Simon Inglis

The publication of this new updated and expanded Design and Development Guide is welcome. The fact that the book is now in its third edition is proof of its value.

It is now a century or so since the first modern stadia started appearing in Victorian Britain, in London, Glasgow, Liverpool and the Midlands. In 1896 the modern Olympic ovement was born in Athens. Since then the stadium has evolved into one of the great public building forms of the twentieth century, regarded, at its best, as an essential and positive element of civic life.

Indeed for many individuals, the stadium and the great performances it encompasses provide the single most important focus of community or national pride.

After a century of gradual change however, the last decade or so has seen the stadium rapidly take on a number of wider and more sophisticated roles.

The edges between sport and leisure have become increasingly blurred. New technology is no longer simply being added to the traditional sports venue (for example, in the form of scoreboards). It is now shaping the structure itself, particularly since the achievement of such breakthroughs as movable roofing and portable playing surfaces.

Social trends and tragic disasters in Europe, meanwhile, have necessitated the rapid introduction to stadia of ideas from other branches of the leisure industry. Some, already well-tried in North American venues, concern crowd management and spectator comfort. A few, such as the application of ticketing, information systems and marketing techniques, have been adapted to suit the more particular needs and wants of sports fans – fans who, unlike regular consumers, do not necessarily 'shop around' but remain steadfastly loyal to their teams and, never let it be forgotten, to their beloved stadia too.

Great stadia continue to reflect well on the towns and cities to which they belong. Increasingly they are seen as valuable tools of urban regeneration and as a focus for wider leisure or commercial developments. Where once perhaps the football or rugby ground, the baseball park or greyhound track were regarded as single entities of limited interest beyond specific social groupings, they are now seen as having the potential to attract different groups at different times for different events.

Overall, the convolution of all these trends and developments has created a new lease of life for the stadium. Even if the high costs of construction and the serious implications of failure have brought design issues into a more critical spotlight than ever before, the rewards for designers remain enormous. Few other buildings allow one to savour (or suffer) so readily and openly the public reaction to one's handiwork.

All the more reason, therefore, for understanding the complexities of the stadium as a building type. Without a deep knowledge or commitment to the form – a commitment wonderfully exhibited within these pages by Geraint John and Rod Sheard – there is always the danger of mediocrity.

Of course a stadium should function properly. As this book shows comprehensively, for this to happen a daunting number of factors need to be considered. But neither should a stadium ever be mediocre.

Geraint John and Rod Sheard are to be congratulated therefore for outlining and clarifying the complex design issues which affect stadia. For this immense task alone I have no doubt their efforts will be widely appreciated for many years to come.

Here are the foundations upon which dreams can be built, for as long as there are dreamers there will surely be stadia.

Simon Inglis

The Sir Alfred McAlpine Stadium, Huddersfield, UK, won the Royal Institute of British Architects Building of the Year Award in 1995. Architects: Lobb Partnership.

Preface

The authors have both been involved in the design of stadia, arenas and grandstands as well as other related sports developments for many years, Professor Geraint John when he was Chief Architect and Head of the Technical Unit for Sport of the Sports Council and as a member of the Football Stadia Advisory Design Council in London; he is now a Visiting Professor of Architecture: Sports Building Design, at the University of Luton; Rod Sheard in private practice as Chairman of the London architectural practice HOK + LOBB Sports Architecture who have specialized in the design of this building type since the early 1960s. During many years of involvement in the field the authors have lamented the lack of an authoritative, comprehensive and practical guide to the design of stadia. For any building type the dissemination of information and experience, both good and bad, eventually leads to a greater understanding and knowledge of the building type – ultimately benefiting society through better designs. All too often this handing on of information is inhibited by commercial judgements. No designer wants to give away the 'trade secrets' of an expertise accumulated over a number of years – particularly when it is through that expertise that further commissions and appointments are obtained.

The aim of this book is to produce that authoritative, comprehensive and practical guide to stadia design, in order to assist all designers, managers, owners, investors, users and other interested parties in understanding one of the most exciting and rewarding building types of today. Stadia can give rise to much enjoyment, enhance a particular sporting event and provide a safe and comfortable environment for a great occasion. At their best they can be elegant and inspiring and at their worst, bleak and deadly. These contrasting results can be caused by lack of funding, but probably more often by bad design, inadequate management and poor maintenance. Throughout the text we make reference to various stadia around the world. In each case there are probably many other examples which could equally have been mentioned, but we have chosen to concentrate on a limited number for simplicity.

We were delighted with the success of the first and second editions of *Stadia*. This new edition has been revised, expanded and updated in order to take account of developments that have taken place in the world of stadia design since the second edition. The additional material includes details and examples of new projects of particular interest to stadia designers.

Geraint John
Rod Sheard

Acknowledgements

The contents of this book are our combined views on the way stadia should be designed and operated based on our observations and experiences over a number of years. We owe a great debt of gratitude to many people who helped us compile the references and photographs as well as guiding our actual methods of approach. The list is too long to name everybody but we would particularly like to thank Edward Gillespie of Cheltenham Racecourse, George Smith formally of Silverstone and Liam Mulvihill of Croke Park for providing information on their respective venues. We are, in addition, both members of various organizations with an active interest in sport and its architecture and we appreciate the assistance and advice these organizations have provided. They include the IAAM (International Association of Auditorium Managers) and the former FSADC (Football Stadia Advisory Design Council) and the AFDM (Association for Facility Development and Management), particularly its Architects Working Group and the IAKS Stadium Working Party.

Most of the drawings were produced by the LOBB Sports Architecture. In some cases they are based on other drawings, particularly the historical plans and sections of past stadia. A great deal of Rod's work was done while enjoying the sun in Biarritz, and the publication would not be complete without a word of thanks to Louis and Helene who effectively serviced its production during this period, and to Cathy, who is an everlasting source of inspiration. Geraint owes a debt to the patience of his wife, Jane. The effort that has gone into this new edition has been generously supported by Rod's practice.

The authors are indebted to Mr TSUNEO ITO of T.M. ITO Ltd. of London and to NIKKEN SEKKEI for their help in providing information on the Japanese Stadia.

Finally, the authors would like to acknowledge the enormous contribution made by Maritz Vandenberg to putting this book together. Professor Terry Stevens of Swansea has made a study of the subject of Stadia & Tourism and the authors are grateful to him for his help and for allowing them to use his material in the chapter Stadia and tourism.

1

The stadium as a building type

1.1 A venue for watching sport

1.1.1 Architectural quality

A sports stadium is essentially a huge theatre for the presentation of heroic feats (Figure 1.1). From such a combination of dramatic function plus monumental scale ought to flow powerful civic architecture. The first great prototype, the Colosseum of Rome, did indeed achieve this ideal, but very few stadia since then have succeeded as well. The worst are sordid, uncomfortable places, casting a spell of depression on their surroundings for the long periods

Figure 1.1 'Sport is theatre where the primal things are in play – courage, passion, perfidy, endeavour, fear; where grace and sometimes incredible gifts pass in front of us' (David Robson, former sports editor of *The Sunday Times*).

when they stand empty and unused, in sharp contrast with the short periods of extreme congestion on match days. The best are comfortable and safe, and offer their patrons an enjoyable afternoon's or evening's entertainment – but even these often fall short of architectural excellence.

Subduing the tiers of seating, the ramps or stairs, and the immense roof structures into a single harmonious and delightful architectural ideal is a challenge that seems almost beyond solution, so that sports stadia tend to be lumpy agglomerations of elements that are out of scale with their surroundings and in conflict with each other, and often harshly detailed and finished.

This book cannot show the reader how to create great architecture. By clarifying the technical requirements to the greatest possible degree, and showing how these problems have been solved in particular cases, it hopes at least to ease the designer's struggles with his brief and leave him better equipped for the really difficult task of thinking his solutions through to the point where they become a fine building.

1.1.2 Financial viability

In the 1950s sports grounds around the world were filled to bursting point at every match and watching live sport was a major pastime for millions. Now, only a few decades later, those same grounds are fighting for financial survival, and owners and managers search for solutions.

The truth is that it is now very difficult for a sports stadium to be financially viable without some degree of subsidy, whether open or covert. The most that can usually be done is to produce a facility that will satisfy a viable combination of the following three factors:

- the required subsidy is not impossibly large;
- the project is sufficiently attractive to public sources of finance to justify investment from the public purse;
- and sufficiently attractive to private sponsors to persuade them to bridge any remaining financial gap.

Anyone who considers the above statements too pessimistic should ponder the American experience. The USA and Canada have highly affluent populations totalling 276 million, are keen on sport and have energetic leisure entrepreneurs and managers very skilled at extracting the customer's dollar. Of all countries the USA and Canada should be able to make their stadia pay, and they have seemingly explored every avenue – huge seating capacities, multi-use functions, adaptability of seating configurations, total enclosure to ensure comfort, retractable roofing to allow for different weather conditions and yet profitability remains elusive, particularly when the huge initial costs of development are taken into account. To take three leading examples:

- The beautifully situated 1968 Three Rivers Stadium at Pittsburgh (unroofed; seating capacity 60 000) has been regularly sold out for every football match but is happy to limit its annual loss, we are told, to under two million dollars (US).
- The management of the 1988 Joe Robbie Stadium in Miami (unroofed; seating capacity 73 000) have optimistically suggested that they are among the first stadia in the USA to be 'turning the corner' thanks to new and aggressive financing arrangements, but observers in the industry are sceptical of this claim, particularly in view of rising interest rates.
- Construction of the famous 1989 Toronto Skydome in Canada (retractable roof; seating capacity 56 000) was funded by a unique system of private sponsorship and public funding, but after three years of use and huge publicity it was said to be struggling with heavy debt problems. As in many cases these were brought on partly by unforeseen interest rate rises – which merely demonstrates how vulnerable such huge projects are to uncontrollable factors.

Just as we cannot prescribe rules which will produce great architecture we cannot give formulae which will guarantee a profitable stadium. Teams of experts must analyse the costs and potential revenues for each individual case and evolve a solution that will be viable – or, at worst, leave a gap that can be bridged by private sponsors or public support.

This book identifies the factors that must be considered. But before getting into such technical details we must make the most important point of all: that sports and leisure facilities are one of the great historic building types, representing some of the very earliest works of architecture (Greek stadia), some of the most pivotal (Roman amphitheatres and thermae), and some of the most beautiful (from the Colosseum in Rome to the Olympic Park in Munich twenty centuries later). Therefore we will start with a brief historic survey.

1.2 History

1.2.1 Greek

The ancestral prototypes for modern sports facilities of all kinds are the stadia and hippodromes of ancient Greece. Here Olympic and other sporting contests were staged, starting (as far as we can tell) in the eighth century BC.

Stadia
Greek stadia (foot racecourses) were laid out in a U-shape, with the straight end forming the start-line. These stadia varied somewhat in length, the one at Delphi being just under 183 m long and that at Olympia about 192 m. Such stadia were built in all cities where games were played. Some, following the pattern of Greek theatres, were cut out of a hillside so that banks of seats with good sightlines could be formed naturally, while others were constructed on flat ground. In the latter

case the performance area was sometimes slightly excavated to allow for the formation of shallow seating tiers along the sides.

Stadia built on the flat existed at Ephesus, Delphi and Athens. The one at Delphi was almost 183 m long by 28 m wide, had a shallow bank of seats along one side and around the curved end, and the judges' seats were at the midpoint of the long side – very much as in a modern facility. The stadium at Athens was first built in 331 BC, reconstructed in AD 160 and reconstructed again in 1896 for the first modern Olympic games. In this form it can still be seen, accommodating up to 50 000 people in 46 rows (Figure 1.2).

Hillside stadia existed at Olympia, Thebes and Epidauros, and their kinship with the Greek theatre is unmistakable: these are essentially elongated theatres for the staging of spectacular physical feats, and from them runs a direct line of development firstly to the multi-tiered Roman amphitheatre and ultimately to the modern stadium.

The civic importance of such sporting facilities in Greek life is demonstrated particularly well at the ancient city of Olympia on the island of Peloponnesus. The site housed a great complex of temples and altars to various deities and, at the height of its development, was a rendezvous for the whole Greek world. There was a sports field situated adjacent to an enclosed training gymnasium, and along the edge of the field a colonnade with stone steppings to accommodate the spectators. As the track became more popular two stands were constructed, facing each other on opposite sides of the activity area. The fully developed stadium consisted of a track 192 m long and 32 m wide with rising tiers of seats on massive sloping earth banks along the

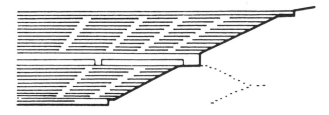

Figure 1.2 The U-shaped sunken stadium at Athens, first built in 331 BC for the staging of foot races, was restored and used for the first modern Olympics in 1896.

sides, the latter ultimately accommodating up to 45 000 spectators. The stadium had two entrances, the Pompic and the Secret, the latter used only by the judges.

Adjacent to the stadium at Olympia was a much longer hippodrome for horse and chariot races, and in these twin facilities we may clearly discern the embryonic forms of modern athletic stadia and racing circuits. The stadium has been excavated and restored and can be studied, but the hippodrome has not survived.

While modern large capacity, roofed stadia can seldom have the simple forms used in ancient Greece, there are occasions when the quiet repose of these beautiful antecedents could be emulated. The essential points are unobtrusive form and use of natural materials which blend so closely with the surroundings that it is difficult to say where 'landscape' ends and 'building' begins.

Hippodromes

These courses for horse and chariot races were roughly 198 m to 228 m long and 37 m wide and were laid out, once again, in a U-shape. Like Greek theatres, hippodromes were usually made on the slope of a hill to give rising tiers of seating, and from them developed the later Roman circuses, although these were more elongated and much narrower.

1.2.2 Roman

Amphitheatres

The militaristic Romans were more interested in public displays of mortal combat than in races and athletic events, and to accommodate this spectacle they developed a new amphitheatrical form: an elliptical arena surrounded on all sides by high-rising tiers of seats enabling the maximum number of spectators to have a clear view of the terrible events staged before them. The term 'arena' is derived from the Latin word for 'sand' or 'sandy land', referring to the layer of sand that was spread on the activity area to absorb spilled blood.

The overall form was, in effect, two Greek theatres joined together to form a complete ellipse. But the size of the later Roman

amphitheatres ruled out any reliance on natural ground slopes to provide the necessary seating profile, therefore the Romans began to construct artificial slopes around the central arena – first in timber (these have not survived) and, starting in the first century AD, in stone and concrete. Magnificent examples of the latter may still be seen in Arles and Nimes (stone) and in Rome, Verona and Pula (stone and a form of concrete). The amphitheatre at Arles, constructed in around 46 BC, accommodated 21 000 spectators in three storeys and despite considerable damage, lacking for instance its third storey which held the posts supporting a tented roof, it is still used every year for bullfighting. The Nimes amphitheatre, dating from the second century AD, is smaller but in excellent condition and also in regular use as a bullring. The great amphitheatre in Verona, built in about 100 AD, is world famous as a venue for opera performances. Originally it measured 152 m by 123 m overall, but very little remains of the outer aisle and it currently seats about 22 000 people. The arena measures 73 m by 44 m.

The Flavian Amphitheatre in Rome (Figure 1.3), better known as the Colosseum from the eighth century onwards, is the greatest exemplar

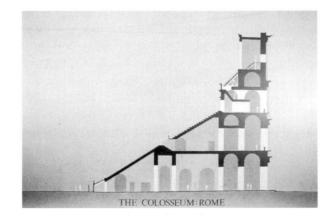

THE COLOSSEUM:ROME

Figure 1.3 The Colosseum of Rome (AD 82) was built for gladiatorial combat and not for races. It therefore took the form of a theatre in which rising tiers of seats, forming an artificial hillside, completely surrounded an arena. The great stone and concrete drum fused engineering, theatre and art more successfully than most modern stadia.

of this building type and has seldom been surpassed to this day as a rational fusion of engineering, theatre and art. Construction began in AD 70 and finished 12 years later. The structure formed a giant ellipse of 189 m by 155 m and rose to a height of four storeys, accommodating 48 000 people – a stadium capacity that would not be exceeded until the twentieth century. Spectators had good sight-lines to the arena below, the latter being an ellipse of roughly 88 m by 55 m bounded by a 4.6 m high wall. There were 80 arched openings to each of the lower three storeys (with engaged columns and encircling entablatures applied to the outer wall surface as ornamentation), the openings at ground level giving entrance to the tiers of seats. The structural cross-section (Figure 1.3), broadening from the top down to the base, solved three problems at one stroke:

- First, it formed the artificial hillside required from the theatrical point of view.
- Second, it formed a stable structure. The tiers of seats were supported on a complex series of barrel-vaults and arches which distributed the immense loads via an ever-widening structure down to foundation level;
- Third it matched the volume of internal space to the numbers of people circulating at each level – fewest at the top, most at the base. The internal ambulatories and access passages formed by the structural arcades were so well-planned that the entire amphitheatre could, it is thought, have been evacuated in a matter of minutes.

The arena was used for gladiatorial contests and other entertainments and could be flooded with water for naval and aquatic displays, thus anticipating modern mass entertainments. Beneath the arena was a warren of chambers and passageways to accommodate performers, gladiators and animals. The amphitheatre could be roofed by stretching canvas awnings across the open top.

All these diverse functions have been smoothly assimilated into a great drum that stands magnificently in the townscape – functional in layout, rational in appearance, yet rich and expressive in its surface modelling. Present-day designers could do worse than to spend some time contemplating the achievements of the Colosseum before tackling their own complex briefs.

Circuses

As the Greek theatre led to the Roman amphitheatre, so the Greek hippodrome led to the Roman circus. These circuses were U-shaped equestrian racecourses with the straight end forming the entrance and accommodating the stalls for horses and chariots. The starting and return courses were separated by a *spina* – a low wall decorated with carvings and statues. Seats rose in tiers along the straight sides of the U and round the curved end, the lower seats being in stone and reserved for members of the upper classes, the upper seats made of wood.

A notable early example was the Circus Maximus in Rome (fourth century BC), followed in 46 BC by a successor of the same name. This was possibly the largest stadium ever built. It was about 660 m long and 210 m wide and offered all-seating accommodation for spectators in three tiers parallel to the track.

Other Roman examples include the Circus Flaminius (third century BC) and the Circus Maxentius (fourth century AD), the latter being the only Roman circus still extant today. Outside Rome were the Byzantium Hippodrome of the second century AD (based on the Circus Maximus) and the Pessimus Hippodrome which was unique at the time in consisting of a Greek theatre and a Roman hippodrome linked at the centre of the hippodrome via the theatre stage. Two events could be staged separately in theatre and hippodrome, or the latter could be used in combination for a single grand event. This building was an obvious ancestor of the modern multi-purpose stadium complex.

1.2.3 Mediaeval and after

As Christianity swept through Europe the emphasis of society shifted to religious salvation, and architectural effort was turned to the building of churches rather than places of recreation and entertainment. No major new sports stadia or amphitheatres would be built for the next fifteen centuries.

Sports buildings inherited from the Roman era became neglected. Some were converted to new uses as markets or tenement dwellings, the amphitheatre at Arles, for instance, being transformed into a citadel with about 200 houses and a church inside it (built partly with stone from the amphitheatre structure); many others were simply demolished.

During the Rennaisance and after, competitions on foot or horseback were held in open fields or town squares, sometimes with temporary stages and covered areas for important spectators rather along the lines of the first Greek hippodromes – but no permanent edifices were erected even though deep interest was taken in classicism and in the architecture of stadia and amphitheatres. The Colosseum was particularly closely studied, but only for its lessons in façade composition and modelling, which were then transferred to other building types.

1.2.4 The nineteenth century

The stadium as a building type saw a revival after the industrial revolution. There was a growing demand for mass spectator events from the public, there were entrepreneurs who wished to cater for this demand and there were new structural technologies to facilitate the construction of stadia or enclosed halls.

A particularly important impetus came from the revival of the Olympic tradition at the end of the nineteenth century. At the instigation of Baron Pierre de Coubertin a congress met in 1894, leading to the first modern Olympic games being staged at Athens in 1896. For this purpose the ancient stadium of 331 BC, which had been excavated and studied by a German architect/archeologist called Ziller, was rebuilt to the traditional Greek elongated U-pattern, its marble terraces accommodating about 50 000 spectators (Figure 1.2). Thereafter, Olympic games were held every four years, except when interrupted by war, and those which produced notable changes or advances in stadium design are noted below.

1.2.5 Twentieth-century Olympic stadia

In 1908 the games were held in London, where the White City stadium was built for the purpose, the architect being James Fulton. It was a functional building accommodating over 80 000 spectators, had a steel frame, and was the first purpose-designed modern Olympic stadium. The arena was gigantic by the standards of today (Figure 1.4), accommodating a multitude of individual sports and surrounded by a cycle track. It was subsequently decided to reduce the number of Olympic sports, partly to give a smaller arena. In later years White City stadium became increasingly neglected and was finally demolished in the 1980s.

Owing to the First World War the 1916 games did not take place, but a stadium with a capacity of 60 000 had been built in 1913 in Berlin in

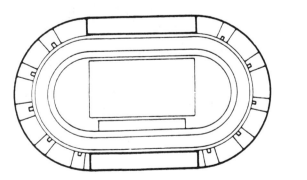
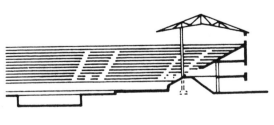

Figure 1.4 White City stadium in London (1908) was the first modern Olympic stadium and accommodated over 80 000 spectators. Its athletics field was encircled by a cycle racing track which made the arena larger than later examples.

anticipation of these games. Its interest lies in its pleasantly natural form: like the theatres and stadia of ancient Greece it is shaped out of the earth, blending quietly into the surrounding landscape and making no monumental gestures. The architect was Otto March, and this stadium formed a prototype for the numerous Sportparks built in Germany in the 1920s.

In 1936 the city of Berlin did finally host the Olympic games. The Nazis had recently assumed power and used the occasion to extend the stadium of 1913 to a great oval structure accommodating 110 000 spectators including 35 000 standees in 71 rows (Figure 1.5). The monumental stone-clad stadium was, unfortunately, used not only for sporting functions but also for mass political demonstrations. In spite of these unpleasant associations the Berlin stadium with its rational planning and powerful columniated façade is a highly impressive design. The architect was Werner March.

The 1948 Olympics returned to London, where the 24-year old Wembley Stadium was renovated by its original designer Sir Owen Williams.

The 1960 Olympiad in Rome marked a new departure. Instead of staging all events on a single site as before, a decentralized plan was decided upon, with the athletics stadium in one part of the city and other facilities some distance away on the urban outskirts, and this was to remain the preferred approach for decades to come. The main stadium, by architect Annibale Vitellozzi, was an uncovered three-storey struc-

ture (Figure 1.6) and bore some similarities to the Berlin stadium. It has an orderly and handsome limestone-clad façade wrapped round its oval shape, to which a roof was added in 1990 when Rome hosted the Soccer World Cup competition. Two of the fully enclosed smaller halls dating from 1960 are architecturally significant: the 16 000 capacity Palazzo dello Sport (Figure 1.7) and the 5000 capacity Palazzetto dello Sport. Both are circular, column-free halls which combine great visual elegance with functional efficiency. The architects were Marcello Piacentini for the Palazzo and Annibale Vitellozzi for the Palazzetto, and Pier Luigi Nervi was the structural engineer for both.

In 1964 the Olympics were held in Tokyo. The Jingu National Stadium, first built in 1958, was extended for the occasion (Figure 1.8) but, as in Rome, two smaller fully-enclosed halls caught international attention. These were Kenzo Tange's Swimming Arena and Sports Arena seating 4000 and 15 000 spectators respectively. The Swimming Arena building was justifiably called 'a cathedral for swimming' by Avery Brundage, the International Olympic Committee (IOC) President. Here, 4000 spectators could sit under one of the most dramatic roof structures ever devised: steel cables were draped from a single tall mast on the perimeter of the circular plan, and concrete panels hung from the cables to form a semi-rigid roof structure. As built the roof forms of the two gymnasia may look natural and inevitable, but both were the result

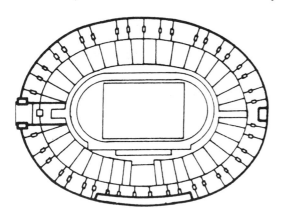

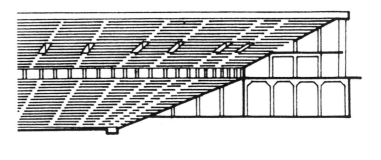

Figure 1.5 The Berlin Olympic stadium of 1936 accommodated over 100 000 people in a rationally planned elliptical layout.

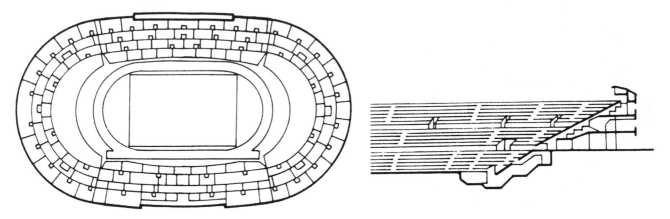

Figure 1.6 The Rome Olympic stadium of 1960, also a colonnaded oval bowl, bears a family resemblance to that of Berlin.

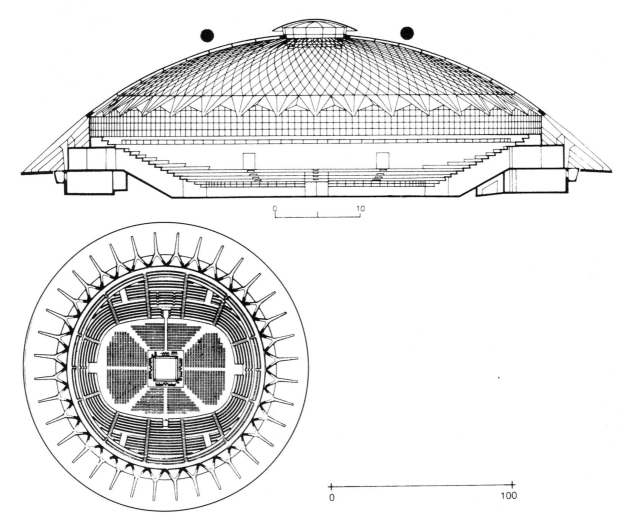

Figure 1.7 A smaller enclosed stadium with column-free interior and of exceptional architectural merit: the Palazzetto dello Sport for the Rome Olympics of 1960. It has a concrete shell roof resting on 36 pre-cast perimeter supports.

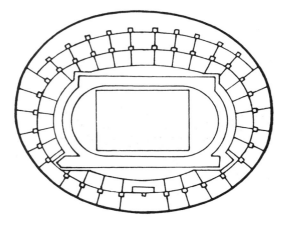

Figure 1.8 The Tokyo Olympic Stadium of 1964.

of very extensive testing and tuning on large-scale models, not merely for structural efficiency but also for visual composition.

In 1968 Mexico City was the Olympic host and rose to the occasion with several notable stadia. The University Stadium, built in 1953 for a capacity of 70 000 spectators, was enlarged in 1968 to become the main Olympic stadium with 87 000 seats (Figure 1.9). Its low graceful form is notable: like the 1913 stadium in Berlin this is basically an 'earth stadium' which barely rises above the natural landscape and uses hardly any reinforced concrete, blending smoothly into its surroundings. It also uses splendid sculptural decoration to enhance its exterior form. More impressive in scale is the Aztec Stadium (architect Pedro Ramirez Vasquez) accommodating 107 000 seated spectators. Most viewers are under cover, and while some are a very long way from the pitch it is a wonderful experience to see this number of cheering fans gathered under one roof. This is said to be the largest covered stadium in the world. Finally, as at Rome in 1960 and Tokyo

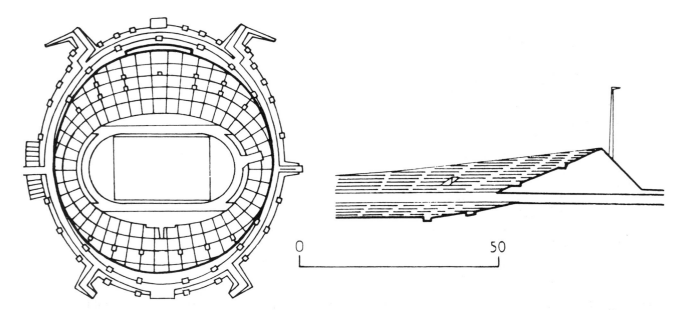

Figure 1.9 The Mexico City Olympic Stadium of 1968 seated spectators in a low, graceful shape sunk into the landscape.

in 1964, there was a fully enclosed indoor arena also worthy of note.

In 1972 the Olympics returned to Germany. The site, formerly an expanse of nondescript land near Munich, was converted with exemplary skill to a delightful landscape of green hills, hollows, meadows and watercourses, and an existing heap of rubble became a small green hill. Perhaps in a conscious attempt to erase memories of the heavy monumentality of the 1936 Berlin stadium, a very expensive but delightfully elegant lightweight roof was thrown over one side of the stadium (Figure 1.10) and extended to several other facilities, creating an airy structure that still holds its age well 20 years later. The arena is embedded in an artificially created hollow so that the roof, which consists of transparent acrylic panels on a steel net hung from a series of tapered masts, seems to float above the parkland, its gentle undulations mirroring those of the landscape below. It must be said that environmental problems have been experienced under the pool section of this plexiglass canopy and that a PVC-coated polyester parasol was suspended under the arena section to shade the area below from the sun. Nevertheless the roof, which is further described in Section 4.8, remains an outstanding achievement: in addition to being beautiful it is the largest to date, covering 21 acres or 8.5 hectares. The stadium designers were architects Günter Behnisch and Partners, and engineers Frei Otto and Fritz Leonardt.

In 1992 Barcelona hosted the Olympics, and the 1929 Montjuic World's Fair stadium was extensively remodelled by architect Vittorio Gregotti, leaving virtually only the Romanesque façades intact, to cater for the majority of track, field and pitch sports. Everything inside the perimeter walls of the stadium was removed, the playing area was lowered to allow twice the previous seating capacity, and a new tunnel system was installed around the 9-lane running track so that members of the press could circulate freely without interfering with the events above. Outside the old gate to the stadium is a new piazza, from which access is gained to four other facilities: the 17 000-seat Palau Sant Jordi gymnasium (architect Arata Isozaki), the Picornell swimming complex, the University for Sport, and the International Media centre. The site is very compact compared to those of most other recent Olympic games.

The stadium built for the 1996 Games in Atlanta was designed to be converted after the games into a baseball stadium.

The best of the above stadia rise to the level of great architecture, most notably perhaps the Rome, Munich and Tokyo buildings. Interesting stadia were built for the games of 1976 (Montreal), 1980 (Moscow) and 1988 (Seoul) but we do not have the space to show them here. Some information on the technically interesting but the problematic Montreal stadium is given in Section 4.4.

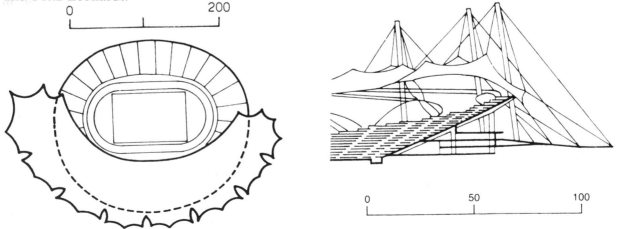

Figure 1.10 The Munich Olympic Stadium of 1972 brought the series of architecturally outstanding stadia of the preceding decades to a climax.

1.2.6 Twentieth-century single-sport stadia

As the above Olympic stadia were being created, increasingly ambitious facilities were also evolving for specific sports such as football (also called soccer in the UK and USA), rugby, American football, baseball, tennis and cricket.

Football

Football stadia predominate in Europe and much of South America, owing to the popularity of the game in these countries. But different traditions in these different regions have led to a variety of architectural types.

In the UK the typical pattern is for each stadium to be owned by a particular football club and to be used only by that club. This dedication to a single sport, combined with very limited income, has helped create a tradition of spectator 'closeness' which takes two forms:

- Firstly there is a tradition of standing terraces in which fans stand closely together. This is no longer acceptable at top division clubs on safety grounds and all standing terraces in the Premier and First Divisions in the UK have been converted to seats – see Chapters 7 and 13.
- Secondly, British football stadia have long been designed to accommodate spectators very close to the pitch. This allows intimate contact with the game but makes it difficult to incorporate an athletics track round the perimeter of the pitch. While this intimate social atmosphere is a much admired aspect of the British football stadium, and one which most clubs would wish to retain, it seems possible that major stadia will increasingly be designed for multi-purpose uses (including athletics in specialist cases).

In European football there is a very different pattern, with each stadium typically owned by the local municipality and used by a large number of sports clubs. The football clubs run their own lotteries, ploughing the profits back into the game; many stadia are also used for other sports, particularly athletics. For all these reasons European stadia have in the past tended to be better funded than British ones and somewhat better designed and built – examples are Düsseldorf, Cologne or the World Cup venue at Turin (Figure 1.11). Dual-use facilities have the drawback that the placement of an athletics track around the pitch pushes spectators away from the playing area, thus reducing spectator/player contact, but such loss of intimacy must be weighed against the advantage of better community use.

The most notable British football stadia are those of the Premier League clubs. Elsewhere there is, sad to say, a depressing tendency for clubs to settle for the cheapest and quickest solution, with little or none of the vision occasionally encountered on the continent of Europe. Exceptions in the UK are Huddersfield and Bolton.

Football is very popular in South America, where there is a liking for very large stadia. The largest in the world is the Maracana Municipal stadium in Rio de Janeiro, Brazil, which has a normal ground capacity of 205 000 spectators, of whom 155 000 may take a seat. It contains one of the first of the 'modern' versions of the dry moat to separate spectators from the field of play, the moat being 2.1 m wide and about 1.5 m deep. This is rather small by current standards (see Section 6.3) but it did establish a trend in player/spectator separation which has been used round the world including, for instance, the 100 000-capacity Seoul Olympic stadium of 1988.

The stadia built for the 1990 World Cup in Italy set very high design standards.

Rugby

One of the most important British examples is Twickenham Rugby Football Ground near London, dating back to 1907. The 10-acre site has undergone considerable development since then. The old grounds are overshadowed by a two-tier South Stand (capacity 12 000) and by three-tier North, East and West stands. The East, North and West stands are linked by a single 39 m-deep cantilevered roof sweeping round three sides of the field and total ground capacity is 75 000, all seated and all under cover. Because the South Stand shades the natural grass turf for part of the day it was given a

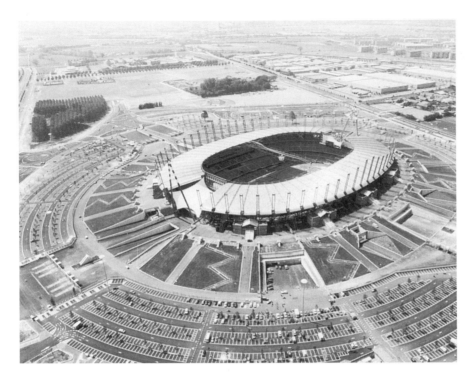

Figure 1.11 Turin Stadium, a World Cup football venue. Architects: Hotter & Ossola. Eng. Majoveski.

translucent roof to allow some transmission of sunlight, including ultra violet radiation, to the pitch (Figure 1.12).

Other British rugby stadia worth studying are the Millennium Stadium at Cardiff Arms Park, Cardiff (which is successfully used for international rugby and soccer) and the Murrayfield stadium in Edinburgh. The latter is an example, like Twickenham, of an entire stadium being rebuilt.

Other leading rugby stadia include the Sydney Football Stadium in Australia (Figure 1.13), the Stade de France in Paris, Lansdowne Road in Dublin, and Ellis Park in Johannesburg.

Rugby has moved increasingly towards stadia shared with football. Examples in the UK include Watford, Reading, and Queens Park Rangers. Greater attention has to be paid to the grass pitch to permit joint use.

American football and baseball

After the First World war the USA broke new ground with a series of pioneering stadia built particularly for two burgeoning national sports – American football and baseball.

Figure 1.12 Twickenham's £4.5 million South Stand (1981) has a translucent roof to allow sunlight to reach the turf. Architects: LOBB Partnership.

Figure 1.13 Sydney Football Stadium for AFL football and rugby is a design of fluidity and grace. Architects: Philip Cox Richardson Taylor & Partners.

To cater for the growing popularity of American football there evolved a new type of single-tier elliptical bowl of vast capacity surrounding a rectangular football pitch. The first was the Yale Bowl at New Haven (1914, capacity 70 000). It was followed by the Rose Bowl at Pasadena, California (capacity 100 000), the Orange Bowl in Miami (1937, capacity 75 000), Ann Arbor stadium in Michigan (capacity 101 000) and others. Stands in the largest of these were up to 90 rows deep, the more distant spectators being so far from the pitch that they could not see the ball clearly.

Baseball became the second great popular sport. Because it requires a very differently shaped pitch and seating configuration than football a series of specialized baseball stadia were built, including the famous Yankee Stadium in New York (1924, capacity 68 000).

Typically the stadia for these two sports were urban stadia, built in the midst of the populations they served, and typically they were open or only partly roofed. After the Second World War there was a new wave of stadium building,

but the typology shifted gradually towards multi-purpose facilities, often fully roofed, and often situated out of town, surrounded by acres of car parking. Between 1960 and 1977 over 30 such major stadia were built, the most impressive being the Oakland Coliseum, John Shea Stadium in New York (1964, baseball and football), and the Busch Stadium in St Louis (baseball). The most recent example is Comiskey Park Baseball Stadium in Chicago (1991), seating 43 000 spectators on five levels.

The Louisiana Superdome in New Orleans, opened in 1975, is the largest of this generation of stadia. It has an area of 13 acres, is covered by one of the world's longest roof-spans with a diameter of 207 m, is 83 m tall and has a maximum capacity of 76 791 for football. One of its most interesting features is a gondola suspended from the centre of the roof, comprising six television screens of 8 m each, showing a range of information including instant action-replays.

Other examples are listed in Table 1.1. Many of these great stadia catered for both American

Table 1.1 Superdomes and other large post-war stadia in North America

	Stadium	City	Roof type	Seating capacities for various functions*	Number of parking spaces
1964	Astrodome	Houston	Closed	66 000 (concerts) 52 000 (football) 45 000 (baseball)	28 000
1965	Atlanta-Fulton County Stadium	Atlanta	Open	60 000 (football) 52 000 (baseball)	6500
1968	Three Rivers Stadium	Pittsburgh	Open	60 000 (not stated)	7000
1971	Veterans Stadium	Philadelphia	Open	67 000 (not stated)	10 000
1972	Hoosier Dome	Indianapolis	Closed	61 000 (not stated)	10 000
1972	Arrowhead Stadium	Kansas City	Open	71 000 (baseball)	24 000 shared by Arrowhead and Royals spectators
1973	Royals Stadium	Kansas City	Open	41 000 (football)	
1973	Silverdome	Pontiac	Closed	93 000 (not stated)	23 000
1975	Louisiana Superdome	New Orleans	Closed	95 000 (general assemblies) 76 000 (sports events)	5000
1976	Giants Stadium	New Jersey	Open	77 000 (football)	30 000
1976	Kingdome	Seattle	Closed	70 000 (not stated)	35 000
1982	Hubert Humphrey Metrodome	Minneapolis	Closed	63 000 (football) 55 000 (baseball) 36 000 (basketball)	500**
1987	Joe Robbie	Miami	Open	73 000 (football)	15 000
1989	Skydome	Toronto	Retractable	68 000 (concerts, boxing) 53 000 (football) 51 000 (baseball)	775***

* Figures for the various stadia may be based on different criteria. Direct comparisons can therefore not be made.
** An additional 23 500 parking spaces are available within a twenty minute walk from the Hubert H Humphrey Stadium.
*** 17 000 parking spaces are available within the city core. But as Skydome is an inner city stadium most spectators come by public transport. A covered walkway links Skydome with the central railway station, allowing rapid dispersal of spectators after events.

football and baseball (and usually other types of activity) in an attempt to maximize revenue. However, as already mentioned, the shapes of football and baseball pitches are so different that it is difficult to provide ideal seating configurations for both, even with movable seating systems as in the John Shea dual-purpose stadium of 1964. The Harry S Truman Sports Complex in Kansas of 1972 therefore separated the two sports: the Royals Stadium has 41 000 seats with excellent viewing over a baseball pitch (Figure 1.14), and its sister Arrowhead Stadium 71 000 seats overlooking a football field (Figure 1.15). Each stadium has its own entertainment facilities, etc. for its particular group of patrons.

Tennis

The world's most famous tennis venue is the All England Lawn Tennis and Croquet Club at Wimbledon in London, home since 1922 of The Championships. The Championship fortnight now attracts about 400 000 people each year. The tournament facilities comprise eighteen grass courts, five red shale courts, three clay courts, one artificial grass court and five indoor courts. Not all of these courts have permanent seats, the major spectator provision being at the following locations:

Centre Court	13 109 seats
No 1 Court	10 000 seats
No 2 Court	2226 seats
No 3 Court	800 seats
No 6 Court	250 seats
No 7 Court	250 seats

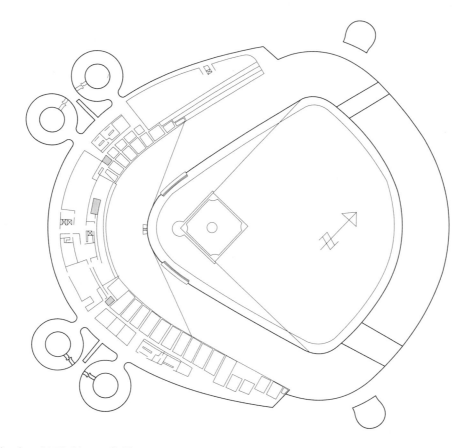

Figure 1.14 In the 1972 Harry S Truman complex in Kansas the Royals Stadium is designed specifically for baseball.

When temporary seating at various other courts is added to the above figures the total capacity is above 30 000. In addition to these tournament facilities there are also 14 grass practice courts in the adjacent Aorangi Park.

To many people 'Wimbledon' means the Centre Court. The stadium surrounding this famous patch of grass was built in 1922 and has been gradually upgraded and renewed ever since. While it suffers from compromised sightlines from some seats, the stadium does in many ways give the most satisfying 'tennis experience' in the world: the tight clustering of spectators round the grass court, under a low roof which reflects the buzz of sound and applause from the fans beneath, creates an intimate theatrical atmo-sphere and an intensity of concentration which are missing from most other venues. To prepare the Club for the next century a comprehensive 20-year master plan for the entire site has been prepared and implemented. It includes a new No 1 court (Figure 1.16) designed to replicate the intimate Centre Court atmosphere.

There are three other international Grand Slam tennis venues which are comparable in scale and complexity to Wimbledon: Flushing Meadows in the USA,[1] Flinders Park in Australia, and Roland Garros in France. They all vary greatly in terms of atmosphere and tradition.

In North America the US Open Championship is played at Flushing Meadows in New

---

[1] Notable non-Grand Slam stadia in the US include the recently-built ATP Championship Stadia in Cincinnati and the Fitzgerald Tennis Centre in Washington, both designed by Browning Day Mullins Dierdorf Inc.

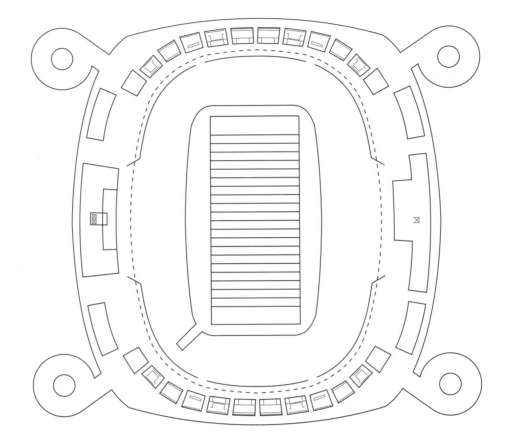

Figure 1.15 The Arrowhead Stadium for American football, in recognition of the very different seating geometries required for good viewing of the two games. Architects: Howard Needles Tammen & Bergendoff (HNTB).

York, where the spectators' attitude to viewing is much more casual than at Wimbledon. This is reflected in the design of the Principal Court where nearly 20 000 spectators sit out in the open under a busy airport flightpath, with the outermost seats too distant to offer good viewing. The sense of detachment seen here is quite characteristic of US stadia which tend to be very large and to be patronized by spectators who are not averse to wandering around getting snacks and drinks while a game is in progress.

Australia's National Tennis Centre at Flinders Park, Melbourne, was constructed on derelict land in 1986–87 (Figure 1.17). It can seat a total of 29 200 spectators at 15 courts, as follows:

Centre court	15 000
Court 1	6000
Court 2	3000
Courts 3 and 4	1000 each
Courts 5 and 6	500 each
Courts 7 to 10	300 each
Courts 11 to 15	200 each.

There are also five indoor practice courts, which are now thought to be too few. The front rows of the Centre Court seats are at a greater distance from the court than at Wimbledon or even Flushing Meadows on the theory that a ball travelling at 180 km/h cannot be seen properly by viewers who are too close to it. The validity of

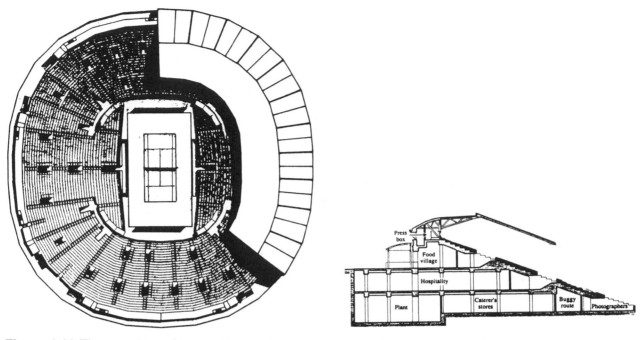

Figure 1.16 The new No 1 Court at the All England Lawn Tennis and Croquet Club in London, with roof partially shown. A seating capacity of only 11 500 ensures the closeness between players and spectators that is one of the strengths of Wimbledon. Architects: Building Design Partnership (BDP).

this approach is contested by those who hold that spectators want to be close to the action, even if that means that the ball is only a blur at times. The 15 000 seats are fed by 20 entrances/ vomitories, and the stadium has a sliding roof which takes 20 minutes to close. Unlike Wimbledon the court has a 'rebound ace' hard acrylic surface which has the advantage of allowing intensive multi-purpose year-round use for other sports and for pop concerts, etc. (around 120 events are staged per annum). However, it is thought by some to be visually 'dead' compared with the Wimbledon grass court.

Since completion of the Flinders Park venue there has been an increased demand, not foreseen at the time, on the hospitality, catering and press facilities in particular. An expansion plan is therefore being undertaken which would double the site area to some 12 hectares and include a full complement of 13 practice courts plus hotel facilities, a merchandising centre, a sports medical centre and more car parking. The existing No 1 Court, which is currently open, would be fitted with a retractable roof.

In France the French Open venue is the Roland Garros stadium in the Bois de Boulogne in Paris, which was established in 1928 and has been gradually upgraded ever since. The 15 acre site contains 16 championship courts, all clay-surfaced, including a Centre Court seating 16 500 and a No 1 Court seating 4500. In atmosphere the Centre Court is closer to Flushing Meadows than Wimbledon, being open to the sky and with greater viewing distances than the tight clustering found at Wimbledon. Current maximum capacity for the site is 30 000 spectators a day, but as at Wimbledon and Flinders Park an expansion plan is underway. This will increase capacity to 36 000 per day. The new No 1 Court accommodates 10 000 spectators with extra provision for players, media, administration and catering, along with two subterranean floors of parking for 540 cars. The number of tournament courts will remain at 16, but 7 practice courts will be added.

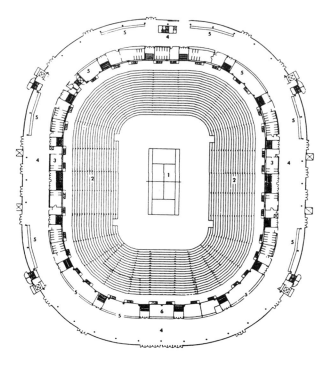

Figure 1.17 The Centre Court of the National Tennis Centre at Flinders Park in Melbourne, Australia, is of a more conventional capacity, seating 15 000 spectators. Architects: Peddle Thorp & Learmonth in association with Philip Cox & Partners.

Cricket

Lord's Cricket Ground in London has been the home of the Marylebone Cricket Club (MCC) since 1814 and is the symbolic centre of world cricket. The 12-acre site (Figure 1.18) has a total capacity of 27 500 spectators accommodated in a variety of open and roofed stands which have gradually grown up round the playing field. The site development policy is to deliberately build on this pattern of individual buildings surrounding a green, instead of moving towards a unified stadium built to a single architectural style. The policy is clearly reflected in the 1987 Mound Stand, which cost approximately £4 million and replaced an earlier stand on the same spot, and the 1991 Compton and Edrich Stands which cost approximately £5 million. The Mound Stand seats 5400 spectators in two main tiers, 4500 at terrace (lower) level and 900 at promenade (upper) level, the upper seating level being sheltered by a translucent tented roof.

A new stand by Nicholas Grimshaw & Partners has been completed on the North side.

The Oval ground in South London, home of the Surrey County Cricket Club, is as well known as Lord's and the site is being master-planned for the future by LOBB Sports Architecture. Also in Britain, a new cricket ground has been built for County Durham by architect Bill Ainsworth. In Australia the leading venue is Melbourne Cricket Stadium (Figure 1.19).

1.3 Current requirements

1.3.1 The spectator

For all of these sports, stand design begins and ends with the spectator, and it is at this much-maligned figure that the planning team must look before anything else. At the outset of a project the first questions to be asked, and answered, must be: *who* are the spectators, *what* are they looking for in the facility, and *how* can their numbers be maximized? Only when these questions are answered will it be possible to examine the technical solutions which will satisfy those users and to do the necessary calculations. This simple methodology should be used for all sports projects.

It must be understood that different people have different motives, and that any crowd will contain a variety of subgroups with different reasons for attending. Some will have a primarily sporting interest, some a social reason for attending, and in some people the two interests are mixed.

The 'sports priority' spectator group is found in the stands and on the terraces for every game. For them 'live' sport at its highest level has an almost spiritual quality, an attitude aptly expressed in a statement once made by the great Liverpool football manager Bill Shankly: 'Football is not a matter of life and death; it is more important than that'. These fans are knowledgeable, respond instantly to every nuance of the action, offer advice to the players, and recognize the form, fitness and style of individual players and the effectiveness of strategies and tactics. Such issues form the basic topics of conversation

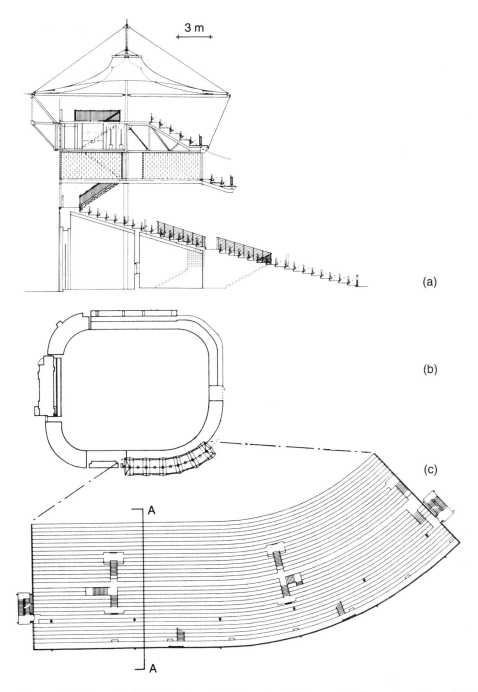

3 m

(a)

(b)

(c)

A

A

Figure 1.18 Lord's Cricket Ground in London is the symbolic centre of world cricket. A variety of stands have been built round the field over many decades with no attempt at a unified style. The Mound Stand was added in 1987. (a) Cross-section A, (b) ground plan and (c) plan of Mound Stand at terrace level. Architects: Michael Hopkins & Partners.

before, during and after the game in the car, pub or train. The motivation and the behaviour of this group sometimes attract negative comment, but this may happen in respect of any group of people sharing some passionate interest – for instance evangelical churchgoers.

The 'social priority' group is found in the clubhouse, dining rooms and private boxes,

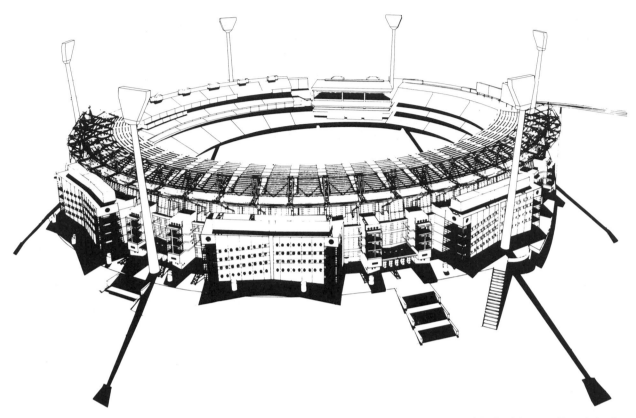

Figure 1.19 Melbourne Cricket Ground in Australia, one of the largest in the world. Architects: Daryl Jackson International.

entertaining or being entertained. The game is 'interesting' but interrupts the personal or business conversations and only briefly becomes the topic of interest. At the end of a game a short post-mortem takes place so that all parties can hint at the depth of their sporting knowledge before resuming the business conversation. This group is usually well dressed because its members will be interacting with other people to whom they must present themselves appropriately, whereas the 'sports priority' group dress casually because their interaction is with the event.

A third group contains elements of the previous two and tends to be fickle: these are the casual supporters who can be persuaded to attend if the conditions are right, but equally easily deterred, as everything depends on their perception of the event. When England was host to the World Cup football, attendances in the UK reached about 29 million per annum, but the figure has declined to around 20 million today. Clubs lose supporters when the team plays poorly, as this group of spectator only attends the game when standards of play are perceived to be high or when 'star' names are playing. These fans are also deterred by discomfort, a perceived risk of violence or lack of safety. Studies carried out well before the disaster at the Hillsborough Stadium in Sheffield (see below) found that football fans in the UK perceived violence from other fans as the most powerful threat to their safety, the risk of being crushed by crowds second and being crushed by mounted police third. All these perceptions will have their effect on attendances.

1.3.2 The player or athlete

After the spectator the next most important person in the stadium is the player or athlete: without these people there is no game or event.

Players' and athletes' needs are covered in chapters 5 and 16, but one matter must be mentioned at this stage because it will influence the proposed stadium in a fundamental way. If players require a natural grass pitch, but other design requirements (such as the need for a multi-use surface, or for a roofed stadium) make a grass surface unviable, then very difficult choices must be made about design priorities.

For some sports a natural grass surface is obligatory – for instance football and rugby. For others it may not be obligatory but is still very much the preferred option for players. In all these cases it is not merely the provision of the grass pitch that is important, but also its condition at time of play. The playing surface is a small ecosystem which actively responds to changes in the environment: it fluctuates in rebound resilience, stiffness and rolling resistance and can alter the trajectory of a bounce or roll so that players talk of the ball 'skidding through' or 'standing up'. All of these minute but critical variations can occur in a relatively short space of time, even during a game. Such uncertainties tend to widen the players' range of skills, both technically and tactically, because they must be sufficiently inventive and responsive to cope with changing conditions. In this way a natural surface may well raise the standard of play, giving a 'bigger stage' for the display of individual talent. But it may be almost impossible to provide a natural grass surface if the brief requires a fully roofed stadium or if the facility requires a multi-use pitch; and in these cases there will be tough decisions to be made.

Such problems are more pressing in Europe and Britain than in North America, partly because the traditional European games of football, rugby and cricket are based on a vigorous interaction between the ball and the playing surface, so that the latter becomes critical, whereas in American football and baseball the ball is kept off the ground at the critical stages of play thus allowing a more tolerant choice of playing surface. American players tend also to be well padded and less likely to suffer injury when falling on a relatively hard surface, whereas lightly clad European players are more vulnerable and have a preference for natural grass. But it is interesting that a preference for natural grass pitches seems to be returning in American football.

For athletics, a synthetic rubber track has become the normal surface with the centre field in grass.

1.3.3 The owner

Assuming players and spectators can be brought together, it falls to the stadium owner to ensure that the physical venue is a going concern – in other words, he must ensure the venue's continued financial viability. As stated in Section 1.1.2 very few stadia produce profits for their owners simply on their sporting functions. In most cases it will be necessary for the planning team to devise a development that will enable the owners to:

- come as close as possible to profitability simply on sporting functions (i.e 'gate income');
- narrow the shortfall by exploiting non-sporting forms of market income ('non-gate income');
- close any remaining gap by means of public funding or other forms of direct subsidy or grant.

Gate income

It will seldom be possible to recoup all costs from 'gate revenue', but this traditionally has been the most important single source of revenue and must be maximized. Investors will require a guaranteed target market of known size and characteristics, a guaranteed number of event days, and a guaranteed cashflow from these sources. To this end:

- An analysis of the market must be made as outlined in Section 1.3.1. It must be established who the stadium is catering for, how many of them there are, how much they will pay, how often they will attend, what are the factors that will attract them, and what are the factors that will deter them.
- Gate revenue can be enhanced by various forms of premium pricing – for instance sale

or rental of private boxes at high prices. The availability of such opportunities should be part of the investigation of the previous item.

- It must be decided which sports types the stadium will cater for. This requires a careful balancing of factors. A facility catering for (say) both football and athletics events will offer the possibility of more 'event days' than one catering for a single sport; but, by trying to accommodate other functions, the facility may be less suitable for its major use, as discussed in Section 1.2.6 above. This is partly because different sports require different pitch sizes and layouts; partly because they require different seating configurations for good sight lines; and partly it is a matter of pitch surface: some sports (like football or rugby) demand a grass surface, but this may be too fragile to stand up to intense use for a variety of sports week after week.
- This question of pitch type also has a bearing on a stadium's overall construction. Just as natural grass is likely to be incompatible with multi-use, so is it also likely to be incompatible with a fully-roofed stadium. Experiments with natural grass under translucent roofs are proceeding, but at present this arrangement is expensive and technically difficult. Where incompatibilities arise and an 'either/or' decision must be taken, priorities will have to be very clear.

Non-gate income

Options for augmenting gate income include sale or rental of hospitality boxes, catering concessions, merchandising concessions, advertising and event sponsorship, media studio rentals, parking rentals and the like. While these can make a vital financial contribution, the planners must not lose their sense of priorities: such forms of income must always be 'supportive', never 'primary'. Increasingly such 'supportive' factors will have a direct influence on stadium design because, for instance, a game watched by 15 000 people from the stands may be watched by 15 million on television – with great cost implications for a sponsor – and these millions must be satisfied. But this influence should not be exerted to the point where the stadium loses its attrac-

tion to its primary patrons – those entering by the gate.

Subsidy

After all the above methods of revenue maximization have been built into the project there may still be a funding shortfall. A final element of support will probably be required from the local municipality, a national grant scheme or elsewhere to make the development viable.

Getting it all together

The key to a successful outcome is clarity of understanding between all concerned. If the stadium developers have a clear understanding of the spectators and players they are aiming for and how to attract them; if the various users have complete clarity about the uses to which the stadium might be put and their compatibility with the stadium design; if the potential providers of a public subsidy and the private developers share the same view of the purpose of the stadium and how it will benefit the local community – then the project may well become a long-term success. But if any of these matters are fudged or left unresolved, or if priorities are put in the wrong order, the stadium is likely to have a very clouded future. Section 5.3 and Chapter 19 deal with some of the above aspects in more detail.

1.3.4 Stadium safety

Safety is such a crucial aspect of the successful stadium that a few paragraphs must be devoted to this subject. Wherever crowds gather, particularly in a context of intense emotion as is the case with sport, mishaps are possible. The wooden stands of the Constantinople Stadium where Roman chariot races were staged were burned down by spectators in 491 AD, 498 AD, 507 AD and finally in 532 AD, when Justinian lost his patience and called in the army to restore order, leading to an estimated 30 000 deaths.

A partial list of recent disasters includes the following:

1996 – 83 people were killed and between 127 and 180 people were injured in a Stadium in Guatemala City when soccer fans stampeded before a World Cup qualifying match. Angry fans kicked down an entrance door, causing spectators inside to cascade down onto the lower levels.

1992 – 17 people were killed in Corsica when a temporary grandstand collapsed in a french Cup semi-final match between Bastia and Marseille.

1991 – 1 person died and 20 were taken to hospital after a stampede when 15 000 fans were allowed into the grounds without tickets just after kick off at Nairobi National Stadium, Kenya.

1991 – 40 people died and 50 were injured after a referee allowed an own goal at a friendly soccer match in Johannesburg, South Africa.

1989 – 95 people died and many were injured during a crowd surge into a restraining fence after kick-off at the Sheffield Hillsborough Stadium, England. (The Lord Justice Taylor Report followed, with a subsequent new edition of the Safety at Sports Grounds Act 1990 and additional tightening of the certification system under the Football Supporters Act 1989 which established the Football Licensing Authority. The football administrators also reacted by setting up the Football Stadia Advisory Design Council in 1991.)

1985 – 38 people died and 100 were injured in a crowd riot at the Heysel Stadium, Belgium.

1985 – 10 people died and 70 were injured in a crush when crowds tried to enter after kick-off through a tunnel which was locked at Mexico University Stadium, Mexico.

1985 – 56 people died and many were badly burnt in a fire at Valley Parade Stadium, Bradford, England. (The Popperwell Inquiry followed, with a subsequent increase in powers under the existing Safety at Sports Grounds Act.)

1982 – 340 people were reported to have died in a crush at Lenin Stadium, Russia.

1979 – 11 people died and many were injured from a 'surge' into a tunnel at a pop concert at Riverfront Stadium, Cincinnati, USA.

1971 – 66 people died after a soccer match at Ibrox Park Stadium, Glasgow, Scotland. (The Wheatley Report followed, with the subsequent Safety at Sports Grounds Act 1975 based upon its findings.)

1964 – 340 people died and 500 were injured after a referee disallowed a goal by the home team in a soccer match in Lima, Peru.

1.4 The future

1.4.1 A new breed of stadium

In view of the many problems facing stadia owners it is easy to see why future stadia will differ from those of the past.

One such change will probably be a trend towards combinations of sports clubs using the same facility, instead of just one club (hitherto the predominant pattern in the UK), thus spreading the burden of construction and maintenance costs. Such shared use is already seen on the continent of Europe. In Italy for instance the Inter-Milan and AC Milan clubs, who are intense rivals on the playing field, share the huge San Siro Stadium (which was extensively modernized for the 1990 World Cup). In the UK, the new Sir Alfred McAlpine Stadium at Huddersfield was the first major venue to accommodate both football and rugby league.

Another trend could be that clubs who wish to improve their grounds will begin to act more aggressively as developers and will finance new facilities either by the sale of surplus land, or by including explicitly 'commercial' uses as suggested in Table 1.2. Good management can increase revenue by exploiting each part of the facility for more than one purpose, a strategy sometimes referred to as 'multi-use' but actually just a matter of maximizing the return from investment. Table 1.2 is only a broadbrush summary of the 'primary' and 'secondary' uses

Table 1.2 Possible multi-purpose uses of sports stadia

Playing area		Support facilities		Additional facilities	
Primary	*Secondary*	*Primary*	*Secondary*	*Primary*	*Secondary*
Football	Concerts	Restaurant	Banquets	Health club	Offices
Tennis	Conventions	Bar	Parties	Other sports	Retail
Rugby	Exhibitions	Private box	Meetings	Hotel	Cinemas
Cricket	Other sports	Lounges	Conventions	Sports retail	Residential

Note: The above are only broad indications of options to be investigated. For actual design it will be necessary to undertake detailed studies using specialist advisers.

which may be possible. More detailed notes will be found in Chapter 10.

If any of these approaches are to be successful in the long term the key to their success will be good creative management. Once stadia management is recognized as a specialist field, as it is beginning to be in the USA, and attracts the best people to the job, it will change the form of stadia for ever. New management ideas are emerging, for instance the concept of added-value tickets, where additional privileges are provided to encourage the whole family to attend. These privileges can include meals, bus rides from outer areas and signed programmes. Family enclosures, which have gained popularity in the UK, are also a relatively new but important trend. Child-minding facilities, baby-changing rooms, family cinemas, museums, tea lounges, quality restaurants with high-chairs and children's play areas are also important to encourage family attendance but very few of these are found in today's stadia. Any facility which attracts a wider cross-section of the family should eventually reap financial rewards, because it is by the inclusion of the whole community that the spectators of tomorrow will be created.

1.4.2 New technology

Technology which is revolutionizing the rest of society will also inevitably find its way into the sporting world. We already expect races to be timed to hundredths of a second, blood samples to be analysed down to particles per million and video play-backs provided instantly. This is only the tip of the technological iceberg. We are already benefiting from improved and faster construction techniques allowing opening roofs, moving seating tiers and soon moving playing areas. The line between natural grass and synthetic pitches may merge with developments in plastic mesh root reinforcement, plastic turf support and plastic granular growing mediums with computer controlled nutrient injection. New hybrid grass types require less light, grow faster and are far more robust. These advances allow a greater number of different types of events to take place in the same venue, making the venue more financially viable.

Sight lines for most modern stadia are calculated on computer; and creation of three dimensional computer models of stadia will allow spectators to see exactly the view they will have from their seat at the time of booking.

The real advances however will be in communication and information technology which will provide the spectator in the stadium with all the advantages of the viewer at home watching the event on television. There can be no guarantee that future generations will find live sport as attractive as the present generation and the move to provide better information to the spectator is essential if attendance at events is to be maintained. Ticket prices are increasing and conditions are often deteriorating while it is relatively free to sit at home and watch the television in comfort. The old argument that only the major events are televised is true at present but with the advent of cable and satellite television more and more sport will be televised. Sport is a comparatively cheap television programme to produce and almost always finds support – for example, the increase in the snooker and bowls audiences in the UK after television decided to cover them on a regular basis.

One answer must be to compete with television on equal terms and, as well as offering facilities at the stadium which are as comfortable, convenient and safe as our own homes, also offer information equal to the professional broadcasters. Replays and information about players and previous matches should be automatic but so should highlights of other events, statistics on the game, expert commentary and perhaps even revenue-generating advertisements. This 'narrowcasting' will be by the stadium's own closed-circuit television (CCTV) network, not just to large video screens but also to small personal receivers with screens a few inches across. These receivers could be part of the ticket price or on hire for the day and would only receive the stadium channel, probably with ear phones and eventually with interactive controls allowing a choice of information. Press the button marked 'statistics', type in your favourite player's name and the career statistics will be displayed; press 'action', type in the date of the match and see the highlights of his match winning performance two years ago.

All this is possible now. The horse racing industry around the world is tending to lead the field, probably because of the large betting revenues which are at stake at racecourses. Pools revenue is also enormous with the annual total in the UK on football alone in the order of two thousand million pounds. In Asia the Hong Kong Jockey Club has developed its own handheld betting device which is about the size of a television remote control and allows the spectator to place a bet on any horse in any race whilst also providing the latest betting information. Their next step is to show the race on the same piece of pocketable equipment.

Technology will revolutionize the management of stadia. Conventional turnstiles may well be phased out in the early part of the twenty-first century and sports clubs will benefit from an 'intelligent' entrance gate linked to the stadium computer system. From these access points,

which will probably look more like the X-ray machines used at airports, full details will be read from the spectator's active pass. Each pass will allow the person access to different areas of the grounds and entitle the holder to other predetermined benefits. The pass will be scanned by monitors at each access or sales point, if the pass is invalid for any reason a warning will sound and the holder advised by synthesized voice of where to go to seek help. The automatic barriers in front which are usually open will close if the person attempts to proceed any further.

In addition to this automatic access and sales control, the computer will store information on the spectators who attend each event including age, sex, address and event preferences. From this data bank of information the club or stadium management will be able to form an exact profile of who attends which events, allowing them to target that exact socio-economic group the next time a similar event is held. This knowledge of the spectator is essential for future marketing; it is amazing how few stadium administrators today can tell you the exact socio-economic profile of the people who attend their venue or even simple statistics like the ratio of male to female spectators. In the future this will be essential information for the survival of the venue.

Technology will be used to improve our comfort level. Seats can be warmed by low voltage trace heating elements or chemical reaction tubes, perhaps even in the concrete structure itself. Cooling can be by chilled air outlets below the seats from high pressure chilled pipes and local fans. Even the seats will be different, being ergonomically designed with soft graded plastics. These will give the effect of a padded seat but in a seamless and therefore weather-proof shell. In one arm will be the sockets for plugging in personal headsets to listen to 'Stadium Radio' or 'Stadium Television' if the receiver is hired. As the average population size increases the seat spacing will also increase and allow for slight adjustment of seat backs to suit the individual spectator. Pockets on the back of the seat in front will contain the free 'Stadium Catalogue' advertising products on

Figure 1.20 The Atlanta Olympic stadium had a configuration for the 1996 Olympics and a post-Olympic configuration for baseball. Architects: Heery Corporation.

sale by post or from the Stadium Retail Centre. Items may be ordered using the hand-held receiver hired for the day, purchases can either be waiting for you at the shop at the end of the match or delivered to your seat at half time.

Support facilities will increase providing amenities for all the family to enjoy as well as other entertainment areas for those not committed to the game. They will eventually include every type of function from business centres to bowling alleys, similar to the range of facilities often found in international airports today. Attractions will be designed to encourage spectators to arrive early and then stay on afterwards perhaps even sleeping overnight in the Stadium Hotel. Tomorrow's stadia will be places of entertainment for the family where sport is the focus but not the complete picture. It will be possible for five members of a family to arrive and leave together but in the intervening period experience five different activities. While the parents 'see' the live game their children 'experience' the live game in the virtual reality studio where images from the 'in pitch' cameras provide close immediate action.

2

Masterplanning

2.1 The need for a masterplan

2.1.1 Basic principles

Sports complexes are often constructed over a period of years (or even decades) for reasons of finance, natural growth or land availability. To help ensure that the ultimate development is consistent in terms of aesthetic quality and functional efficiency, and to avoid abortive work, a comprehensive plan for the entire development should be evolved at the very outset. This allows successive phases of the development to be carried out by different committees or boards over a period of time in the safe knowledge that their particular phase will be consistent with the whole.

As one example of the kind of planning that is involved, Figure 2.1 shows in schematic form the 20-year masterplan drawn up in 1993 for the All

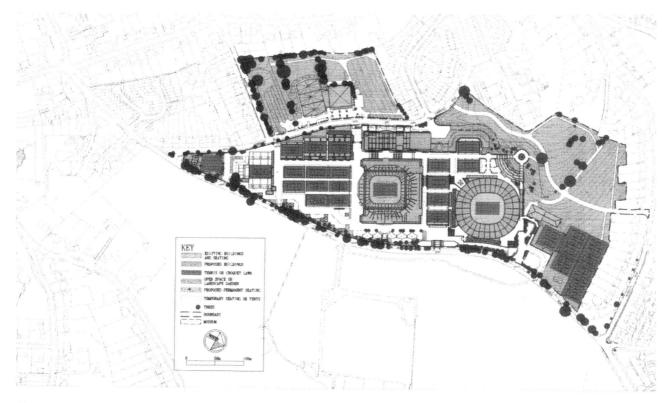

Figure 2.1 The 1993 20-year masterplan for the All England Lawn Tennis and Croquet Club, Wimbledon, in schematic form.

England Lawn Tennis and Croquet Club. The objectives of this plan were to provide for better tennis watching, better facilities, a better ambience, and benefits for the site's neighbours (such as less congestion in surrounding streets).

The art of planning large stadium sites hinges on the correct zoning of the available land and the separation of incompatible uses which must be accommodated within the site boundaries. These uses include not only the direct sporting functions but also very substantial parking areas, pedestrian and vehicular circulation routes, etc.

2.1.2 Sequence of decisions

All design must set out from the following determining factors.

Pitch/central area

The starting point of design is the central area or playing field. Its shape, dimensions and orientation must enable it to fulfil all the functions required of it (see Chapter 5).

Seating capacity

Next comes the seating capacity. If the pitch is to be of variable size to cater for very different activities then the design capacity should be stated as two figures: the number of seats around the *maximum* pitch size (perhaps football or athletics) and the maximum capacity around the *smallest* space user (perhaps the performers in a pop concert, or a boxing ring). The stadium owners will have very strong views on seating capacities as these form the basis of their profitability calculations.

Orientation

Pitch orientation must be suitable for the events to be staged (see Section 2.2 below), and the masterplan must be structured around this.

Zoning

Finally, a discipline for the arrangement of all the elements of the stadium, from the pitch at the centre to the parking spaces outside, is provided by the need for safety zoning as explained in Section 2.3 below.

2.2 Orientation

2.2.1 Design factors

The orientation of the playing field will depend on the uses to which it will be put, the main factors being:

- the hemisphere in which the stadium is located;
- the period of the year in which the designated sports will be played;
- the times of day these events will be played;
- specific local environmental conditions such as wind direction.

All the advice below applies to open stadia in temperate zones in the northern hemisphere, and readers should make the necessary adjustments for stadia in other situations.

2.2.2 Football and rugby

Football and rugby in Europe are played during the autumn and winter months, in the early afternoon. This means that the sun is low in the sky and moving from south-south-west to west. An ideal orientation for the playing area is to have its longitudinal axis running north–south, or perhaps northwest–southeast. With these orientations the sun will be at the side of the stadium during play, and the early morning sun will fall on the greatest area of the pitch, thus helping any frost in the ground to thaw before play commences. Figure 2.2 summarizes the situation.

2.2.3 American football and baseball

The sun should be at the side of the pitch during play. This suits the players, the spectators and the TV cameras.

2.2.4 Athletics

Field and track sports in Europe take place mostly during the summer and autumn months. Runners and hurdlers approaching the finishing line should not have the sun in their eyes and

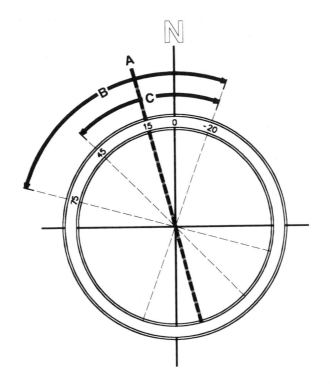

Figure 2.2 Recommended pitch orientations in northern Europe for principal sports. The underlying principle is that runners in athletics and sportsmen in ball games should never have the late afternoon sun in their eyes. A – Best common axis of orientation for many sports. B – Range acceptable for football and rugby. C – Best range for track and field and pitch games.

nor, ideally, should spectators. The ideal orientation in the northern hemisphere is for the longitudinal axis of the track to run 15 degrees west of north (Figure 2.2). The same applies to the stadium, which should be situated on the same side as the home straight and as close to the finish line as possible.

Sometimes it is difficult to achieve the above track orientations while also conforming with the requirements for wind direction. Where possible, alternative directions should therefore be provided for running, jumping and throwing events.

2.2.5 Tennis

The longitudinal axis of the court should run north–south. Diverging by up to 22 or 23 degrees in either direction is acceptable, and diverging by 45 degrees is the limit. If matches are to be played in early morning or late evening the orientation becomes more critical.

2.3 Zoning

2.3.1 Planning for safety

Having set the orientation the next priority is to plan the position of the stadium on the site, and to start thinking about the interrelationship of its major parts; and this is best done by identifying the four zones which make up the safety plan (Figure 2.3). The size and location of these zones are critical to the performance of the stadium in an emergency, and they are:

Zone 1   the activity area (that is the central area and/or pitch on which the games take place).

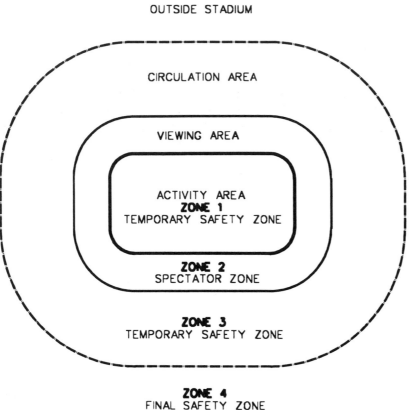

OUTSIDE STADIUM

CIRCULATION AREA

VIEWING AREA

ACTIVITY AREA
ZONE 1
TEMPORARY SAFETY ZONE

ZONE 2
SPECTATOR ZONE

ZONE 3
TEMPORARY SAFETY ZONE

ZONE 4
FINAL SAFETY ZONE

Figure 2.3 Zoning diagram showing the four 'safety zones' which form the basis for a safe stadium.

Zone 2   the spectator terraces and concourses surrounding the activity area.

Zone 3   the circulation area surrounding the stadium structure and separating it from the perimeter fence.

Zone 4   the open space outside the perimeter fence and separating it from the car parks.

The purpose of such zoning is to allow spectators to escape from their seats, in an emergency, to a series of intermediate safety zones leading ultimately to a place of permanent safety outside. It provides a clear and helpful framework for design not only for new stadia but also for the refurbishment of existing facilities.

A tragic example is provided by the fire which killed 56 people at the Valley Parade Stadium in Bradford, UK in 1985. The stand was an old one, built of framing and timber steppings. On

11 May 1985 a fire started in the accumulated litter under the steppings and spread rapidly through the antiquated structure. Most spectators fled from the stands (Zone 2) to the open pitch (Zone 1) and were safe; but many made their way back through the stand towards the gates by which they had entered. Because there was no Zone 3 in the Valley Parade Stadium these gates formed the perimeter between the stadium and the outside world and management took the view that they needed to be secure – therefore the escaping spectators found them locked. Hundreds of people were trapped here, the fire and smoke soon caught up with them, and 56 people died.

Two lessons came out of this experience, one for managers and one for designers.

- Managers must ensure that gates offering escape from the spectator terraces to places of safety must be manned at all times when the stadium is in use, and easily openable to let spectators escape in case of emergency.

- Designers must recognize that management procedures such as the above can never be foolproof, and the stadium must be designed on the assumption of management failure. There should, where possible, be a Zone 3 *within* the outer perimeter to which spectators can escape and where they will be safe even if the perimeter gates are locked, cutting them off from the outside world.

More detailed design notes follow below, starting with Zone 4 (the area of 'permanent safety') and proceeding to Zone 1 (a place of 'temporary safety').

2.3.2 Zone 4

The stadium should ideally be surrounded by car parks, bus parks and access to transport. The car park (well-designed, to avoid bleakness) should ideally surround the stadium on all sides so that spectators can park their cars on the same side of the stadium as their seats and then walk straight to an entrance gate and to their individual seats without having to circumnavigate.

Between this ring of parking areas and the stadium perimeter there should be a vehicle-free zone usually described as Zone 4, which can serve several useful purposes:

- From the point of view of safety, it is a so-called 'permanent' safety zone to which spectators can escape from the stands via Zone 3, and safely remain until the emergency has been dealt with. It should be possible to accommodate the whole of the stadium population here at a density of 4 to 6 people per square metre.
- From the point of view of everyday circulation, Zone 4 provides a belt of space in which spectators may circumnavigate the stadium to get from one entrance gate to another, assuming their first choice of gate was wrong (see Section 13.3.1). Every effort should be made to ensure that people are directed from their cars (or other points of arrival) to the appropriate gate for their particular seat, but

mistakes will always be made and there should be an easy route round the stadium to allow for this.

- Retail points, meeting points and information boards can also very usefully be located in this zone of open space. To serve this social function the surface and its fittings (kiosks, information boards, etc.) should be pleasantly designed, not left as a bleak band of tarmac.
- The above point can be taken further with Zone 4 serving as a pleasantly landscaped buffer zone between the 'event' and the outside world. Stadium performances (whether they be sport, music or general entertainment) are essentially escapist, and their enjoyment can be heightened by visually disconnecting the audience from the workaday outside environment.

2.3.3 Zone 3

The stadium perimeter will form the security line across which no one may pass without a valid ticket. Between this line of control and the actual stadium structure is Zone 3, which may have two functions:

- From the point of view of safety, it is a place of 'temporary safety' to which spectators may escape directly from the stadium, and from which they can then proceed to permanent safety in Zone 4. It is therefore a kind of reservoir between Zones 2 and 4. If the pitch (Zone 1) is *not* designated as a temporary safety zone, then Zone 3 should be large enough to accommodate the whole stadium population at a density of 4 to 6 people per square metre. But if Zone 1 is so designated Zone 3 may be reduced appropriately. In all cases the number of exit gates, and their dimensions, must allow the necessary ease and speed of egress from one zone to another (see Section 13.6).
- From the point of view of everyday circulation, Zone 3 is the main circumnavigation route for people inside the stadium perimeter (i.e. who have surrendered their tickets and passed the control points).

The importance of Zone 3 can be seen from the Valley Parade fire. Because that stadium had no such zone, management felt that the link between Zones 2 and 4 had to be secure. The gates were therefore locked, inadequately supervised, and many people died horribly. Had there been a Zone 3 and good signposting many lives could have been saved even with the outer gates being locked.

2.3.4 Zone 2

This comprises the viewing terraces, the internal concourses, and the social areas (restaurants, bars, etc.). It is the zone which must be evacuated in case of emergency, and is situated between Zones 1 and 3. It must be designed for easy and safe escape from each individual seat, first to a place of temporary safety (Zones 1 or 3) and thence to permanent safety (Zone 4).

There is often a second line of security between Zones 2 and 3 where tickets are checked, with perhaps a final check inside Zone 2 for individual seat position, and there will often be a fence or moat along the inner periphery, where the stands meet the pitch (see below). These barriers must not impede people trying to flee from a fire or other emergency.

2.3.5 Zone 1

The pitch or event space forms the very centre of the stadium. Along with Zone 3 it can serve the additional purpose of being a place of temporary safety, on the following conditions:

- The escape routes from the seating areas to the pitch must be suitably designed – i.e. escape will not be an easy matter if there is a barrier separating pitch and seating terraces (see Chapter 6).
- The surface material of the pitch must be taken into account. The heat in the Valley Parade fire was so intense that clothing of the police and spectators standing on the grass pitch ignited: had the pitch been covered with a synthetic material that too might have ignited. These matters must be thoroughly discussed with the fire authorities at design stage and it must be ensured that management cannot take decisions many years later to change the pitch surfacing without being aware of the implications for safety.

2.3.6 Barriers between zones

In all cases the number of exit gates, and their dimensions, must allow the necessary ease and speed of egress from one zone to another. The principles involved are given in Section 13.6.

2.4 Conclusion

The matters above represent merely the first few decisions in a process that will ultimately involve hundreds of design judgements. But these are controlling decisions, and once they have been rationally made there should be regular checks to ensure that the evolving design never contradicts or moves away from them.

3

External planning

3.1 Location

3.1.1 Past and current trends

Traditionally the sports stadium was a modest facility with a capacity of perhaps a few hundred, serving a small local community and forming part of the social fabric along with the church, town hall and drinking house.

As communities grew larger and more mobile, with ordinary people able and willing to travel great distances to follow their favourite sports, stadia became larger and much of the new capacity was needed specifically for visiting spectators. The presence of multitudes of 'away' supporters created problems in crowd control for which no one (whether the local communities, their police forces, or stadium managers) was adequately prepared. We tend to think of this as a recent problem, but it goes back many decades. Evidence can be found in any book of social history, or in an account such as this, made all the more astonishing by its source:

along the track . . . were returning coaches. We conscientiously demolished them with stones. We had broken everything breakable in our own train. The trains that followed, hastily pressed into service and waiting behind us in a straggling queue, were inspired by our methods. We also demolished the signals. Towards four o'clock the massed officials of the suburbs mobilised the firemen to intimidate us . . . the mob, one knows, generally becomes inspired when it is necessary to take action. As our train did not leave and other trains arrived in the night, filled with would-be spectators . . . we set to work to demolish the station. The station at Juvisy was a big one. The waiting rooms went first, then the station-master's office . . .

The passage describes events at an aircraft show in France in 1933 and was written by the famous architectural visionary, le Corbusier.[1] Even allowing for the habitual hyperbole of the author it shows that the destructive impulse which may arise in crowds of otherwise civilized sporting fans is, alas, nothing new.

Crowd control proceeded on a 'trial and error' basis, and many mistakes were made; but we have finally begun to evolve a more systematic understanding which can be applied both to the design of stadia and their management. The lessons for stadium design are incorporated in the various chapters of this book; but an additional response has been a locational one – to move major stadia away from town centres to open land on the town periphery.

Large out-of-town stadia

A major trend of the 1960s and 1970s was the building of large stadia on out-of-town locations where crowds, whether well or badly behaved, would create less disturbance to the everyday lives of people not attending events. Such locations would also reduce land costs and increase ease of access by private car. The largest developments of this kind are to be seen in Germany, where advantage was taken of post-war reconstruction opportunities, and in the USA, where high personal mobility and the availability of open land made it easier to locate

[1] *Aircraft*, Le Corbusier, Trefoil Publications, London.

stadia away from the communities they were meant to serve and provide the amount of car parking required. Leading examples of a cross-section of types include:

- The Astrodome at Houston, 1964, a dome stadium for both football and baseball. It seats 66 000 spectators for concerts, 52 000 for football and 45 000 for baseball. There are 28 000 parking spaces in total.
- The Arrowhead and Royals Stadia at Kansas City (Figure 3.1), 1973, a complex which provides separate facilities for football and baseball. Arrowhead Stadium for baseball seats 71 000 spectators and the Royals Stadium for football seats 41 000. There are parking spaces for 24 000 cars and 300 buses.
- The Giants Stadium at New Jersey (Figure 3.2), 1976, is a dedicated stadium for football only and seats 76 700 spectators. It has parking spaces for 30 000 cars and 400 buses.

These stadia tended to cater for a variety of activities to make them financially viable, had huge spectator capacities, and were surrounded by acres of car parking. They were built in a period when spectator sports were attracting markedly increased followings, probably owing to the influence of television; but even so they found it difficult to show a profit. Recovering their vast development costs would have been problematical anyway, but there were two aggravating factors. First, television coverage had improved to the point where people could stay at home and follow the action very satisfactorily in their living rooms; and second, the stadia of the late 1970s and early 1980s were all too often barren places with little by way of spectator comforts.

There was also a growing number of violent incidents in various parts of the world (resulting from crowd misbehaviour, fire or structural collapse) which probably reinforced people's growing preference to watch from the comfort and safety of their living rooms.

Large in-town stadia

The next significant step in the development of the stadium occurred in 1989 with the opening of the Toronto Skydome in Ontario, Canada. The public authorities in Toronto had recognized the problems of out-of-town sites and decided to take a brave step by building their new stadium in the very centre of their lakeside city (Figure 3.3).

The stadium is within walking distance of most of the city centre and uses much of the transport and social infrastructure of Toronto. They had also learned the lesson of poorly serviced facilities and incorporated many spectator services designed to enhance comfort and security.

But in spite of all these efforts, and an ingenious funding arrangement, Skydome's financial viability has unfortunately proved no better than previous attempts – see Section 1.1.2.

Current trends

In Britain, following an inquiry by Lord Justice Taylor into the disaster at the Hillsborough Stadium in Sheffield (where 95 people died in a crowd surge) there has been a formal report recommending major changes to sports stadia to improve their safety. This document has caused many British clubs to question whether it would be best to redevelop their existing, mostly in-town grounds or to relocate to new sites out of town with all the transport and planning problems entailed. Existing in-town sites have the advantages of being steeped in tradition and being situated in the communities on whose support they depend, but the disadvantage of being so physically hemmed in that it may be difficult or impossible to provide the safety, comfort and variety of facilities which are necessary. There are proving to be numerous town-planning difficulties in finding new sites.

The situation elsewhere in the world is equally ambiguous. Everywhere there is a preoccupation with the intractable problems of financial viability, everywhere there is pressure towards greater comfort and greater safety, and everywhere the refurbishment of old stadia is gaining ground . . . but these vague generalizations are about the only 'trends' that can currently be identified.

Figure 3.1 The Arrowhead and Royals Stadium at Kansas City overcomes the difficulty of providing good viewing for the contrasting configurations of baseball and football by giving each sport its own dedicated stadium. Architects: Charles Deaton, Golden in association with Kivett & Myers.

3.1.2 Locational factors

Today it is technically feasible to build a safe, comfortable and functionally efficient stadium in any location (town centre, open countryside, or anywhere in between) provided that there is sufficient land and that the stadium's use is compatible with the surrounding environment. The deciding factors are itemized in the following paragraphs.

Client base

Any stadium must be easily accessible to its 'client base' – the people whose attendance will

Figure 3.2 The Giants Stadium at New Jersey caters only for American football. The two major tiers, separated by a 'club level concourse' for private boxes and press seats, is characteristic of recent American stadia. Architects: Howard Needles Tammen & Bergendoff (HNTB).

generate the projected revenues; this is usually the primary motive for looking at a particular site. To test feasibility a careful analysis must be made of who the projected customers are, how many they are, where they live, and how they are to get to the stadium. All these criteria must be satisfied by the proposed stadium location.

Land availability
A new stadium can require around 15 acres of reasonably flat land just for the stadium and ancillary facilities, plus car parking space at 25 square metres per car (see Section 3.3.1). It may be difficult to find this amount of space.

Land cost
Land costs must be kept to a minimum and this is why sports facilities are frequently built on low-grade land such as refuse tips or reclaimed land that is too poor for residential or industrial use (but which may then lead to additional structural costs as noted in Section 4.5.1).

Land use regulations
Local or regional planning legislation must be checked to ensure that the proposed development will be allowed in that area.

3.1.3 The future

Taking all these factors together, wholly independent, stand-alone stadia may increasingly have to share their sites with commercial and retail complexes. Examples of such developments include:

- in the USA, the Hoosier Dome in Indianapolis of 1972;
- in Canada, the Skydome in Toronto (Figure 3.3) of 1989;
- in the Netherlands, the Galgenwaard Stadium in Utrecht (Figure 3.4);
- in Norway, the Ulleval Stadium of 1991;
- in the UK, the Sir Alfred McAlpine Stadium in Huddersfield, West Yorkshire. This state-of-the-art 25 000-seat stadium will cater for both football and rugby and share its site with a 60-bedroom hotel, a 500-seat banqueting hall, a golf driving range and dry ski slope, and numerous shopping and eating facilities. Figure 3.5 shows the site layout.

3.2 Transportation

3.2.1 Spectator requirements

If the journeys involved in getting to a sporting event seem excessively difficult or time-consuming, the potential spectator may well decide not to bother – particularly if alternative attractions are available, as tends to be the case nowadays. There may be a sequence of journeys involved, not necessarily just the journey from home on the morning of the match. This sequence may start from the moment when the decision is taken to buy a ticket, possibly weeks or months before the event, and involving pre-planning the actual match day with details such as:

Figure 3.3 In contrast to the previous three out-of-town examples the Skydome is in the very centre of Toronto. Architects: Rob Robbie. Engineer for roof, Michael Allen.

- Will I be travelling with a friend or on my own?
- Will I be travelling by car, bus or train?
- Where will the transport leave from, and when?
- How do I get to and from the transport?
- What are the things which can go wrong with the above arrangements, and what alternatives do I have?

The transport infrastructure of a major stadium should offer ways of getting to (and away from) an event which are relatively quick, unconfused and trouble-free, otherwise attendance and revenues will undoubtedly suffer.

3.2.2 Public transport

Any large stadium should be close to a well-served railway and/or metro station, preferably with paved and clearly defined access all the way to the stadium gate. If the stadium cannot be located near to an existing station, it may be possible to come to a financial arrangement with the transportation authorities whereby they open a dedicated station for the stadium. In the UK this is the case with the existing Watford and Arsenal football stadia, and it is hoped that a new metro station may be established as part of the development plan for the Wimbledon Tennis Court complex in London.

Figure 3.4 The Galgenwaard stadium in Utrecht combines shops and other commercial uses, located in the corners and on the street side, with the sports function.

3.2.3 The road system

The road system must allow easy access into, around and out of a major stadium complex. There must not only be adequate roads, but also adequate electronic monitoring and control systems to ensure that any build-up of traffic congestion in the approach roads can be identified well in advance and dealt with by police and traffic authorities (see Section 17.2.1).

3.2.4 Information systems

Before major events, advice can be mailed to spectators with their tickets and car parking passes; some information can be printed on the tickets themselves. In the run-up to the event, information giving the choice of routes and the most convenient methods of transport should be thoroughly publicized via local, regional or national media (including radio, television and the press).

On the day of a major event every effort should be made to ensure an orderly traffic flow. Local radio and newspapers can be used to illustrate preferred routes and potential problem areas. Dedicated road signs, whether permanent or temporary, should start some distance away from the stadium and become increasingly frequent and detailed as the visitor approaches the venue. Near to the stadium information and directions should be particularly plentiful and

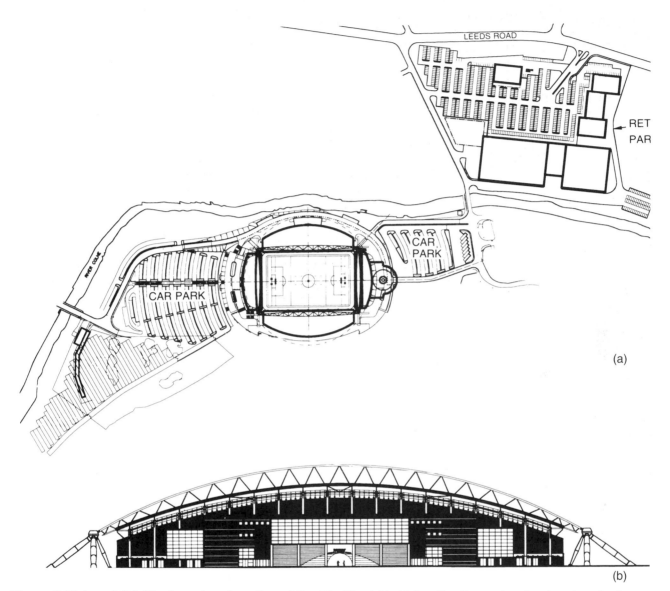

Figure 3.5(a) and (b) Site layout and section of the Sir Alfred McAlpine Stadium, showing hotel and other commercial facilities facing on to Leeds Road. Architects: HOK + LOBB.

clear with 'close-in' information indicating whether car parks are full, and identifying meeting points and train and bus stations. The same amount of effort should be made to ensure a smooth flow of people and cars away from the stadium after the event: it cannot be assumed that people will find their own way out, and a clear sequence of exit directions should be signposted.

3.3 Provision of parking

3.3.1 Types of provision

Parking is most convenient if located in the area immediately surrounding the stadium, and at the same level as the exits/entrances. But this tends to be an inefficient use of land – which is both scarce and expensive in urban areas – and the vast expanses of tarmac have a deadening effect on the surrounding environment unless extremely skilfully handled. Four alternative solutions follow.

Multi-level car parking

Building the stadium over a covered car park, as in Cincinatti in the USA or the Louis IV Stadium in Monte Carlo, helps to reduce the amount of land required and avoids the barren expanses of car park. But such a solution is very expensive and its viability may depend on the next option.

Shared parking with other facilities

A stadium may share parking space with adjacent offices or industrial buildings as at Utrecht, or even (as is the case with Aston Villa Football Club in Birmingham, UK) with superstores or shopping complexes. But problems will arise if both facilities need the parking space at the same time. This is quite likely in the case of shops and supermarkets which stay open in the evenings and at weekends. In the case of Aston Villa there is a condition in the agreement that the store cannot open during first team home matches. Therefore careful planning is required.

On-street parking

This is not encouraged by the authorities. However, stadium sites in green parkland (like Cologne) can allow parking to be distributed over a large area.

Park and ride

This term refers to car parking provided at a distance from the venue, with some kind of shuttle service ferrying spectators between the parking area and the stadium. It is mainly used on the continent of Europe, especially in Germany. In the UK, Silverstone motor racing circuit and Cheltenham racecourse have helicopter park and ride services, both of which are usually fully booked.

3.3.2 Access roads

It is essential to provide the right number of parking spaces and to ensure that they are efficiently accessed, because nothing is more likely to deter visitors from returning than lengthy traffic jams before or after an event. There must be a clear system of routes all the way from the public highways via feeder roads into the parking area, and an equally clear way out. Arrivals will probably be fairly leisurely, possibly spread over a period of two hours or more before start time, whereas most spectators will try to get away as quickly as possible after the event. Such traffic patterns must be anticipated and planned for. It may also be possible to change these patterns of use. For instance, visitors can be enticed to stay longer and leave more gradually, thus reducing traffic congestion, by providing restaurants and other social facilities and by showing entertainment programmes on the video screens before and after the event (see Chapters 9 and 10 and Section 17.2.2).

Parking spaces, and the routes feeding them, must not encroach on areas required for emergency evacuation of the stadium, or for fire engines, ambulances, police vehicles, etc.

3.3.3 Spectator parking

Vehicular parking can account for more than half the total site, and the quantity and quality of parking provided will depend on the types of spectators attending. Table 3.1 gives data for a variety of existing stadia – not as guidelines to be followed, but purely to give a 'feel' of provision that may be required in various situations.

In the USA, where the shift from public transportation to travel by private car has gone furthest, the trend has been towards stadia located out of town, not served by any significant public transportation network but surrounded by huge expanses of parking spaces.

In Europe, by contrast, most stadia are well served by public transport. Land is not easily available for large parking lots and it is quite common in European cities, where the majority of European stadia are still located, for only a handful of parking spaces to be provided for officials and for there to be no on-site parking for fans. A rural facility, such as the UK's Silverstone Circuit for motor racing, which

Table 3.1 Examples of car parking provision at major stadia

Stadium and city	Capacity	Number of car parking spaces	Number of coach spaces	Comments
North America				
Skydome, Toronto	68 000	775	Not stated	This is an inner city stadium and 17 000 additional parking spaces are available within the city core. But most spectators use public transport. A covered walkway links Skydome with the central railway station.
Hubert H Humphrey Metrodome, Minneapolis	63 000	500	Not stated	There are an additional 23 500 parking spaces within a 20-minute walk of the stadium.
Arrowhead and Royals Stadia, Kansas City	71 000 (Arrowhead) 41 000 (Royals)	24 000 shared by both stadia	300	The parking has proved rather limited for large crowds and Arrowhead stadium managers now think that a ratio of one car per 2.5 to 3.0 spectators would have been more suitable.
Atlanta-Fulton County Stadium, Atlanta	60 748	6500	Not stated	
Houston Astrodome, Houston	66 000	28 000	Not stated	
Joe Robbie Stadium, Miami	73 000	15 000	Not stated	The 15 000 reserved spaces on the site are augmented by off-site parking. It is stated that 'off-site parking is limited, and fans without reserved spaces have experienced problems'
Lousiana Superdome	95 000	5000	Not stated	
Europe				
Bari Stadium	55 000	9000	158	There is a bus service
Turin	70 000	4000	100	There are fast tram and bus services
Munich	69 300	4500 (including coaches)		There are two rail links plus bus routes
United Kingdom				
Wembley Stadium London	80 000	7500	50 (approx)	There are two metro lines, one rail link, bus routes, and park and ride.

Note: Figures for the various stadia may be based on different criteria. Direct comparisons can therefore not be made.

caters for 98 000 spectators and provides parking for 50 000 cars, is definitely the exception.

In the design of a new stadium parking requirements for spectators should be estimated from an analysis of the following considerations.

Stadium seating capacity

It would be wasteful to provide car parking for every seat in the stadium as the maximum seating capacity will only rarely be achieved. A 'design capacity' should be calculated by assessing a typical programme of events over a season, and estimating a typical attendance for each event.

Programme and types of events

Each event type generates its own particular pattern of demand for parking. Some spectators will come by public transport, some by private car and some by specially hired fleets of coaches; the ratios between them will vary from one type of event to another (in the UK, for instance, national football club finals are likely to draw a higher proportion of coach travellers). The amount of parking space required will therefore be based upon:

- The ratios between the various categories.
- The occupancy rate of coaches and cars. It may be estimated, for example, that an average car carries 2.5 people and an average coach 50 or more.
- The amount of parking space needed per car or coach. As more fully described below, car parking may require about one hectare per 50 cars, and coach parking perhaps one hectare per 10 coaches.

By researching the above data for a particular stadium and multiplying the various factors a reasonable 'design capacity' and parking area may be deduced.

Rival demands for parking space

Some of the available parking spaces may occasionally be taken out for other uses, for instance by television service coaches, which must be parked immediately adjacent to the stadium (see Section 14.2.1). As many as ten vehicles, needing standing spaces of up to 12 m by 4 m each plus working space, may be needed for several days at a stretch. This may greatly reduce the planned car parking capacity near the stadium.

Cars: public parking

For preliminary estimation purposes, and subject to the computations suggested above, the following formulae may be helpful:

- a minimum of one parking space to every 10 to 15 spectators;
- if FIFA recommendations are to be followed, one space to every six spectators;
- if recent German recommendations are to be followed, one space to every four spectators. It must be said that this will very seldom be possible in European urban situations.

An area of about 25 square metres per car (including circulation space) may be assumed in the UK and Europe. Exact dimensions will depend on national codes of practice.

Cars: private parking

Private box holders and their guests, VIPs and similar private visitors should have special clearly identified parking areas, separate from the mass parking, and close to the entrances giving access to private hospitality suites (see Chapter 9).

Buses and coaches

FIFA suggests one bus space per 120 spectators, but this is quite an onerous standard and will in any case depend on other factors (for example number of cars expected and access to public transportation); we suggest that one bus per 240 spectators may be quite reasonable for preliminary estimation purposes.

An area of 60 square metres per bus (including circulation space) may be assumed in the UK and Europe.

Motorcycles and bicycles

Provision will depend very much on national and local characteristics and must be determined as part of the brief. The demand for bicycle parking is likely to be greatest in Asian countries, very much less in the UK and Europe, and least in North America and Australasia.

Spectators with disabilities

In the absence of more specific requirements one per cent of car parking spaces should be set aside for spectators with disabilities. These should be the spaces closest to the stadium entrance gates, with easy access to ramped pedestrian routes.

3.3.4 Other parking

Players

Parking space for team buses should be provided for each team of players. Usually between two and six bus spaces may be required, but FIFA recommends at least two bus spaces plus ten car spaces: the specific figure will depend on the sport involved and should be researched. These spaces should always be secure and separate from other parking areas and from each other, and give direct access to the players' changing areas without coming into contact with the public (see Section 16.2).

Officials

Directors, sponsors and stadium staff should have parking in separate, clearly identified and secure areas, under close supervision and control, including closed circuit television (see Section 17.2.1). Sometimes this area is inside the perimeter fence of the grounds, which is acceptable if the zone inside the fence is large enough and out of reach of the circulation routes used by the public. Often this is not possible, when it is recommended that all official vehicles (except for emergency and essential service vehicles) be kept outside the main perimeter fence.

The media

Extensive areas must be provided for the increasing numbers of television and broadcast vehicles. As many as ten may be required for a single event, and factors to be taken into account are not merely their standings but also the widths of access roads and radii of turning circles required by these large vehicles. Their parking spaces may be incorporated into the general parking areas, provided they are adjacent to the cable access points provided (see Section 14.2) and able to bear the weight of the heavy technical support trucks. Provision must be made for catering, toilet and similar support vehicles adjacent to the technical vehicles, as media crews may spend long periods at the stadium before and after events. These areas must be fenced or protected.

Provisionally a space of 24 m by 4 m should be allowed per vehicle, and a level surface capable of supporting up to 15 tonnes.

Service and deliveries

A modern stadium complex requires heavy goods access to many delivery and service points (catering, cleaning, etc.) and these must be identified in the brief so that direct and unobstructed access can be built into the scheme at the earliest stages and not come as an afterthought.

3.3.5 Parking layout and services

Dimensions

Dimensions of parking bays should meet national standards, but for preliminary planning a space of 2.4 m by 4.8 m per car is reasonable.

Zoning

All user groups should have independent and easily identifiable zones in the parking area, which should be divided into blocks of roughly 500 to 1000 cars. These blocks should be instantly recognizable by signs, numbering systems – devices such as colour-coded tickets coordinating with colour-coded signs – and by attractive landmark elements which can be seen and easily recognized from a distance. Varying surface treatments can also assist in partitioning the car park into separate zones.

When making these decisions bear in mind that spectators may arrive during daylight hours but start looking for their car after dark when everything looks very different; that evening games under floodlights mean arrival and departure in darkness, requiring good lighting of all parking areas.

Pedestrian routes

On leaving their cars, spectators should be able to proceed directly to a safe pedestrian passage which feeds through the car park to the stadium entrance gates. This distance should preferably be no more than 500 metres, or an absolute maximum of 1500 metres. If distances become too great there should be an internal transport system of regular pick-up and drop-off buses, in which case waiting areas must be provided, and (as above) very clear signs provided so that spectators do not get confused.

Signage

The importance of signs has been raised in the preceding paragraphs and a summary might be useful.

At each entry point to the parking area there should be signs guiding visitors to their individual parking positions. When they have parked and left their cars or coaches there should be further boards telling them where they are, and guiding them towards their viewing positions. The correct perimeter access point must be clearly identified. Similar provision should be made for spectators leaving the stadium to guide them back to their vehicles quickly.

Public transport waiting areas

An efficient internal transport system around the car parks reduces overcrowding of the spaces close to the stadium, and allows visitors to leave the parking area more easily and quickly. There should be highly visible waiting areas, sheltered, provided with information boards and well lit. If possible communication links with the transport control centre should be installed.

Kiosks

The routes followed by visitors as they walk from their cars towards the stadium should be well provided with kiosks where food, beverages, programmes and perhaps even tickets may be bought well before the entrance gates are reached. Such decentralized sales points in the car parking area help reduce congestion at the entrance gates; they should be of an eye-catching design to ensure that they are noticed. Such kiosks, if well-designed, can add to the leisure atmosphere and even serve as 'markers' to help people memorize where their cars are parked.

Lighting

All parking areas should be uniformly lit, with no dark patches, to allow easy ingress and egress and to create a safe environment. High mast lighting is likely to be chosen for this purpose, provided it is aesthetically acceptable and does not cause annoying overspill into adjacent residential areas.

Separate pedestrian walkways, designed into the parking layout to provide clear walking routes between stadium gates and distant parking spaces, should be well lit, probably with low-level local luminaires chosen particularly for their suitability to this purpose.

Telephones

There should be a good provision of public telephones along the outer periphery of the car park in case of vehicular breakdown.

Overspill

If the site is unable to accommodate the total number of cars required, or if certain individual events demand a greater number of spaces, additional parking facilities should be identified in the locality. These can include fields, parks and play areas. The effects of cars parked on these surfaces should be considered, particularly in open-field conditions during the winter or in wet weather.

3.3.7 Parking landscape

Car parks can be barren-looking places casting a spell of bleakness on their surroundings and detracting from the spectators' enjoyment of their visit unless very great care is taken. A comprehensive landscaping plan must be devised to reduce the visual impact of these great expanses and to give them some humanity. At the same time, a well thought out scheme can help to define the parking zones and the vehicular and pedestrian routes which intersect them.

The key to success is mental attitude: stop seeing the car park as a piece of ground to be covered in asphalt, but see it rather as a great outdoor floor that must be planned and designed as carefully as the stadium itself. The following suggestions may help to achieve this:

- The paved surface could be subdivided into areas that would form a neat and attractive pattern as seen from above – perhaps a radial configuration centred on the stadium. One element in the formation of such a pattern could be a geometric layout of paved driveways and walkways set into the lower-cost general surface and contrasting with it, say, bricks or interlocking pavings set in an asphalt surface. Another might be the planting of regular rows of dense car-height shrubs or trees between adjacent blocks of car parking spaces to soften the space when observed from eye-height. A third might be rows of tall, slender trees lining the main radial access roads and marking their positions for drivers. Where climate allows, grass surfaces can with great advantage be incorporated in such a surface pattern (Figure 3.6).

- Each of the paved areas formed by such subdivision should be flat and true, separated (if the site contains substantial differences of level) by neat ramps and low retaining walls; it should not be a great undulating expanse of tarmac untidily following the natural ground contours, as is all too often seen.
- For rainwater run-off each paved area should be laid to fall to gulleys or drainage channels. The ridges and valleys should express the pattern established by the first suggestion above, instead of zigzagging across the site along the lines of least resistance.
- Changes of level should be designed to pedestrian rather than vehicle standards, and there should be no risk of tripping owing to uneven surfaces or sudden changes of level, particularly at danger points such as drainage gulleys and channels. Routes used by disabled people must avoid steps.
- Details at edges and verges should be particularly carefully designed, and formed in good quality materials.
- The materials and construction methods should be selected to minimize maintenance,

Figure 3.6 Where climate allows, as in the Joe Robbie stadium in Miami, the use of grass can greatly soften the carparking landscape. Architects: Hellmuth, Obata & Kassabaum (HOK).

offer a good walking surface, and look attractive. Tarmac is commonly used and is cheap, but it will not give an acceptable result unless carefully subdivided, articulated and trimmed at the edges. Bricks and interlocking pavings offer a superior (but more expensive) finish but even they will not give an attractive result without careful design.

- Part-concrete, part-grass surfaces for vehicles combine the visual benefits of grass with the load-bearing strength of a road. One type uses pre-cast concrete units with large openings through which the grass grows, these units being laid like ordinary pavings. A second type is formed by lightweight, air-entrained concrete being cast *in situ* around polystyrene formers which are then burnt away leaving apertures for the grass to grow through. These surfaces are usually best where use is occasional (for example access roads) rather than continuous, because oil drips and heavy use may kill the grass.

3.4 Stadium landscaping

3.4.1 The stadium in its surroundings

Stadia are major developments which can enhance the surrounding environment or blight it. Attitudes to such environmental impact vary around the world, with the most protective approach found in Europe – partly no doubt because of its limited amount of green space.

Most countries now have environmental protection legislation for both town and country. They also have increasingly aware and assertive communities who will vociferously object to bulky-looking new buildings (particularly if these are likely to generate traffic and noise) perhaps even preventing their construction, or at least forcing expensive modifications to the design. Therefore, not only must very careful attention be given to the form of the stadium and the way it is blended into the landscape, but additionally, officials and community representatives should be consulted and involved from an early design stage and 'carried along' as the design develops, with the problems and the preferred solutions explained to them in jargon-free language. To do otherwise is to risk a refusal of planning permission entailing a heavy loss of time and money.

3.4.2 Planting

There are stadia, particularly in the USA, which have virtually no planting as a conscious part of the overall site philosophy. Pontiac Silverdome in Michigan is one. Another is the Three Rivers Stadium in Pittsburgh where the approach has been to allow the structure to be seen for miles around. The siting of the Three Rivers Stadium at the junction of the rivers which flow through Pittsburgh is certainly one of the most striking to be found anywhere, particularly when approached from across the river.

On the other hand, planting can greatly ameliorate the problems of scale and un-friendly-looking finishes sometimes associated with sports stadia and can make almost any stadium look better. The 35 000-capacity Cologne Stadium in Germany (Figure 3.7) is set inside a large sports park and is completely surrounded by foliage so thick that it is possible to be beside the building and virtually not see it. The effect is very pleasing and could be emulated with advantage elsewhere.

However, planting is expensive both in initial cost and in maintenance, particularly in places (such as sports stadia) where vandalistic behaviour may occur from time to time, and few stadia can afford large maintenance bills just for the care of plants. Possible precautions include:

- planting mature trees and shrubs and protecting them for as long as possible with frames;
- establishing a plant nursery on the site (assuming there is enough space) which is

Figure 3.7 Cologne Stadium is almost totally screened behind lush foliage. The effect is very pleasant and could be emulated more widely. Architects: Dyckerhoff & Widmann AG.

inaccessible to the public and where plants may grow unhindered until they are strong enough to risk the attention of the crowds;

- concentrating the planting in those areas where it will be most effective, as discussed below.

Above all landscaping and planting should not be left as an afterthought at the last stages of a project, as happens all too often. They should be part of the masterplan, planned and adequately budgeted for from the very beginning. The ideal is a landscaping masterplan in which trees which will take several years to grow to maturity are planted immediately, protected during their vulnerable years, and are fully effective when the stadium comes into use. Mature trees can also be purchased from nurseries, transported to the site and planted, but this is expensive.

In summary, it is difficult to have too many trees on a stadium site, but we very frequently see too few. In some cases the planting becomes the focus of our attention: who would think of the Championships at Wimbledon, for example, without a mental image of the green virginia creepers covering the main elevations of the buildings? They are as much a part of Wimbledon as the singles finals, and the development plan which is to take this venue into the twenty-first century very consciously retains and builds on this image.

The following are particularly effective locations for plants.

Site boundary planting

Site boundary planting can soften the visual impact of a large stadium development on its environment, making the buildings seem smaller and perhaps less gaunt. Such planting can also help protect the stadium from the neighbours and the neighbours from the stadium, and form the transition between the outside world and the stadium precinct while also highlighting the positions of the entrances.

Car park planting

As drivers approach the car park, tall slender trees lining the main radial access routes can help them find their way in; and once they are inside and walking towards the stadium tall rows of trees can similarly help them locate the pedestrian routes. Lower, denser rows of planting can be used to separate adjoining blocks of parked cars from each other, softening the view as one looks across the acres of hard, bare landscape. These configurations of tall and low planting should add up to a functional and pleasing total design, as suggested in Section 3.3.7.

Buffer zone planting

The principal buffer zone is the transition between the stadium building and the car parking area – Zone 4, as described in Section 2.3.2. At least part of it should be hard paved or grassed to act as an assembly area if required, but the remainder can be trees, shrubs or even flowering plants, the latter particularly near the main entrances.

Concourse planting

Concourse planting is used inside the stadium perimeter to help define circulation patterns and to help screen the structure. Because these areas will be crowded with people we recommend planting that is hardy, with no foliage lower than about two metres. In addition to being less prone to damage, trees or shrubs with foliage only at higher levels do not obstruct vision, which is an advantage in circulation areas.

Figure 3.8 The Hong Kong Stadium, built on the site of an existing stadium. Architects: HOK. Photo: Kerun Ip.

4

Form and structure

4.1 The stadium as architecture

4.1.1 The ideal

As suggested in the Introduction, sports stadia are essentially large theatres of entertainment which ought to be as pleasant to visit as a cinema, opera house or play theatre, whilst also being social and architectural landmarks in their towns and cities.

The designers of pre-modern stadia rose to this challenge with admirable skill. The Colosseum and the circuses of Rome, the amphitheatre in Verona, and similar buildings throughout the Roman empire played central roles in the civic lives of their communities. Based on the circle and the oval, they were also wonderfully successful in translating functional requirements and the known building technologies of the time into noble architectural form. The profile of the Colosseum (Figure 1.4) solves at a stroke the challenges of clear viewing, structural stability and efficient circulation, the latter allowing the building to be cleared of thousands of spectators in a matter of minutes; whilst the outer façade is related to the human scale by the colonnaded arcades of its composition. So powerful and inventive was this unprecedented façade that it became a primary source of inspiration for the architects of the Renaissance fourteen centuries later.

Whilst the basic form of the modern stadium remains very similar to those of antiquity (stepped tiers of seats facing a central arena) brick and stone have largely been replaced by concrete and steel, and it must be said that architectural standards have fallen: all too many current stadia are banal at best, anti-human at worst.

Design excellence is achieved in stadia when structure, enclosure and finishes express at all scales – from overall form right down to the smallest detail – a single concept which functions well, is rich and expressive, and avoids jarring conflicts. There are current examples of excellence, such as the Bari Stadium in Italy by the architect Renzo Piano, but complete success is rare: the first step towards higher architectural standards must be the identification of those particular problems which make it so difficult to achieve functional and beautiful stadium design nowadays.

4.1.2 The problems

Because sports stadia are so closely geared to onerous functional requirements (clear sightlines, efficient high-volume circulation, etc.) this is a building type where 'form' follows fairly directly from 'function'; unfortunately 'delight' is more elusive – for the reasons which follow.

Inward-looking form
Stadia naturally look inward towards the action, turning their backs on their surroundings. The elevation facing the street or surrounding landscape tends therefore to be unwelcoming, often made even more forbidding by security fences and other crowd control measures.

Car parking
They must often be surrounded by acres of car and bus parking which are not only unattractive

in themselves but tend to cut off the stadium from its surroundings.

Gigantic scale

Whilst the huge physical scale of a major stadium may not create problems in an out-of-town environment it is more difficult to fit happily into a town setting. Reconciling the scales of stadia with those of their surroundings is a difficult challenge.

Inflexible elements

A stadium is composed of elements (seating tiers, stairs and ramps, entrances and roof forms) which are inflexible and sometimes difficult to assimilate into a traditional façade or compositional scheme. And even if traditional rules of composition are abandoned and innovatory architectural forms sought these stiff elements resist being bent or smoothed or tucked away to achieve the grace, harmony, and apparent effortlessness that makes good architecture. They tend to obstinately assert themselves, and the resultant form often simply does not 'look right'.

Tough finishes

Turning from form to finishes, stadia must have tough and highly resilient surfaces able to stand up, without much maintenance effort, to the worst that weather, uncaring crowds and deliberate vandalism can do to them. All too easily the requirement of 'resilience' tends to translate into finishes which are read as 'tough', 'brutal' and 'anti-human'.

Periods of disuse

Stadia tend to stand empty and unoccupied for weeks at a time, casting a spell of bleakness and lifelessness on their surroundings; then for short periods they are so intensively used as to overwhelm their environment. This pattern of use, almost unique among building types, inflicts upon the stadium and its surroundings the worst effects of both under-use and over-use.

4.2 Structure and form

4.2.1 Introduction

It is impossible to lay down a neat set of design rules which will guarantee good stadium architecture, but three suggestions may be helpful regarding architectural form:

- First, designers should think very hard indeed about each of the matters identified above, which are the key architectural problems.
- Second, they should look at existing stadia in which these (or other) problems have been solved with conspicuous success, and try to identify precedents relevant to their own case. There are very few entirely original building concepts in the history of architecture: much good design is an intelligent modification of an existing model that has been shown to work, and there is no shame in learning from the past.
- Third, the approaches outlined below may prove helpful. They are not intended as prescriptive rules but only as suggestions, intended to prompt designers into clarifying their own thoughts, and should be read in this spirit.

4.2.2 Low profile

Many stadia would look best with a profile kept as low as possible. Two techniques which help achieve this are dropping the pitch below ground level (Figure 4.1) and raising the surrounding landscape by means of planted mounds.

4.2.3 Roof and façade

In roofed stadia, which are becoming more common (particularly in Europe), the most important step towards a satisfying and harmonious architectural solution is to avoid having an assertive façade competing with an equally assertive roof. If one of these elements is dominant, with the other subdued or completely invisible, the composition may immediately become easier to handle.

Figure 4.1 Barcelona Olympic Stadium, remodelled for the 1990 Olympic Games, shows the level of the pitch sunk beneath ground level. This reduction in apparent stadium height often improves appearance. Architect: Gregotti.

Dominant roof

A successful example of a 'dominant roof' design is Gunter Behnisch's complex of sports buildings in the Olympiapark, Munich. In these buildings the wall has been virtually eliminated and the stadia reduced visually to a series of graceful roof forms hovering over green landscape (Figure 4.2). The playing surfaces are recessed below ground level.

Where the walls cannot be eliminated altogether it helps to reduce them to submissive, horizontal elements of 'built landscape' over which floats a separate graceful roof.

Dominant façade

A successful example of the 'dominant façade' approach is the Mound Stand at Lord's Cricket Ground in London by Michael Hopkins &

Partners (Figure 4.3(a)). This stadium façade can genuinely be called successful. It maintains an urban scale, follows the streetline, contains variety and grace; and there is a satisfying progression from the heavy, earthbound basecourse to the light pavilion-like tent roof at the top.

Dominant structure

In large stadia there could be a third approach: to make the structure dominant. For instance, both façade and roof could be visually contained behind a dominant 'cage' of vertical structural ribs. Examples include the Chamsil Olympic Main Stadium at Seoul and the Parc des Princes in Paris. This may work best on large open sites where the building is mostly seen from a distance.

Figure 4.2 Visual conflict between roof and façade can be resolved by eliminating the wall and reducing the building profile to a graceful roof hovering above the landscape. An excellent example is the 1972 Olympic Stadium at Munich. Architect: Günter Behnisch. Structural engineers: Frei Otto and Fritz Leonardt.

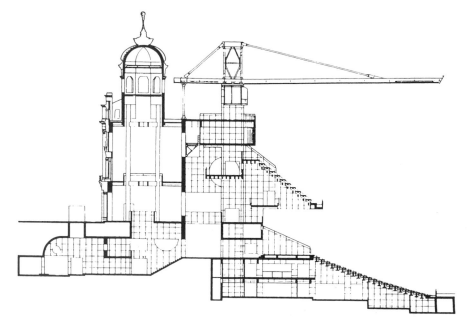

Figure 4.3 (a) Barcelona Olympic Stadium. Architect: Gregotti.

Figure 4.3 A converse strategy, often the most suitable approach in urban contexts, is to have a dominant façade with the roof either hidden or subdued. The Mound Stand at Lord's Cricket Ground, London (b) has a light roof floating above a dominant and well-composed façade. Architects: Michael Hopkins & Partners. (c) and (d) Arsenal Stadium in a built-up north London location also has a strong façade forming a satisfying vertical boundary to the street. Architects: LOBB Partnership.

Kenzo Tange's twin gymnasia for the 1964 Tokyo Olympics provide supreme examples of structural expressionism of a different kind. Both have organically-shaped roofs suspended from cables which in turn are anchored to massive concrete buttresses. The horizontal sweep of the seating tiers and the upward-curving spirals of the suspended roofs obey few of the traditional canons of architectural composition and yet look magnificent – but it has to be said that few designers could handle such unorthodox forms so successfully.

Appropriate choice: open sites

Stadia situated in open parkland can make a positive contribution to the environment if the form rising above the landscape is genuinely attractive and well-composed. If these qualities cannot be achieved, for whatever reason, then there is no shame in hiding the stadium completely behind landscaping; it is a perfectly valid strategy.

Achieving a form that blends with the surroundings is usually not too difficult in the case of an open stadium. Roofed stadia present a greater challenge. Sinking the playing field below ground level and/or surrounding the stadium with planted mounds to reduce the apparent height are useful devices, and could enable the stadium almost to melt away into the landscape.

Appropriate choice: urban sites

If a stadium is situated in a town or city the façades will probably be dominant, partly to allow the site to be exploited right up to its perimeter at all levels, and partly to maintain rather than disrupt the rows of façades which form the streetscape on either side of the stadium. It may then be desirable to subdue the huge stair ramps, and the backs of the seating tiers with their horizontal or sloping geometry, to blend with a surrounding streetscape of closely-spaced, vertically-accented building façades.

One approach, exemplified by the Mound Stand in London, is to adopt a structural pattern for the stadium that enables the rhythm, scale, materials and details to harmonize with the surroundings, and to ensure also that the façade smoothly follows the street line (Figure 4.3(a)).

The other, exemplified by the Louis IV stadium in Monte Carlo, is to place a row of shops, restaurants, a hotel or some other 'orthodox' building type between stadium and street as part of a multi-purpose development. In addition to its architectural merits such a solution would help bring life to the street and could have economic benefits for the stadium as explained in Section 19.4.

4.2.4 Turning the corner

When stands are placed on three or four sides of a pitch the problem of gracefully 'turning the corner' where they join has defeated many designers, particularly with roofed stadia. Each individual seating terrace may be elegant in itself and be fitted with an equally elegant roof – but how to bend these stiff forms round the corners?

Some stadia, such as the one at Dortmund in Germany or Ibrox Park in the UK (Figure 4.4) simply dodge the problem: four rectangular 'sheds' are placed on the four sides of the pitch and the corners are left as gaps. This may be inexpensive and may avoid awkward structural and planning problems, but the effect is visually unhappy and the geometry sacrifices potentially revenue-earning corner seating, as pointed out in Section 7.34. One solution is to infill the corners with towers, with the side and end stands spanning between them. The stadium in Genoa (architect: Vittorio Gregotti), which is in tight urban surroundings, is an example of this approach. Such towers could accommodate offices or other functions depending on the local context.

Satisfying results have also been obtained by designs in which both the stands and roofs are swept round the pitch in some form. Examples include the Stadium of the Alps in Turin. This approach may be difficult on tight urban plots, partly because of insufficient space, partly because it may be desirable that the stadium façades follow the street line, and partly because swept forms may 'look wrong' in some contexts. But there is Philip Cox's elegant Sydney Football Stadium to prove it can be done (Figure

Figure 4.4 At Ibrox Park stadium, Glasgow, four separate stands meet awkwardly at the corners. Architects: Miller Partnership & Gareth Hutchinson.

EAST ELEVATION

Figure 4.5 Millennium Stadium or the new Cardiff Arms Park is Britain's first opening roof stadium and one of the largest in the world. Architects: HOK + LOBB.

Figure 4.6 Sydney Football Stadium in Australia is a well-resolved overall design. The stands are deepest and highest where most people want to sit, and the roof sweeps gracefully round the field. Architects: Philip Cox Richardson Taylor & Partners.

4.6). As in so many successful designs the playing area is submerged below ground (about 5 m in this case) which usefully lowers the stadium profile. The original design had the fluidly-shaped roof floating free above the seating structure – soaring high along the sides of the pitch, where most people want to sit and where the depth of seating extends back furthest

and highest; and swooping down close to ground level at the pitch ends, where there are fewer and shallower seating tiers. This dip towards ground level also reduced the apparent scale where the stadium approached a residential area. But the gap between the roof and the rear of the spectator tiers proved too great and offered insufficient weather protection, a problem which had later to be rectified by a multi-million dollar contract to fill in the gaps.

The projected designs for the Manchester Commonwealth Games Stadium, designed by Arup Associates, with HOK + LOBB are a further example of the same design theme.

4.2.5 Assimilating circulation ramps

Ramps are overtaking stairs as the preferred means of escape for the valid reasons given in Section 13.7.3, but their enormous scale (a circular ramp will probably have an internal diameter of around 12 m) makes them difficult to handle with elegance. Relatively successful examples include the San Siro stadium in Milan and the Joe Robbie stadium in the USA (Figure 4.7).

Figure 4.7 Joe Robbie stadium in Miami, USA, handles the difficult architectural problem of escape ramps, with their huge scale and unorthodox shape, better than most. Architects: Hellmuth, Obata & Kassabaum (HOK).

4.2.6 Assimilating the structure

Lattice-like structures
Massive columns, beams and cantilevers are often difficult to assimilate into a coherent design concept, and a very useful trend in recent years has been the increasing use of more delicate lattice or tension structures to replace (wholly or in part) these assertive structural elements.

These concepts do not automatically solve all problems or guarantee aesthetic success, but they do offer help towards shapely and graceful structures which are related to the human scale. Good examples include:

- Sydney Football Stadium by Philip Cox Richardson Taylor & Partners (Figure 4.6).
- The forward-looking proposal 'A Stadium for the Nineties' by LOBB Partnership, the Sports Council and YRM Anthony Hunt Associates (Figure 4.8). See also Section 4.9.2 and Figure 4.25.
- The roof of the Prater Stadium in Vienna (Figures 4.9, 4.10, 4.11).

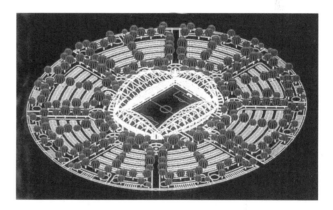

Figure 4.8 Lattice structures offer the possibility of light, graceful stadium designs. This example is the British 'Stadium for the Nineties' proposal by Lobb Partnership in association with the Sports Council. Structural engineers: YRM Anthony Hunt Associates.

Massive structures
The alternative 'brutalist' approach of powerfully expressed large-scale structural elements fascinates architects, but alas, for every masterpiece of sculptural concrete there are a dozen cruder examples, deeply disliked by the public. The sheer scale of a modern stadium is part of the problem. As an indication, the 110 m-long

Figure 4.9 The Vienna Prater Stadium was built as an open stadium in 1928–31 and fitted with a column-free compression/tension ring-type roof in 1986. Architects: Erich Frantl and Peter Hoffstätter. Structural Engineers: Conproject & Partners.

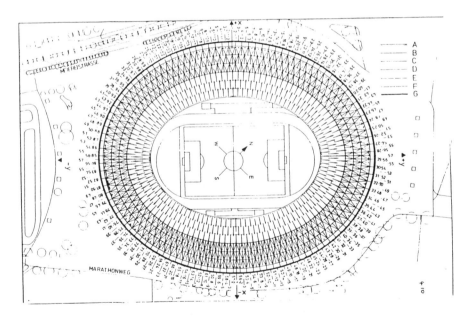

Figure 4.10 Plan of Vienna Prater Stadium roof. The outer perimeter forms an ellipse of 270 m by 215 m.

girder spanning the North Stand at Ibrox Park stadium (Figure 4.4) is large enough to hold four double-decker buses.

If massive concrete forms are to be used they ought possibly to be 'softened' by heavy planting, as in the Cologne stadium in Germany. This is set in a large sports park and is most attractively surrounded by a screen of extremely lush trees and shrubs (Figure 3.7).

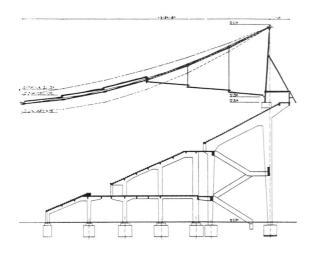

Figure 4.11 Cross-section showing the inner half of the roof decking resting on top of the structure while the outer half is suspended beneath it, thus forming a flat saddle roof.

4.3 Materials

4.3.1 Visual aspects

Finishes

Unfinished concrete has many functional virtues and is widely used in stadium design. But it is disliked by the general public, tends to weather unattractively, and should be used with great caution. The following suggestions may be helpful.

- Exposed concrete finishes are best avoided in rainy climates, particularly in urban or industrial locations where the rainwater becomes contaminated by pollutants which then stain the concrete as the water runs down the surface. In theory the staining can be avoided by surface treatment, by well-designed drip mouldings and the like, but in practice these measures are seldom completely effective. Also, in theory, the staining of concrete can be positively exploited by carefully planning and guiding the patterns of water-flow to produce a pre-designed effect, but it is difficult to think of any examples where attractive results have been achieved.

- If exposed concrete must be used in these situations then expert advice should be sought and the greatest care taken (both in design and workmanship) to avoid surface staining. Aggregates, sand and cement should all be very carefully specified and be of high quality. The increasing use of pre-cast concrete, which can be manufactured under more controlled conditions than *in situ*, helps towards the achievement of higher quality finishes.

- Painting the concrete can also help, and several existing stadia (including Wembley Stadium in London and the Seoul Olympic stadium) have been treated in this way. But it poses a very great maintenance burden.

The above problems are reduced in locations with unpolluted air (where the rainwater is therefore cleaner and less liable to soil the concrete) and in dry climates with low or very intermittent rainfalls. An example of success is Renzo Piano's Bari Stadium in Italy.

Finally, concrete surfaces that are close to people should if possible be clad with brickwork, timber or some other 'friendly' material. This will do much to make for more popular sports stadia, though admittedly it will be expensive.

Colours

Tempted by the enormous range of colours now available for stadium seats, claddings and synthetic pitch surfaces, and trying to overcome the bleakness of the average stadium (particularly when it is half-empty, without crowds of people to give colour and variety to the terraces), designers may fall into the trap of producing gaudily coloured stadia. Imagination controlled by the strictest discipline may give the best results.

4.3.2 Technical aspects

Stadia have been built of every conceivable material. The ancient Romans built theirs in brick and stone, and modern Romans refurbished their existing Olympic stadium in concrete, steel, aluminium and plastic fabric roofing for the 1990 World Cup in football.

Cost is a major factor because structure, as discussed in Chapter 19, is a larger proportion of total cost in the case of stadia than in most other building types. Cost comparisons between all the alternative structural materials are therefore vital, with particular attention to the roof as discussed in Section 4.8 below.

Other performance characteristics such as durability, fire resistance, etc. must be just as thoroughly investigated – and then balanced against the less quantifiable but equally important qualities of user-friendliness, grace and beauty. Stadia can prosper only if they attract spectators, and increasingly people will stay away if the facility is rough or sordid-looking – no matter how technically correct the specifications.

4.3.3 Concrete

Reinforced concrete competes with steel as the most commonly-used structural material for stadia. It has the great advantage of being naturally fire-proof and cheaper than steel in some countries, but it has the disadvantage of being unpopular if left unfinished (which is usually the case). By and large it is the only practical material for constructing the seating profiles of the stadium. Concrete may either be cast *in situ* or applied as pre-cast units, and both types are frequently used together.

In situ *concrete*

The plastic properties of *in situ* concrete have been exploited to produce some very dramatic stadia, for instance the shell canopies of the Grandstand at Zarzuela racetrack near Madrid (Eduardo Torroja, 1935); in Rome the Palazzetto dello Sport (Annibale Vitellozzi and Pier Luigi Nervi, 1957) and the Palazzo dello Sport (Pier Luigi Nervi and Marcello Piacentini, 1960); and in the composite structures of the Hockey Rink at Yale University, Connecticut (Eero Saarinen, 1958) and the National Olympic Gymnasia in Tokyo. Recently such use has diminished in favour of more lightweight structures.

Pre-cast concrete

Pre-cast concrete, like steel, has the advantage over *in situ* concrete that structural members can be prefabricated away from the site well in advance of site possession, thus greatly reducing construction time. This is important when construction must be planned to minimize disruptions to the season's fixtures. Such is often the case with sports stadia in the UK, which must to be constructed in phases during the few months between one season and the next. This practice is not yet common in the USA where stadia tend to be constructed in one operation, but even here stadia owners are beginning to experience the difficulties Europe has had for decades, of clubs not wanting to move from the stadium while necessary redevelopment or upgrading work takes place.

Pre-stressed and post-tensioned concrete

Pre-cast concrete is widely used for the tread and riser units which form the seating platform. These stepping units are often pre-stressed so that they can be thin and light, but their jointing can cause problems. Choice of materials and detailing of junctions is as important here as for roof construction, particularly if the spaces below are to be as usable rooms. Waterproofing especially will be very important.

When using pre-cast framing, thought should also be given to the future uses of the stadium. If stadia are used for pop music concerts the spectators can set up rhythms in time to the music which may affect the structure, and some stadia in Germany have had to be temporarily propped for concert use to compensate for this phenomenon.

Both pre-stressing and post-tensioning are useful techniques in stadium construction – pre-stressing for reasons of lightness, and post-tensioning for offering a reduction (or even absence) of movement joints through the structure. This is an important advantage because many stadia are 100 m or more in extent, and normally such a length of concrete structure should be built as two independent units with a clear expansion gap between. In a post-tensioned structure the thermal movement still occurs but is greatly reduced by the enormous tension placed on the reinforcing rods. The entire structure is held together like a string of beads pulled together by a thread – the threads in this case being steel rods stressed to a hundred tons or more.

Two examples of stadia which exploit these techniques, both in the UK, are the South Stand at Twickenham Rugby Football Ground and the West Stand (also known as the Sir Stanley Rous Stand) at Watford Football Club. Both were built entirely of pre-cast, post-tensioned concrete both designed by the LOBB Partnership with engineers, Jan Bobrowski & Partners.

4.3.4 Steel

Steel is cheaper in some parts of the world than concrete and it allows prefabrication off-site, which can be a great advantage for the reasons given above.

It is of course lighter than concrete, both physically and aesthetically. This offers functional advantages, such as cheaper footings on bad soil, and the possibility of slender, graceful structures. Steel is an obvious choice for roof structures, two examples of excellence being the Olympic Stadium in Rome (Figure 4.12) and the

Prater Stadium in Vienna (Figures 4.9, 4.10 and 4.11), both of which were given new steel roofs over the existing stadia.

Fire regulations will probably require steel members below the roof to be fire-proofed by encasing, spraying with mineral fibre or vermiculite cement, or by thin-film intumescent coating (which detracts least from the appearance of steel profiles). This could cause steel to lose its cost advantage over concrete. But fire safety regulations are changing as the emphasis shifts towards 'fire-engineered' solutions, and unprotected steel seems likely to become more widely acceptable provided certain additional measures are taken. These include:

- Ensuring that people can escape from the stadium within a defined time, as discussed in Section 13.6.2, and reach safety well before structural failure commences. This should not be a major problem because the main danger with fire in stadia is not that of structural collapse but of smoke suffocation. The Valley Parade stadium in Bradford, where 56 people died and many were badly injured in a fire in 1985, had an old pitched roof which effectively contained the smoke and flames.

Figure 4.12 The new compression/tension ring roof added in 1990 to the Rome Olympic Stadium. Structural engineer: Prof. Ing. Massimo Majowiecki.

- Installing a sprinkler system. New UK fire regulations do allow unprotected steelwork if sprinklers are installed, a concession that may in some cases tip the economic balance from concrete to steel in the UK. On the other hand the effects of a sprinkler downpour on an already panicking crowd have yet to be seen.

4.3.5 Brickwork

In a large stadium, brickwork is more likely to be used to clad a structure than to act as a structural material in itself. Its use would be particularly apt at 'people level' throughout the stadium to humanize otherwise brutal surfaces, or at street level to help the stadium blend in with the surrounding townscape.

4.4 The playing surface

4.4.1 Level

The level of the playing surface is often sunk below the ground line so that part of the front seating tier can be rested directly on the natural ground (Figure 4.1). This device may offer a saving in construction costs and give the aesthetic benefit of reducing the apparent height of the building. But constructing viewing terraces directly on the ground is not always as straightforward as it may sound: poor soil conditions (see Section 4.5.1 below) could create problems which cancel out the envisaged savings.

4.4.2 Surface

Chapter 5 deals in detail with playing surfaces: here we merely wish to point out that certain stadium forms will rule out (or at least have an adverse effect upon) certain playing surfaces.

Natural grass
Natural grass is the preferred surface for many sports, but the feasibility of installing it will depend on the degree to which the stadium is enclosed. The current situation is as follows.

Completely open stadia: these will accept any playing surface, including grass.

Partly roofed stadia: these may have natural grass playing surfaces, but a combination of shading from sunlight and reduced airflow at pitch level could damage the grass. Therefore expert guidance must be sought, sun-path diagrams used to determine the shadow effects of the structure, and wind effects studied by means of models and wind tunnels – as there are, as yet, no reliable mathematical formulae for predicting wind conditions.

Totally permanently enclosed stadia: at present these cannot have natural grass pitches, and the use of synthetic turfs must be investigated as discussed in Chapter 5.

Experiments to make natural grass pitches feasible in enclosed stadia have so far either proved unsuccessful or very expensive, and cannot be wholeheartedly recommended. For the record, they include:

- Maintaining the grass surface in the open air outside, and then sliding it into the stadium when needed. An example is the Robbie/Allen Roll-in/Roll-out pitch proposed for Toronto's Skydome: in its 'outside' position this grass field can be used for open-air events seating up to 20 000 spectators. The stadium at Arnhem is a recent example.
- Raising the grass surface on jacks into the roof area between games. An example is the 'Turfdome' concept produced by Geiger Engineers in New York, which allows the grass pitch to be raised or lowered to various levels, each serving a different purpose. This is a technically expensive and difficult solution, as yet unbuilt.
- Supplementing a permanent translucent roof with artificial light. Studies of which have been undertaken by HOK + LOBB.
- Using an openable roof structure to provide sufficient light. The foremost examples of opening roofs are to be seen in Canada, probably a result of the climatic extremes experienced there. One is the 1989 Toronto Skydome which has an ingenious system of rotating and sliding roof segments (Figures 3.4 and 4.13), and the other is the 1976 Montreal

Figure 4.13 The Toronto Skydome uses rotating and sliding roof segments.

Olympic Stadium which had a movable fabric roof pulled up on a cable structure from a very high tower (Figure 4.14). But the enormous cost of the Skydome, and the fact that the Montreal Olympic Stadium roof (which was completed only in 1988) will never be operated again suggest that these designs may not be widely emulated.

Synthetic surfaces
The chosen stadium form is unlikely to have any adverse effect on synthetic playing surfaces. Table 5.1 should be followed with regard to choice, and the advice in Sections 5.1.4 and 5.1.5 with regard to installation.

4.5 Foundations

4.5.1 Poor soil

The only foundation design factor applying specifically to stadia is that sports facilities are often sited on soil too poor to be used for any other kind of development – reclaimed land from disused refuse tips, old mine workings, drained marshland, etc. Much of the construction budget in these cases goes on ground improvement operations such as vibro-compaction, anti-methane treatment and garbage removal.

As soils of low or variable bearing capacity always carry the risk of expensive foundations, a full geotechnical report should be commissioned in all suspect cases before the final construction budget is agreed.

4.6 Seating tiers

4.6.1 Geometry

This is covered in detail in later sections. Here we merely wish to give the designer a clear picture of the key influences on overall stadium form and structure.

- Spectators should preferably not look into the sun while following a match: see Section 2.2 regarding orientation.
- Spectators should be close enough to the pitch to see the movement of the ball. For large-capacity stands this may be difficult or impossible, particularly if the ball is small and fast-moving (as in tennis), in which case compromises must be made; see Section 7.3.
- All spectators should be given a clear view of the pitch over the heads in front of them, which means that seating terraces must be 'raked' to angles which must be very carefully calculated; see Section 7.4.2.
- At the same time the stands must not be so steep as to be dangerous or induce vertigo: about 34 degrees will normally be the maximum; see Section 7.4.3.
- There must be no obstructions such as columns or excessively low roof edges to interfere with spectators' views of the pitch; see Section 7.5.

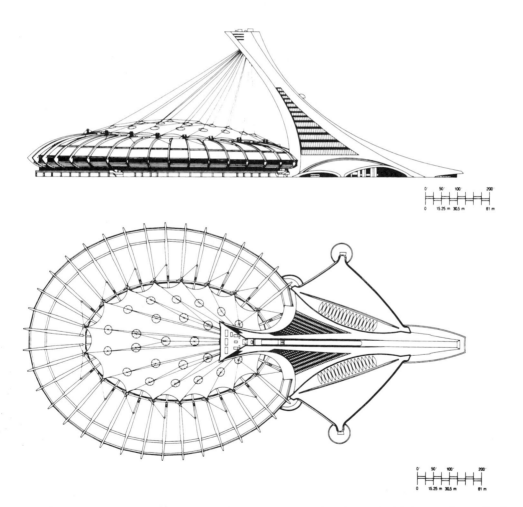

Figure 4.14 The Montreal Olympic Stadium had a fabric roof which may be pulled up from a high tower. This proved awkward in use, and has been replaced with a fixed permanent roof.

4.6.2 Construction

As stated in Section 4.3.2, seating tiers are most commonly constructed in pre-cast concrete. Steel as a material will be cheaper in some countries, but not necessarily after the members have been fire-proofed.

4.7 Concourses, stairs and ramps

4.7.1 Geometry

As with seating tiers this is covered in detail in later sections and we wish here only to give the designer a picture of the key influences on overall stadium form and structure.

- The pattern of concourses, stairs and ramps must allow for the smooth inflow of spectators, without people losing their way or getting confused, as outlined in Section 13.5; and a similarly smooth outflow after the end of the match, as outlined in Section 13.6.1.
- Most critically, the layout must allow for fast, safe emptying of the stadium in panic conditions; see Section 13.6.3.
- Planning must also facilitate easy access to toilets as discussed in Chapter 11 and catering facilities as discussed in Chapter 10. As a general rule no seat should be more than 60 m from a toilet, preferably on the same level.
- The circulation routes will probably be planned in a way that subdivides the total seating capacity of the stadium into sectors of about 2500 or 3000 spectators each, to allow for easier crowd control and a more even distribution of toilets, bars and restaurants; see Section 13.2.2.
- In each individual seating area the circulation routes will consist of vomitories fed by lateral gangways (running parallel with the side of the pitch), and radial gangways (which will be stepped). A pattern of few vomitories served by long gangways usually leaves less space for seats, while a larger number of vomitories fed by shorter gangways gives better space usage, and easier egress in panic conditions. A balanced solution should be aimed for.

4.7.2 Surface finishes

Stadia likely to be patronized by well-behaved crowds who will not abuse the building can be finished in the same way as any other public building, and no special notes are needed here. This is the trend in recent UK and North American stadia, which may have polished marble concourse floors, toilets finished to hotel standard, and luxuriously appointed social areas to attract patrons.

In Britain a recent example of a stadium finished durably but elegantly is Richard Horden's 5000-capacity Queen's Stand at Epsom Downs racecourse, Surrey. This building, opened in 1992, is not so much a stand as a private box viewing area and therefore exceptional – but it shows what can be achieved. Another example in the UK is the North Stand at Arsenal Football Club, north London, completed in 1993. All seats are padded and with arms; and circulation, toilets and amenity features are finished to cinema standard.

But where crowds have a record of being boisterous and ill-behaved, and where large parts of the building are exposed to wind and weather, finishes must be tough enough to stand up to intense wear and tear, regular abrasive cleaning, and the effects of sun, rain and temperature change.

Concrete surfaces are widely used and relatively inexpensive, can be very durable if treated with additives and sealants, but are associated with precisely the image that the modern customer-winning stadium would like to avoid – of a rough, mean place where one would prefer not to linger. They are also less easy to keep clean than smoother surfaces, and this adds to their negative image. More positively, the colour and stain additives as used at places such as Euro Disney are likely to become popular in the future.

Natural concrete block surfaces with anti-graffiti coatings are serviceable; but for the public they have the same utilitarian image as unfinished concrete.

Natural brick walls promote a better image than concrete, and can be treated with anti-graffiti coatings.

Wall and floor tiles or mosaics in ceramics and terracotta are expensive initially but are hard-wearing and, if properly used, pleasing in feel and appearance.

Coated steel claddings have improved greatly in recent years and are now very durable. They are easily cleanable, the choice of colour and pattern is wide, and this cladding type offers the possibility of handsome yet eminently practical concourse wall-surfaces.

Studded rubber floor tiles and sheeting are available in improved forms and although relatively expensive initially they are hard-wearing and available in attractive colours. They have been successfully used in the concourse areas of Wembley Stadium in London.

4.7.3 Details

In all cases correct detailing is as important as correct choice of materials:

- Careful positioning of doors and openings reduces confusion and aids circulation.
- The use of rails along walls can protect the wall face from abuse by keeping people at a safe distance.
- Balustrades set back from the edges of landings and concourses help reduce the danger of objects being accidentally dropped on people below. Similarly, floor edges in these positions should be upturned to prevent objects rolling over the edge.
- Upper surfaces of rails and balustrades should be sloping to make it difficult for fans to stand on them.
- Corners can be protected from damage by catering trolleys and other service vehicles by fixing metal guards, or by having rounded profiles.
- High ceilings help to create an open, airy atmosphere and are beyond reach of deliberate damage.
- Toilets should have surfaces and edge details, etc. which allow the complete washing down of walls and floors.
- All dangerous projections and sharp edges should be avoided.

4.8 Roof

4.8.1 Degree of enclosure

Open or partially covered stands are still common in less wealthy regions such as Central and South America and Africa, and are found even in countries with relatively robust climates such as Canada and Russia. But spectators are increasingly demanding some form of protective cover and in colder climates (especially northern Europe, North America and Japan) where sporting events take place in winter roofs are becoming a standard requirement. The trend towards enclosure has gone furthest in the USA and Japan, where most new stadia are entirely covered. Designers should note that this decision, as pointed out in Section 4.3.2, has a dramatic effect on the playing surface.

Shading from the sun
For afternoon matches, which are the majority, the main stand should face east with a minimum of spectators having to look into the sun from a west-facing stand.

In all cases the efficacy of a roof in shading its occupants from the sun, and the extent of shadow it casts upon the pitch at different times of the day and year, must be studied by computer modelling (Figure 4.14). Such modelling should proceed in parallel with wind tunnel testing, especially if the playing surface is to be natural grass, because 'it is now generally accepted that a combination of shading from sunlight and reduced airflow at pitch level has an adverse effect on the durability and quality of grass', to quote Britain's Football Stadia Advisory Design Council.

Shelter from wind and rain
As far as plan shape is concerned, designers should note Rudolf Bergermann's advice that continuous roofs arranged in a circle or ellipse, as opposed to separate roofs with gaps between, normally have a calming effect on the air inside the stadium. This creates more comfortable conditions for spectators and performers – experience at the Don Valley Stadium in the

UK actually suggests that such improved conditions can measurably enhance the performance of athletes. One disadvantage is that too little airflow in wet climates may give inadequate drying of a grass pitch after rain, which may argue in favour of open corners between the stands. A balance must be struck between such differing and possibly contradictory factors.

As far as cross-sectional shape is concerned, very approximate rules of thumb are given in Figure 4.15.

These simple parameters are only a starting point for design, and detailed studies should be made using scale models and wind tunnels. Factors to be included in the investigations are:

- prevailing wind directions and velocities;
- prevailing air temperatures, and whether winds at match times are likely to contain rain or snow;
- local patterns of air turbulence caused by surrounding buildings and, of course, by the proposed stadium design itself;
- conflict between the needs of spectators (wanting protection from wind and sun) and the desirability of a natural grass pitch.

Obstruction to viewing
The roof edge must be high enough that the majority of spectators keep sight of the ball when it rises high in the air, and spectators' views of the pitch should not be obstructed by roof support columns.

4.8.2 Design life

Different elements will have different design lives. The loadbearing structure (columns, beams and trusses) will always have the longest replacement cycle, usually 50 years unless otherwise decided; roof coverings 15–20 years or more depending on type; and finishes will have the shortest cycle, the actual length depending on the type and quality of finish and standard of maintenance. These periods must be discussed and decided with the cost consultants at briefing stage as part of the 'whole-life costing' of the stadium.

Elements which have shorter life cycles than the loadbearing structure, such as claddings, must be designed for reasonably easy replacement; and a definite maintenance cycle for the

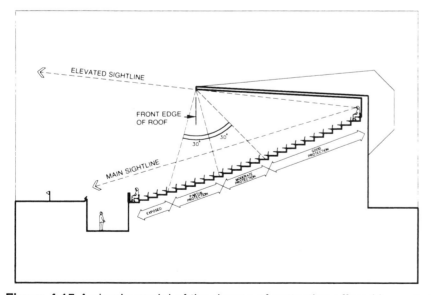

Figure 4.15 A simple model of the degree of protection offered by a stadium canopy. For actual design more detailed studies are needed taking into account factors such as orientation, prevailing wind direction and local patterns of turbulence.

roof must be decided on and spelt out in an Owners' Manual as discussed in Section 18.1.1.

4.8.3 Designing for wind uplift

When considering alternative forms of roof structure it must be remembered that holding the roof up is not the only structural problem. Wind pressure under the roof may at times create a much more serious problem of holding the roof down – and it is worth noting that more grandstand roofs have failed from destructive uplift than from collapse. This uplift condition is often transitory and may introduce a further complication by setting up an oscillation in the roof beams which must be dampened by the structure.

The problem is particularly great in lightweight structures which have insufficient mass to naturally dampen the 'bounce'. Increasing the weight of the structure specifically to resist conditions of uplift is a possible solution, but an expensive one because these conditions may apply only occasionally. An alternative approach is to adequately stiffen the lightweight structure, partly with special braces and partly by deliberately enhancing the structural potential of elements which are normally non-load-bearing (cladding panels, fascia panels and the like), so that they are able to play a part in transferring loads to the more massive elements and help to control vibration.

The use of wind tunnel testing is recommended in these cases, even though this may require sophisticated models, take two to three months, and possibly cost a lot of money. To get maximum value for this expenditure, testing for structural stability can be combined with testing for environmental impact (for example deleterious effects of wind on a grass pitch, or the creation of unpleasant gusting conditions in surrounding properties). Environmental impact testing is becoming a standard requirement anyway.

4.8.4 Roof types

We summarize below eight principal structural forms which can be used to resolve the many

forces acting upon a stadium roof, some of them working best as complete bowls, others as individual stands, as noted below. The list is not exclusive: there are other forms, and many variations and combinations of the basic options.

Throughout Section 4.8 we have drawn on the information contained in *Stadia Roofs*, published in 1992 by the Football Stadia Advisory Design Council (of which both the present authors were members until the Council's demise in early 1993), and we wish to give full acknowledgement to the editors and contributors who produced that publication. *Stadia Roofs* is an essential reference for stadium designers, as are all the publications of the FSADC.

i Post and beam structures

This structural system comprises a row of columns parallel to the pitch, supporting a series of beams or trusses which in turn carry the roof.

Advantages

The post and beam system is cheap and simple (though these attributes tend to be overrated: currently the cost of a column-free roof in a new stand is likely to increase total stadium costs by only about 2–4 per cent over the costs of a roof with columns).

Disadvantages

The row of columns along the pitch obstructs spectator viewing to an unacceptable degree. We believe that there are no circumstances in which this outdated form of roof construction can now be recommended.

If cases do arise where a post and beam roof is the only feasible option, owing perhaps to space constraints or the nature of the existing structure, then it is worth noting that the further back the columns are placed the less obstruction they cause. Seats behind such obstructions may have to be left unused or sold at reduced prices.

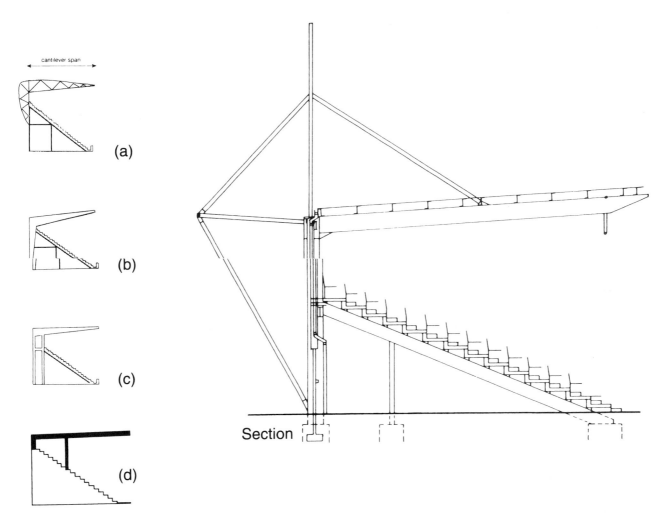

Figure 4.16 Various cantilever configurations; (d) is a 'propped cantilever', which reduces the span but has the disadvantage of obstructing vision.

ii Goal post structures

This is like a post and beam roof with posts only at the two ends, and none between (Figure 4.17), the entire length of the roof being spanned by a single girder. An example may be seen in Figure 4.4. A girder depth of about one twelfth of the length is normally economical (i.e. a beam that spans 120 m will be 10 m deep). Regular inspection and maintenance is especially important for this system because the entire roof structure depends upon a single girder.

Advantages
- Unobstructed viewing, particularly if the two uprights are situated at the ends of the playing field, with the entire length of the pitch left clear of columns.
- Moderate cost.

Disadvantages
- The system works best when little or no corner seating is required, thus placing a restraint on the seating layout as discussed in Section 7.3.
- The goal post system tends, from the visual point of view, to create a 'boxy shed' that cannot be coaxed round a curve or corner with any degree of grace, and is difficult to link smoothly with adjacent stands.

Figure 4.17 Goal post structures are column-free and comparatively cheap, and best suited to rectangular stadia of simple, shed-like character. Computer design by Lobb Partnership.

Figure 4.18 Watford Football Club Stadium in Britain, an example of a powerfully projecting cantilever roof. Architects: Lobb Partnership. Structural engineers: Jan Bobrowski & Partners.

This system is therefore most likely to be appropriate where separate stands are required on the sides of a playing pitch, with no intention of extending the roof other than in a straight line.

Examples
The goal post system is widely used in the UK, and examples include Ibrox Park in Glasgow (Figure 4.4).

iii Cantilever structures
A cantilevered roof is held down by weight or otherwise securely fixed at one end while its other end, facing the playing field, hangs free and unsupported. A variation of the above is the propped Cantilever (Figure 4.16).

Advantages
- Such a structure can provide completely unobstructed viewing for virtually any length of stand while spanning depths of 45 m or even more, the limiting factor being cost rather than technology. As examples the north stand at Twickenham Rugby Football Ground, London, has a clear depth of 39 m; the new north and south stands at Murrayfield Rugby Stadium, Edinburgh, a clear depth of 43 m, and the Husky Stadium, Seattle, a clear depth of 48 m.

- Cantilever roofs can be very dramatic, exploiting the excitement engendered by structure with no apparent means of support (Figure 4.18).
- The cantilever is as suitable for continuous bowl-shaped roofs as for isolated stands. In bowl stadia the individual frames can be arranged as a closely-spaced series of vertical elements fluidly following a circular or elliptical plan form – as in the Parc des Princes in Paris – which is a great planning advantage.

Disadvantages
- Where the rear seating rows must be very distant from the playing field the cantilever becomes markedly expensive and it may be found that a roof of the goal post type, for instance, can be built more cheaply. Whether the cost factor will be enough to outweigh other considerations (such as aesthetics) is a matter for careful evaluation.
- The reversal of forces caused by wind uplift can be particularly destructive in the case of a cantilevered roof (though less so if it is a bowl stadium, where the curved plan provides a stiffening effect). If slender 'holding-down' stays were envisaged at the back of the cantilever, to create a light and graceful

Figure 4.19 An elegant structure in Germany. Architect: Verene Dietrich.

structure, it may be found that these must become more massive to cope with the compression forces set up when the roof is lifted, thus creating a heavy structure where the desire was for a light one.

- A cantilever roof rises to its highest point at the back of the stand – the 'street side' as it were – and may therefore appear taller and more intimidating to passers-by than alternative forms of structure enclosing a similar seating capacity. The East Stand at Stamford Bridge football stadium in London, while being an admirably heroic and exciting design, also demonstrates the colossal visual impact that a large cantilevered structure may have. Not every site can absorb such a dramatic intrusion, particularly on the street side, where the stadium must relate to the scale of much more ordinary buildings.
- Related to the above point, a cantilevered roof thrusting boldly out into space without any visible means of support provides not only an aesthetic opportunity but also a risk. Great

care and some self-restraint is required if an obtrusive, out-of-scale result is to be avoided.

Examples
The East Stand at Stamford Bridge football stadium in London is not without problems: its construction costs were high, the upper seats seem a long way from the pitch, the lower seats are uncomfortably exposed to wind and rain, and there are difficulties with cleaning. Nevertheless its design has 'presence' and architectural power. Other examples include the Bari Stadium in Italy, Twickenham RFU and Seoul Olympic Stadium.

iv Concrete shell structures

Shells are thin surface structures which are curved in one or two directions, deriving their strength from the geometric shape rather than the thickness or firmness of the material (just as a flimsy sheet of paper may become capable of carrying a load if correctly curved). They include cylindrical, domed, conoid and hyperbolic shapes and offer the possibility of very elegant roof forms. A shell as thin as 75 mm or 100 mm may easily span 100 m.

Advantages
- Shell structures have the potential of great visual elegance. This does not, however, come automatically. Such innovative forms require very thorough testing of architectural character, using both computer modelling and physical scale models, if absolutely 'right-looking' results are to be obtained.
- If carefully detailed, shells can be self-finished both underneath and on the upper surface. The latter requires sufficiently steep drainage falls to ensure rapid and complete disposal of rainwater.

Disadvantages
- Specialist designers must be used, as the mathematics involved are advanced.
- If *in situ* concrete is used the formwork costs will be very high since a 'birdcage' or similar type of scaffold will be required. A pre-cast concrete solution should be considered, or a combination of pre-cast and *in situ* concrete.

Examples
The grandstand at Zarzuela racecourse near Madrid (1935) by Eduardo Torroja, the Palazzetto dello Sport in Rome (1957) by Annibale Vitellozzi and Pier Luigi Nervi, and the Palazzo dello Sport in Rome (1960) by Marcello Piacentini and Pier Luigi Nervi are the best-known examples of shell construction in sports buildings.

v Compression/tension ring

Such a roof consists of an inner tension ring and an outer compression ring, the two being connected by radial members which maintain the geometry of the overall doughnut-shaped structure and carry the roof covering.

Advantages
- Very great stand depths can be spanned with comparative ease: the new roof to the Vienna Prater Stadium (Figures 4.9, 4.10 and 4.11) spans a distance of 48 m between the inner and outer rings, and the recently added new roof to the Olympic Stadium in Rome (Figure 4.12) a distance of 52 m.
- As can be seen from the above examples, this roof type lends itself both technically and aesthetically to the problem of retro-fitting a new roof to an existing bowl stadium.
- The inner perimeter is completely column-free, so that there are no obstructions whatever between spectators and pitch.
- The roof has a light, weightless appearance as seen from the stadium interior and is unobtrusive or even invisible when seen from the outside. The latter can be a particular advantage in many situations as discussed in Section 4.2.3.
- Both the overall roof form and the structural details have inherent qualities of harmony and grace, and do not resist the designer's attempts to produce beautiful architecture. This contrasts with some other structural types which are technically efficient but aesthetically difficult to handle.
- Transparent or translucent roof coverings are possible, as in the Olympic Stadium in Rome.

- Some types permit the addition of a permanent or temporary roof cover over the playing field.

Disadvantages
- This structural system can be used only with bowl stadia.

Examples
The Prater Stadium in Vienna was built in 1928–31 and extended in 1956, and the new roof retrofitted in 1986 with no need for any additional reinforcement to the existing concrete structures. The pitch itself has been left open, while the surrounding stands seating 63 000 people are entirely covered by a continuous oval roof, the outer perimeter forming an ellipse of 270 m by 215 m. The roof covering consists of galvanized and plastic-coated corrugated steel sheets, while the structure comprises an inner tension ring and an external compression ring (both of these being box girders) with a connecting framework of steel tubes. The latter have a structural function and also support the steel covering plates. Special ties hold down the lightweight structure against wind uplift. Roof depth, front to back, is 48 m, and the overall roof area over 32 000 m^2. Floodlights are mounted on the inner ring and TV camera stands, public address systems and other services are integrated into the roof.

A more recent and even larger example is the open stadium in Rome which was used for the 1960 Olympic Games and then retro-fitted with a roof for the 1990 Soccer World Cup Competition. In this case roof depth is 52 m from front to back, and the roof covering consists of translucent Teflon, allowing some light to penetrate to the seats below.

vi Tension structures

These are roofs in which all the primary forces are taken by members acting in tension alone, such as cables. They are always more economical in material (though not necessarily in costs) than other forms of structure, but must be very carefully stabilized and restrained against any deformation which could cause parts of the system to go into compression. There are three principal forms – catenary cable, cable net and membrane.

Catenary cable structures

These consist of a compression arch (or arches) supporting one or more cables hanging in catenary shape, which in turn support a roof structure.

The beautifully shaped roof of Eero Saarinen's hockey rink at Yale University, New Haven (1958) is formed by cables suspended from a rigid arched keel. At Tokyo, seven years later, Kenzo Tange roofed the twin gymnasia for the 1964 Olympic Games with concrete slabs hung from massive steel cables to create two of the most dramatic architectural forms of the century.

These are very heavy forms of tension structure compared with the types below.

Cable net structures

As above the supporting structure is separated from the roof covering. The structure consists of a three-dimensional net of cabling (probably steel), and the covering probably of plastics (acrylic, PVC or polycarbonate). Glass reinforced plastic has been used but it tends to become brittle and less translucent with age. Suitable plastics for coverings are listed in Table 4.1, published by kind permission of the Football Stadia Advisory Design Council and the Sports Council.

An excellent example of a cable net roof is the Olympic Stadium complex at Munich (Figures 1.10 and 4.2) where a covering of transparent acrylic panels is supported by a web of steel cables. Because the covering in this case was designed to be relatively rigid, deformation in the cable system had to be minimized by very powerful pre-tensioning, leading to high costs for the masts and other anchoring members.

Membrane structures

Unlike the preceding two types, the roof covering material forms both the structure and the enclosure. Suitable fabrics include:

- PVC-coated polyester fabric. This is cheaper initially than the next type below, and easy to handle. But it has a life of only about 15 years, the fabric tends to sag with time, and the surface becomes sticky with age and requires frequent cleaning.
- Teflon-coated glass fibre fabric (also known as PTFE-coated glass fibre fabric). This is an expensive roof by any standards but it has a longer life than the type listed above and, being Teflon, it is to some degree self-cleaning. Use of this material is limited or banned by some authorities because of a tendency to produce toxic fumes in a fire. But as fire is not normally a hazard in stadium roof situations the material ought to be acceptable in this context. Use of an expert designer is essential, together with a fire engineering approach.

Examples in the UK include the Mound Stand at Lord's Cricket Ground, London of 1987 (translucent PVC-coated woven polyester fabric with PVDF top coat), the Sussex Stand at Goodwood Racecourse of 1990 and the Don Valley Stadium at Sheffield of 1991 (Figure 4.20) in 1991. The Riyadh Stadium in Saudi Arabia is an example of a complete stadium roofed in fabric.

Advantages

- Cable net or fabric roofs can be designed to lend an airy, festive appearance to a stadium, especially when seen from a distance. Given the aesthetic difficulties discussed in Sections 4.1 and 4.2 this can be a valuable attribute.
- If a translucent membrane is used the spectator spaces underneath may have a lighter, more open feel than with opaque roofs. It may also reduce the shading of the pitch which causes problems for grass growth, as discussed in Section 4.4.2, and for television coverage as discussed in Section 17.1.4.
- Tension structures can be adapted to many stadium layouts, and do not dictate a particular plan form.

Disadvantages

- Very sophisticated design is needed for all tension structures, and it is best to use structural engineers with previous experience and a track record of successful designs.

Table 4.1 Comparative properties of roof covering materials

	Profiled metal sheeting		Concrete	PVC		Acrylic	GRP	Polycarbonate		Fabric	
	Steel	Aluminium		Single glaze	Double glaze			Single glaze	Double glaze	PVC-coated	PTFE-coated
Relative cost factor (supply and fix) as at 1992 in the UK	1.0**	1.2	2.5 to 8.0	2.4 to 4.0	3.0 to 5.0	2.4 to 4.0	1.5 to 3.5	4.5 to 7.0	6.0 to 8.0	3.0 to 5.0	5.0 to 8.0
Durability	Good	Good	Good	Medium	Medium	Medium	Medium	Good	Good	Medium	Good
Flame retardancy	Incombustible	Incombustible	Incombustible	Self-extinguishing		Class 1 (when edges are protected)	Class 1	Self-extinguishing		Approx Class 1 equiv.	Class 0
Transparency	Opaque		Opaque	Transparent: 70% to 85% light transmission, which lessens markedly with time.		Translucent or transparent: 50% to 70% possible light transmission, which lessens moderately with time	Opaque	Transparent: 80% to 90% visible light transmission, which lessens slightly with time.		Translucent	

Figure 4.20 Another fabric-roofed stadium: the 25 000-capacity Don Valley Stadium at Sheffield, the largest athletics stadium in the UK. Architects: DBS Architects. Structural engineers: YRM Anthony Hunt Associates.

- More systematic and intensive maintenance is required than with other structural forms.
- Fabric roofs require very careful detailing of rainwater guttering.

vii Air supported roofs

An air supported roof consists of a plastic membrane which forms an enclosure, either on its own or in combination with a wall structure, and is supported by positive internal pressure provided by fans. These membranes are commonly formed in PVC polyester, sometimes with cable reinforcement in the case of larger roofs.

Advantages

Air supported roofs are relatively low in cost.

Disadvantages

- Full enclosures are vulnerable to damage.
- Design life is relatively short.

Examples

The leading air-supported roofs are mostly in North America. Those in the USA are the Hoosierdome in Indianapolis (1972) with a seating capacity of 61 000 and the Silverdome in Pontiac (1973) with a seating capacity of 80 000. The latter is shown in Figure 4.21. The leading Canadian example is BC Place in Vancouver (1983) with a seating capacity of 60 000. All these roofs are of fibreglass. The best-known Japanese example is the so-called 'Big Egg' in Tokyo.

Figure 4.21 The 80 000-capacity Silverdome in Pontiac, USA, with a roof of Teflon-coated Fiberglass supported entirely by internal air pressure and restrained by a diagonal network of steel cables. The roof membrane is 6 per cent translucent. Architects/engineers: Howard Needles Tammen & Bergendoff (HNTB).

viii Space frame

A space frame is a grid of structural members which is three-dimensional in shape and also stable in three dimensions, unlike, for instance, a roof truss, which is stable only in its own plane. Such frames can be constructed of any material but are commonly of steel.

Advantages
- Capable of spanning large distances.
- Suitable for all-over roofs with only perimeter support.

Disadvantages
- A space frame is efficient and sensible only if spanning in two directions. Plan proportions should therefore be roughly square, and preferably not have a length-to-width ratio greater than 1.5 to 1. This structural form will therefore not be appropriate for normal stand roofs unless the sections of roof between structural supports can be of these proportions.
- Space frames tend to be expensive.

Examples
The San Siro Stadium in Milan (Figure 4.22) is roofed over by an aluminium deck supported from steel lattice beams. The roof covering is translucent polycarbonate sheeting. It must be said that this was a very expensive solution

which has not functioned as well as expected (the main failure being that the grass on the pitch is struggling to survive, probably as a result of excessive shading, though that is no criticism of space frame roofs as such). Other examples include the stadium at Split in Croatia (Figure 4.23).

4.8.5 Roof coverings

We can best summarize the many requirements of roof coverings by quoting the authors of *Stadium Roofs*: 'Materials used for roof covering need to be lightweight, tough, water-tight, incombustible, aesthetically acceptable, cost-effective and durable enough to withstand the effects of outdoor weathering, including ultra-violet light. They should also be strong and stiff enough to span between primary and secondary elements, supporting snow and other super-imposed loads, including wind forces. Over the facility areas ... such as private boxes, kitchens, restaurants and toilets, the roof construction may require additional thermal and/or acoustic insulation.'

Opaque coverings

Profiled metal sheeting is cheap, easy to fix, and very commonly used. Steel sheets generally come in galvanized, plastic-coated or painted form. Aluminium sheets are lighter and inherently

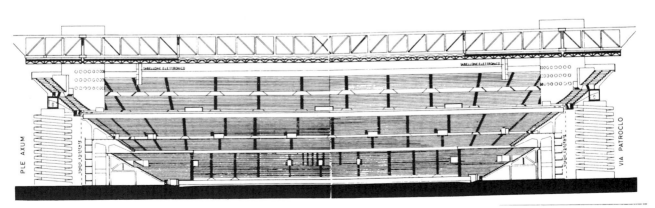

Figure 4.22 San Siro stadium in Milan is an example of a space frame roof. Structural engineer: Prof. Ing. Leo Finzi.

Figure 4.23 The roof of the stadium at Split, Croatia, shows a curved space frame structure. Architect: Prof. Boris Magas

resistant to atmospheric attack, but have less impact resistance and will suffer electrolytic corrosion when in contact with other metals or with concrete, and chemical attack when in contact with wood that is subject to wetting: in both cases separating membranes must be used at all contact points.

Concrete is so heavy that it will seldom be used as a roof covering as such, but where the roof structure is also the covering (for example a shell or slab) the chosen material may well be concrete. The problems which must then be addressed are likely to be excessive weight (which may be reduced by using lightweight aggregates) and the unattractive weathering that is associated with concrete surfaces. Silicone treatments may help reduce the latter, but if the stadium is to be built in a climate that is both rainy and polluted the concrete should preferably be given a finish such as tiling. If this is unaffordable then it will be very difficult to avoid the concrete gradually becoming stained and unattractive-looking, as discussed in Section 4.3.1.

Translucent coverings

Rigid plastics include acrylic (of which perspex is one variant), PVC and polycarbonate sheeting.

These materials are waterproof and strong, can withstand reasonably large deformations without damage, and have reasonable impact resistance. Examples of rigid translucent roofs include the 1972 Olympic Games stadium in Munich (Figure 4.2) which uses acrylic panels; the stadium at Split in Croatia which uses tinted 'lexan' sheeting; and the recently completed Rous Stand at Watford Football Stadium which uses pink-tinted triple-skinned PVC vaulted shells to give a warmer ambience to the light entering the upper tier.

Non-rigid plastics include PVC-coated polyester and PTFE-coated glass fibre. Examples are those already mentioned: the Mound Stand at Lord's Cricket Ground, the Sussex Stand at Goodwood Racecourse, and the Don Valley stadium in Sheffield.

A particularly innovative example of a translucent roof was seen in the stadium designed in 1993 by Arup Associates for Manchester's bid for the 2000 Olympics. Its elegant roof is graded from clear transparency at the front, via several stages of translucency further back, to complete opaqueness at the rear.

Table 4.1 gives guidance to both rigid and non-rigid types of translucent roofing.

4.8.6 Completely enclosed stadia

Stadia with permanent roofs over the playing area are to be found in the USA in particular, where they are known as 'domed' stadia. Examples in order of size are the Louisiana Superdome, New Orleans (capacity 95 000); the Silverdome, Pontiac (capacity 93 000); the Astrodome, Houston (capacity 66 000); the Hubert H. Humphrey Metrodome, Minneapolis (capacity 63 000) and the Hoosier Dome, Indianapolis (capacity 61 000).[1]

Many of these structures use translucent coverings. Such a covering gives a welcome effect of visual lightness, a pleasant open ambience, and it does assist television broadcasting by reducing contrast between sunlit and shadowed areas.

---

[1] It should be pointed out that the larger capacities in this list are generally for non-sporting uses such as concerts. See Table 1.1 for more detail, including sports capacities.

But even the best-performing translucent roofs will not permit grass to grow on the playing field below. If this is not important (as tends to be the case in the USA, where the great national sports do not require a natural grass surface, and where intensive multi-use favours hardwearing synthetic surfaces) the decision between an open or enclosed stadium becomes a relatively straightforward matter of balancing the relative costs and revenues of the two options against each other. But in Britain and Europe, where both soccer and rugby require natural grass pitches, the fully enclosed stadium will usually be ruled out in principle.

4.9 A stadium for the future

4.9.1 Background

Following the disaster at Britain's Hillsborough stadium in 1989, in which nearly 100 spectators died, the Taylor Report of January 1990 severely criticized most existing British football stadia and recommended sweeping improvements.

There followed an uncertain period among British football clubs in which an urge to rebuild was inhibited by lack of money and lack of clarity on how rigidly the authorities would implement the new recommendations. It seemed all too possible that a wave of cheap, functional 'tin sheds', whose only merit was that they obeyed the new regulations, would start springing up on football grounds all over Britain to meet the demands of clubs.

To aid debate and raise standards of expectation three organizations combined to design a theoretical 'stadium for the nineties': the Technical Unit for Sport at the UK's Sports Council, the LOBB Partnership (architects) and YRM Anthony Hunt Associates (structural engineers).

4.9.2 A stadium for the nineties

Their plan (Figure 4.24) hypothesized a 20 000 all-seater stadium with spectators distributed around the pitch in accordance with their known preference (the greatest number around the

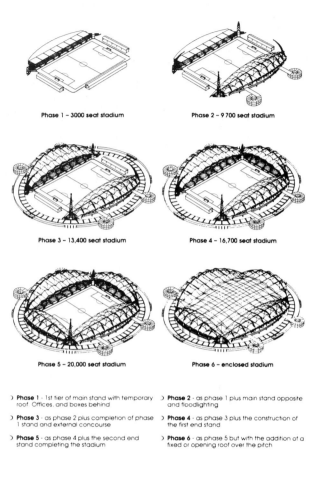

Phase 1 – 3000 seat stadium

Phase 2 – 9 700 seat stadium

Phase 3 – 13,400 seat stadium

Phase 4 – 16,700 seat stadium

Phase 5 – 20,000 seat stadium

Phase 6 – enclosed stadium

〉 **Phase 1** - 1st tier of main stand with temporary roof. Offices, and boxes behind

〉 **Phase 2** - as phase 1 plus main stand opposite and floodlighting

〉 **Phase 3** - as phase 2 plus completion of phase 1 stand and external concourse

〉 **Phase 4** - as phase 3 plus the construction of the first end stand

〉 **Phase 5** - as phase 4 plus the second end stand completing the stadium

〉 **Phase 6** - as phase 5 but with the addition of a fixed or opening roof over the pitch

Figure 4.24 The British 'Stadium for the Nineties' proposal by Lobb Partnership in association with the Sports Council. Structural engineers: YRM Anthony Hunt Associates.

halfway line and behind the goals) and with no spectator further than 90 m from the centre spot.

A seating row depth of 800 mm, and a line-of-sight clearance over the head of the spectator in front of 120 mm, are optimal and of a standard rarely to be found in existing British stadia. The pitch is protected all round by a moat rather than the more usual, and unpopular, fence.

The all-important roof design uses translucent Teflon-coated glassfibre membranes which are self-cleaning and with good fire-resistance, supported on four graceful longitudinal steel arches each of which spans clear across the stand beneath.

Figure 4.25 The roof at Selangor Turf Club, Malaysia, is mainly designed for protection from the sun. Architects: T. R. Hamzah & Yeang Sdn. Bhd in association with LOBB Partnership. Structural engineers: Tahir Wong.

Figure 4.26 The Alamo dome USA is a covered stadium with a clearly articulated structure. Designers: HOK. Photo: R. Greg Hursley Inc.

Figure 4.27 The Comiskey Park in the USA is a new example of the stadium in the streetscape. Architects: HOK. Photo: Scott McDonald, Hedrich-Blessing.

To meet the financial capacity of the club the stands can be constructed in five phases seating first 3000, then 9700, then 13 400, then 16 700 and finally 20 000 spectators. A sixth phase, if desired and affordable, would be the addition of a fixed or opening roof over the pitch.

There is generous provision for private function rooms and executive suites of the kind now regarded as essential for financial viability.

The scheme is a notional one, but it satisfies most of the functional criteria which have been set out in this chapter, does so within an elegant form, and contains many features that would be of interest to clients and design teams.

5

Activity area

5.1 Playing surfaces

5.1.1 History

Informal sport has been played on grass fields, city squares or open ground for hundreds of years but it was not until the middle of the last century that sports became organized and conditions were defined under which the sport could be played fairly. These early, rather loose, conditions later became rules and eventually the laws of sport were born. A notable exception is tennis which had its origins as an indoor sport and only later took to the outdoors. The surface to be played upon was often specified in these rules, as it was recognized that the nature of a game differed when the surface it was played upon changed.

The established rule of ball sports being played on natural surfaces was unchallenged until 1966 when the Houston Astrodome opened. This was the first completely covered stadium in the world and was designed, using the best technology at the time, with a transparent roof and natural turf playing surface. Unfortunately, the grass did not grow below the transparent roof for a number of reasons, one of which was that the steel structure holding up the solid roof was substantial and hindered the natural light from penetrating to the playing surface. No transparent or translucent roof has yet permitted the growth of natural turf suitable for playing ball sports.

In order to avoid this show case stadium turning into a disaster, a manufactured synthetic grass was woven using green plastic and laid over the existing ground. This product was called 'Astroturf' after its host venue, the 'Astrodome' and variants of this original synthetic grass have covered many other sports surfaces around the world. Synthetic sports surfaces have been developed over time into more sophisticated constructions, all with the enormous advantage to a stadium manager that he can hold different events on the same playing surface, one after the other. Although players and team coaches tended to prefer a natural grass surface for its playability, artificial surfaces were approved for American football and spread quickly through the USA.

5.1.2 Current requirements

Table 5.1 shows the playing characteristics of tennis court surfaces, reproduced with the permission of the Lawn Tennis Association.

5.1.3 Natural grass surfaces

Advantages
Natural grass remains the most user-friendly of surfaces, and the only permissible choice for some sports. The advantages of natural grass are:

- it is aesthetically attractive;
- it gives a speed of rebound and a degree of rolling resistance that is just about right for most ball sports;
- it provides reasonable (though variable) purchase for players feet when dry or wet;
- it gives a surface that is neither excessively hard nor excessively soft for comfortable running;

Table 5.1 Playing characteristics of tennis court surfaces

Surfaces	Ball–surface interaction					Player–surface interaction		
	Speed of court	*Height of bounce*	*Trueness of bounce*	Spin		*Sliding/firm footing*	*Traction (slip or non-slip)*	*Resilience (hardness)*
				Topspin	*Slice*			
Grass	Fast	Low	Variable	Little	Yes	Firm footing with partial slide	Slip	Soft
Synthetic turf	Fast	Medium to low	Variable	Little	Yes	Firm footing	Mainly non-slip	Medium to soft
Impervious acrylic	Medium	Medium	Uniform	Yes	Yes	Firm footing	Non-slip	Hard to medium
Porous macadam	Slow	High	Almost uniform	Yes	Little	Firm footing	Non-slip	Hard
Shale	Medium	Medium	Variable	Yes	Yes	Sliding	Slip	Medium to soft
Continental clay	Slow	Medium	Almost uniform	Yes	Yes	Sliding	Non-slip	Medium to soft

Source: *Tennis Courts*, published by the LTA Court Advisory Service. Reproduced by kind permission of Christopher Trickey.

- it is less injurious to players who fall than most alternative finishes;
- if irrigated it is a relatively cool surface in hot climates.

Disadvantages

The major limitation to the use of grass surfaces is that they cannot be used in roofed stadia, and are difficult to keep healthy even under partial cover. The reason is that grass needs ample light for really healthy growth, and air movement, humidity and temperature levels need to be kept within fairly strict parameters. To date it has proved impossible to arrange all these matters satisfactorily in a totally enclosed stadium, even using the most transparent roofing materials. In theory supplemental artificial lighting does help but there are no real-life applications to demonstrate the effectiveness of this solution, and in any case the energy costs of such lighting may be prohibitive.

Even in a partly-roofed stadium the size of the roof aperture, the shadow-effects of the surrounding structure and other such factors may lead to disappointing results. One example of failure is the San Siro Stadium in Milan which was redeveloped to accommodate 80 000 specta-tors for the soccer World Cup in 1990. Only the spectator seating areas are roofed, with a central opening over the playing area. Even though this aperture is approximately the size of the football pitch below the grass is struggling to survive. The reasons are not clear, but the lesson to designers must be one of caution.

A second limitation is that grass cannot survive the same intensity and frequency of punishment as most artificial surfaces. This relative fragility will inevitably conflict with the stadium's need to maximize the number of event days per annum for profitability.

The 'pitch replacement' concept

One response to the problems outlined above is the concept of 'pitch replacement' on an organized and systematic basis. The principle is to remove the grass when not needed, to allow other events to take place on an artificial surface underneath. There are many removal techniques: (i) a Canadian method of growing the turf in large boxes which can then be moved out of the stadium on rails; (ii) a German method of growing the turf on pallets 4 m square which are then moved on the hovercraft principle; and (iii) a Dutch concept of leaving the natural grass in place and constructing above it a new platform supported on remote-controlled hydraulic legs. In the UK, Odsal Stadium in Bradford has used a simple system of restoring the corners of a football pitch which had been cut off by a speedway track around the pitch: grass was grown on wooden pallets with a reinforced plastic mesh sub-base, and these were moved away to storage by forklift truck before speedway events. Further notes on this topic are provided in Section 4.4.2.

Installation

Planting and maintaining a grass pitch is a task for specialists. All the advice given below is for general background understanding only: a specialist consultant should be retained from the outset to give advice, draw up a detailed specification, invite tenders and supervise the work.

Figure 5.1 shows the elements of a typical grass-turfed surface, and should be studied in conjunction with the following notes.

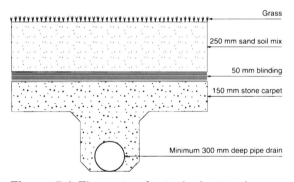

Figure 5.1 Elements of a typical natural grass playing surface.

For bowling greens and croquet the upper grass surface must be smooth, true and absolutely level, necessitating very good subsoil drainage arrangements. For other sports the grass surface can be less exacting but should be smooth and free from surface unevenness, and possibly laid to a slight fall for water disposal. Maximum permissible gradients must be checked before design with the relevant governing bodies, because such rules are constantly

being upgraded, and the main fall should ideally be from the centre to both sides of the pitch and not in the direction of play.

The species of turf grass must be carefully chosen for the correct playing characteristics, resistance to wear and disease, and suitability for its particular climatic and physical environment and the season of play. An appropriate cultivar or mix of cultivars will be specified by the consultant and supplied by specialist growers. 'Fescues' and 'bents' are commonly chosen species. As an instance, the famous grass surface of Wimbledon Centre Court is resown every year with 66 per cent Troubadour perennial rye grass, 17 per cent Bingo chewings fescue, and 17 per cent Regent creeping red fescue. This is the best mix for the specific soil, drainage and other conditions found at Wimbledon, but other situations will demand other specifications.

Immediately beneath the grass surface is a layer of topsoil, often consisting largely of sand, with a depth of not less than 100 mm and usually averaging about 150 mm. This layer must contain no stones or injurious material, must be permeable enough for water drainage, and must be uncontaminated and well-fertilized for healthy growth. Using some local suitable-seeming soil will not be good enough: the material will almost certainly be obtained from specialist suppliers to the precise specification of the consultant, and will probably contain a large quantity of graded sand.

Beneath the topsoil is a blinding layer of fine material (ash, crushed stone or the like) to fill the voids in the surface below and provide a smooth base for the topsoil.

Beneath the blinding layer is a zone of graded stone to ensure that all excess water can drain away freely to pipes laid in trenches below. There may be sheets of tough water-permeable membrane laid between the foundation layer and the formation surface to prevent soil from being forced up into the foundation layer and obstructing the free flow of water. This decision, the depth of the graded stone layer, and the layout and fall of the drains will depend on subsoil conditions and will all be decided by a specialist.

Drainage

Adequate drainage is a necessity, and the above methods may need to be supplemented to avoid standing pools of surface water after heavy rainfall and to minimize expensive 'down-time' in wet weather. There are basically two methods of drainage – passive and active.

The *passive* approach relies on gravity to drain away the water, and one method of enhancing the basic system described above would be the cutting of deep 'slit drains' into the subsoil by specialist machine, and filling these with sand or fine gravel to help surface water flow down quickly into the land drains. This is quite expensive and needs to be carefully costed before a decision is taken.

The *active* approach uses pumps, usually activated by water-sensing electronic devices in the field, to literally suck the water off the pitch and into underground storage chambers, thus clearing the surface very quickly and maximizing the availability of the pitch for revenue-generating activity. Special drainage pipes may be laid for this purpose, or alternatively cellular technology may use the same underground network of pipes both for irrigation and drainage simply by reversing the direction of flow by computer control.

Irrigation

Traditionally grass pitches have been watered by sprinklers, usually of the pop-up kind, but these are being challenged by underground water delivery systems. Using special porous low-pressure water supply pipes (or possibly the underground drainage system with the direction of flow reversed by computer control as suggested above) which allow a uniform 'weep rate' along the whole length of the pipe, a steady supply of water – possibly mixed with fertilizer and weed-control additives – seeps directly to the grass root zone. The advantages that are claimed for sub-surface irrigation include:

- a lusher, tougher growth of turf grass than overhead watering, which tends to create a stressful cycle of drought and flood conditions;
- a deep root system rather than a shallow one;

- less tendency for the soil to compact (this being a major problem with intensively-used pitches);
- probably less water-loss by evaporation than would be the case with surface irrigation;
- similarly, a conservation of fertilizers, insecticides and herbicides.

Underground irrigation pipes are normally laid between 150 mm and 350 mm below the surface, spaced from 450 mm to 900 mm apart; but specialist advice must be sought.

Heating

Many major stadia in cold climates use some form of under-pitch heating, the most common type being based on a system of hot water pipes operated by gas boilers and thermostatic sensor controls. The most important aspect of this type of installation is the laying of the pipes, which must be high enough to heat the pitch but low enough not be damaged by pitch aeration and other surface works. A free-draining pitch is essential if heating is to be considered.

Maintenance

Day-to-day maintenance operations are discussed in Section 18.2.1.

5.1.4 Synthetic grass surfaces

In completely enclosed stadia artificial turf will almost certainly be chosen in preference to natural grass for the reasons given in Section 5.1.3 above.

For other situations, while synthetic grasses have great virtues and will undoubtedly become more widely used, specifiers must not see them as a magically everlasting, maintenance-free answer to all problems. Capital outlay is high (which means such pitches need to be fairly intensively used to justify the initial cost); the surface is not everlasting, six to eight years being a typical life expectancy; the surfaces may need to be watered before play to keep dust down and keep them cool in summer; sand-filled turfs need periodic re-sanding; markings need replacement two to four times a year; and regular cleaning and repair are essential.

But having made these cautionary remarks it must be said that synthetic turfs have very great advantages in terms of their ability to endure intensive use in virtually all weathers. There are three basic categories of permanent surfacing.

Non-filled turf

This is made of nylon, polyester or polypropylene, is available in water-permeable or impermeable types, and comes in the form of a turf-carpet with an underlying shock-absorbing layer of foam, the latter available in various densities and thicknesses. The turf and the underlayer may be supplied already bonded, or they may be supplied separately and bonded together on site. Turf and underlayer are laid by specialists on a smooth asphalt substrate which in turn rests on a base of broken stone, sand, and gravel designed to suit the particular situation. Various pile-types and pile-lengths (typically 10 to 13 mm) are available to suit individual sports and conditions.

In the past it was said that artificial turf caused more skin-burn than natural grass in sports such as rugby, but manufacturers claim that this need no longer be true. On this, as on choice of turf, design of substrate, and general installation, up-to-date specialist advice must be sought.

Filled turf

This is a variant of the previous type, consisting in most cases of polypropylene with an upright pile that is longer and more open than the non-filled type, backfilled with sand up to 2 or 3 mm from the surface. As described here it has become a very popular surface for club tennis courts because the playing characteristics are not dissimilar to natural grass, but the court remains usable throughout the year including winter. The finish takes two to three months to settle in, and needs brushing two or three times a week plus regular top-dressing to maintain its condition. This type of artificial turf is specifically suited to outdoor use and usually carries a 5-year guarantee, though the life may well be longer.

Sand-filled turf has had a reputation of causing injuries when players fall, but this is probably no longer the case: if in doubt the advice of the relevant sports governing bodies should be sought. Occasional watering after a prolonged period of dry weather will help reduce the risk of friction burn.

Combined natural and synthetic turf

Natural and artificial surfaces have begun to merge, and systems are now available in which plastics are used to reinforce the root structure of grass – for instance in the form of a plastic webbing through which the natural grass grows. By this means the user-friendliness of a natural grass surface is combined with the superior durability of artificial turf, hopefully giving stadium managers the best of both worlds.

As practical experience of these combined systems increases and the technicalities are perfected they may well become the compromise of the future, offering a cost-effective, multi-use natural playing surface. In that case sporting authorities will soon have to face some interesting decisions as to whether these systems are to be classified as 'natural' or 'artificial'. Because of climatic difficulties, the Ulleval stadium in Norway has used such a system for many years.

Temporary synthetic turf surfaces

It is possible for a synthetic turf carpet to be kept in a store near the pitch, and then rolled out over the pitch for events needing that kind of surface. The carpet can simply be rolled out manually, or, in some systems, air jets are used to float the carpet over the pitch with a minimum of weight, drag and friction. In this case six men can carry out the operation in three hours or less, allowing for a quick change of events.

5.1.5 Synthetic hard surfaces

Synthetic surfaces are expensive to lay but offer the possibility of all-weather high-intensity use and much reduced maintenance. They have therefore become very popular for athletics tracks. There are two categories.

Impervious finishes

These may take the form of a 'wet-poured' layer of continuous sheeting (either permanent or temporary), or of a tiled finish laid on a substrate of bituminous macadam, concrete or both. In the case of athletics tracks, gradients for water run-off must be less than 1:100 and the direction of fall must be towards the inside lane, with a drainage channel to dispose of the water. The thickness of the finish must be related to the length of the spikes on athletes' footwear, or else punctures will allow water to penetrate to the substrate, causing problems.

Porous finishes

These finishes are of the same types as above, but 'stipple-bonded' to a porous substrate (porous bituminous macadam or no-fines concrete) so that water can filter through the surface and drain away. In theory the surface can be completely level, but a cross-fall of 1:100 is advisable in case the surface loses permeability as a result of pollution.

5.1.6 Markings

In the case of grass the line markings may consist of a temporary powder containing lime. In the case of hard surfaces the markings can either be inlaid strips of coloured material (the most expensive in first cost but also the most durable method) or simply be painted on to the surface (and requiring regular repainting).

Governing bodies will give guidance on correct line widths and colours, and whether the width of the line includes or excludes the playing area – a crucial matter. But as a general guide line widths are mostly 100 mm, and white and yellow the most common colours.

5.1.7 Protective coverings

If the surface cannot be removed and is vulnerable to damage there are protective covers which will preserve it when the stadium is used for concerts or other activities which make use of the playing area. Natural grass especially needs protection, but covers can usually be left down for only about two days before the grass beneath starts to suffer damage. There are cases where grass pitches have been covered for up to two weeks and survived, suffering only discoloration, but a natural grass pitch would not be ready for immediate sporting use after such an experience.

For grass protection, Wembley Stadium in London has in the past used a resilient underlay covered with a stiff hardwearing rubber layer above, these materials being stored in large rolls outside the stadium and transported to the ground in special vehicles. More recently Wembley have assisted in the development of a new system which consists of translucent tile squares (actually 1 m by 1 m boxes about 50 mm deep) which lock together to provide a good even surface for concert usage, but allow the grass below to grow and survive.

5.2 Pitch dimensions, layout and boundaries

5.2.1 Dimensions and layout

Figures 5.3 and 5.14 set out the basic dimensions of the playing areas plus surrounding safety zones for the major sports. Some of these are simplified versions of more complex official requirements too detailed to fully reproduce here, and many may become out of date within the lifetime of this book. Therefore these diagrams must be checked with the relevant governing bodies before final design.

The following summaries of advice for specific sports are taken with due acknowledgement from the *Handbook of Sports and Recreational Building Design* (Vol. 1, 2nd edn.) published by the Sports Council in Britain.

Football

Pitch dimensions for Association Football (more commonly known as football or soccer) are shown in Figure 5.2. Safety margins should be 6 m wide behind the goal line and 3 m along the side touch-lines and the grass surface should extend beyond the touch lines by at least 3m and 2m respectively. A natural turf pitch is recommended by the governing bodies and is the only surface allowed for some competitions, but the use of artificial surfaces may become more widely accepted.

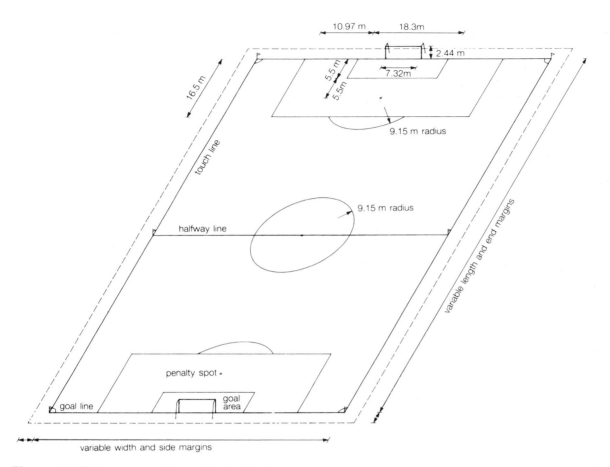

Figure 5.2 Pitch size and layout for football or soccer.

Rugby league football
Pitch dimensions are shown in Figure 5.3. There should be a margin of at least 6 m at each end of the pitch and at least 2 m, but preferably 6 m, at each side. Natural grass is currently the only accepted surface. Markings are in white, 76 mm wide, and are not included in the playing area.

Rugby union football
Pitch dimensions are shown in Figure 5.4, and there must be no obstruction such as fencing within 5 m of the touch-line. Natural grass is currently the only accepted surface except that rubber-crumb or synthetic turf is acceptable for training. Markings are in white, 76 mm wide, and are not included in the playing area.

American football
Pitch dimensions are shown in Figure 5.5, and there must be a safety margin of at least 1.83 m,

but preferably twice that, all round the field. Both natural grass and synthetic turf are acceptable. Markings are in white or failing that yellow, 100 mm wide, and the playing area excludes the side lines but includes the end lines.

Australian Rules football
Pitch dimensions are shown in Figure 5.13, and a surrounding gap of 3 m is generally recommended between spectators and the oval boundary line. The game is played on grass only. Markings are in white, 100 mm wide, and are included in the playing area.

Gaelic football
Pitch dimensions are shown in Figure 5.7, and a margin of 1.5 m is required on all four sides. Pitch surface may be grass, synthetic turf (sand-filled) or shale. Markings are in white, 50 mm wide, and are included in the playing area.

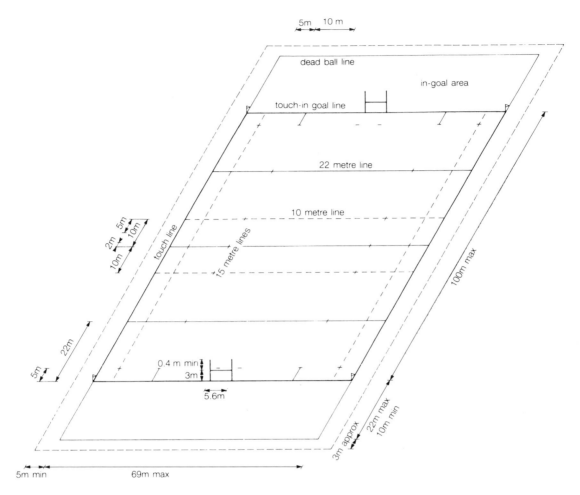

Figure 5.3 Pitch size and layout for rugby union football.

Hockey
Pitch dimensions are shown in Figure 5.8. The surface may be grass or synthetic. Markings are in white or yellow, 75 mm wide, and are included in the playing area.

For a grass pitch it is currently recommended that there should be margins of at least 3 m along both sides and 4.57 m at both ends, but preferably more, so that the pitch can be shifted from time to time to minimize wear; and for a synthetic pitch there should be a minimum of 5 m between the end line and any obstruction, with the synthetic grass extending at least 3 m all round the pitch. All these regulations are subject to change and advice must be sought. If sand-filled synthetic turf is used there must be two large-capacity water hydrants near the pitch to allow for watering.

Hurling
Pitch dimensions are shown in Figure 5.9. Margins of 4.57 m are required at each end, and margins of at least 3 m along each side. Markings are in white, 50 mm wide, and are included in the playing area.

Baseball
Pitch dimensions are shown in Figure 5.10, and the surface may be grass or synthetic turf. A batting cage is strongly recommended. Markings are in white, 127 mm wide, and are included in the playing area.

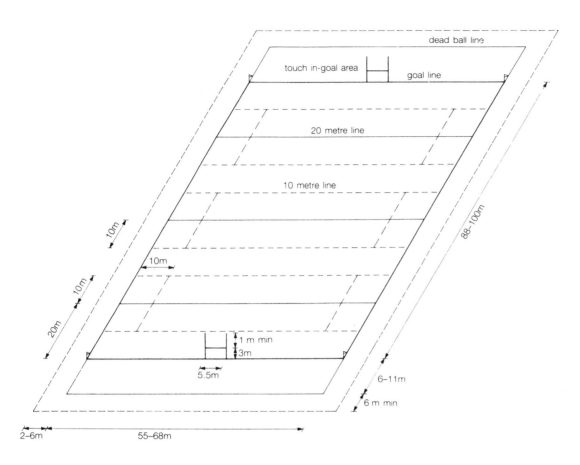

dead ball line

touch in-goal area

goal line

20 metre line

10 metre line

88–100m

10m

10m

10m

10m

20m

1 m min

3m

5.5m

6–11m

6 m min

2–6m

55–68m

Figure 5.4 Pitch size and layout for rugby league football.

Cricket

Pitch dimensions are shown in Figure 5.11, and the surface may be natural turf or any of several synthetic finishes as recommended by the governing body.

Athletics track and field

Figure 5.12 gives guidance on layout, but different arrangements are possible to suit different circumstances. Table 5.2 gives a guide to lane provision, and in the UK a common choice is a six-lane, 400 m track together with indoor training facilities. Lanes are always 1.22 m wide to the centre of markings. Whatever the layout, the central area must have a natural grass surface because this is obligatory for field throwing events. The running tracks on the other hand may be surfaced with a variety of synthetic materials. On this and all other aspects of athletic track and pitch design the governing

bodies must be consulted for precise and up-to-date information.

Lawn tennis

Pitch dimensions are shown on Figure 5.6 and in Table 5.3, and the characteristics of alternative surfaces summarized in Table 5.1. All markings are in white and between 25 mm and 50 mm in width except the centre service line which must be 50 mm and the base line which may be up to 100 mm wide.

5.2.2 The playing area surround

The detailed design of the zone surrounding the playing area must be verified with the governing bodies and safety authorities. Such requirements cannot safely be given here: they vary from sport to sport and from country to country, and are subject to change. Purely as an example of the

Table 5.2   Recommended lane provision in athletics tracks

Standard of use	*Number of lanes* recommended	
	Synthetic all-weather surface	*Hard porous (waterbound) surface*
Minimum standard international competitions; British Athletic Federation Area and Regional competitions and below	6 lanes	7 lanes
International competitions	6 lanes with 8-lane straight(s)	8 lanes
Full standard international competitions	6 lanes with 8-lane straight(s)	7 lanes with 9-lane straight(s)
Major international competitions	8 lanes with 10-lane straight(s)	

* All lanes are 1.22 m wide to the centre of markings.

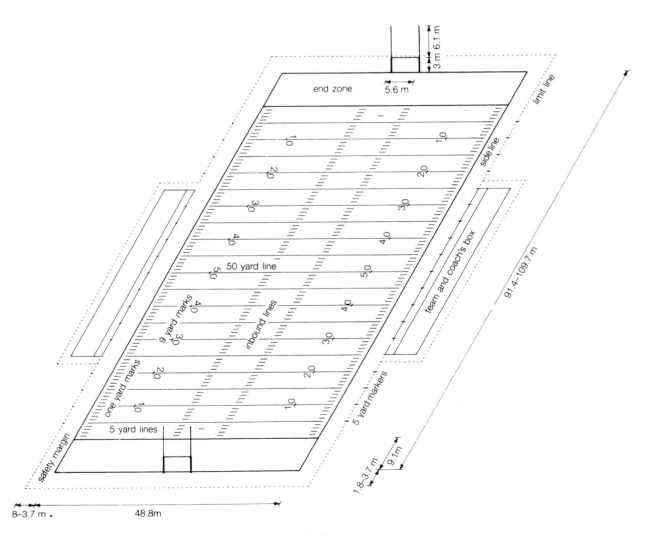

Figure 5.5 Pitch size and layout for American football.

Table 5.3 Tennis space requirements

Marked out playing area	International and National Championships		Club and County		Minimum recreational standard	
	m	ft	m	ft	m	ft
Court length	23.77	78	23.77	78	23.77	78
Court width	10.97	36	10.97	36	10.97	36
Length of net (doubles)	12.80	42	12.80	42	12.80	42
Runback at each end	6.40 (1)	21 (1)	6.40	21	5.49	18
Side run out, each side	3.66 (1)	12 (1)	3.66	12	3.05	10
Side run between aligned courts without separate enclosure	ND	ND	4.27	14	3.66	12
Overall size of enclosure(s)						
Length	36.58 (1)	120 (1)	36.58	120	34.75	114
Width for one enclosed court	18.29 (1)	60 (1)	18.29	60	17.07	56
Width for 2 courts in a single enclosure			33.53	110	31.70	104
Width added for each additional court			15.24	50	14.63	48

Note (1): May need increased overall dimensions for court officials, furniture and sponsorship boards.

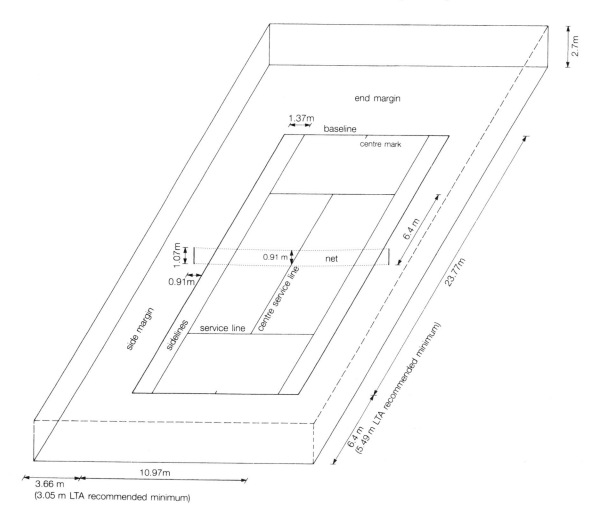

Figure 5.6 Pitch size and layout for lawn tennis.

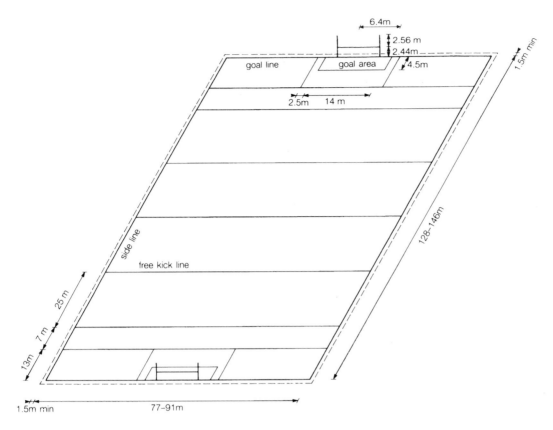

Figure 5.7 Pitch size and layout for Gaelic football.

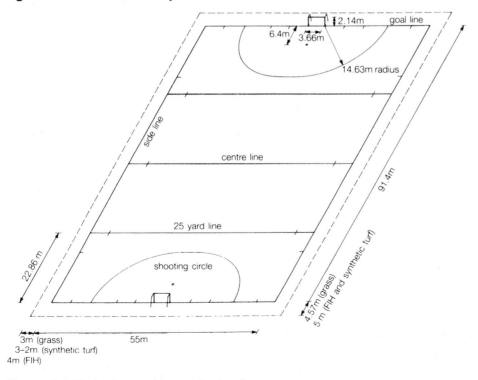

Figure 5.8 Pitch size and layout for hockey.

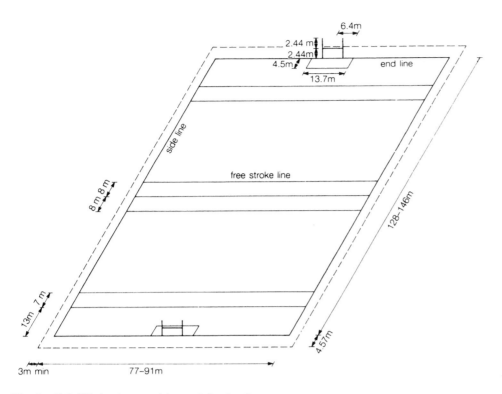

Figure 5.9 Pitch size and layout for hurling.

provisions that might be required, the following criteria are laid down by FIFA and UEFA for football pitches:

- There should be two units of seating, accommodating ten people each, on the two sides of the centre line. They must be at ground level and protected from the weather.
- Advertising boards must never obstruct spectators' sight lines, must under no circumstances be located where they could endanger players, and must not be constructed in any fashion or of any material which could endanger players. They must not be higher than 900 mm and must be located at least 6 m behind the goal, at least 5 m behind the side lines and at least 3 m behind the corner flags.

5.2.3 Perimeter walls and barriers

All sports require some kind of barrier between the pitch and the spectators, and the requirements for these are laid down not only by the governing bodies for the sports concerned, but

also by local safety authorities and police. Detailed advice is given in Chapter 6.

5.3 Multi-purpose use

5.3.1 Europe

In continental Europe there has been a tradition for a city to establish a 'municipal' stadium for the use of its citizens playing and watching a wide range of sports. The facility is often initially funded by the city authority and supported by a football club, which may run its own lottery and plough the profits back into the stadium. Often the stadium accommodates an athletics track around the pitch and thereby provides a multipurpose facility although one which is heavily weighted towards football financially. In the UK the separation of the spectators from the playing field by the running track, effectively pushing everyone away from the action by 10 or 12 m, has never gained acceptance. British football clubs pride themselves on providing a close

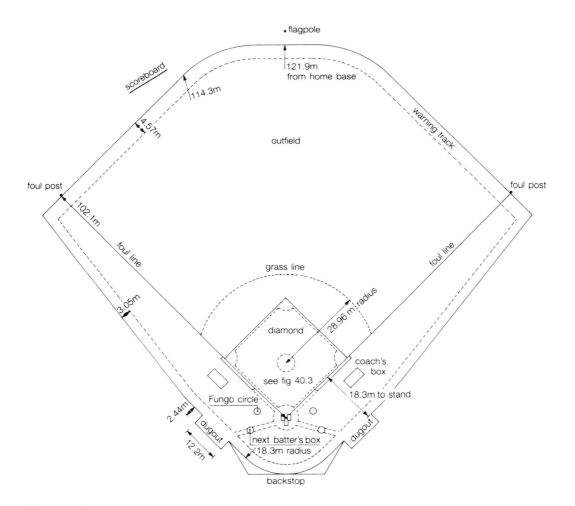

Figure 5.10 Pitch size and layout for baseball.

concentrated atmosphere to watch the game and consequently forego the possibility of sharing their grounds with an athletics club. It is possible that by using movable seating tiers and other devices, the close football atmosphere and athletics can be made to work together.

5.3.2 North America

In the USA several different approaches have evolved which combine functions on the same site. The two major stadium sports in the USA of American football and baseball do not coexist easily in a stadium unless the basic plan configuration can change. Solutions sought are either as a dual use venue with movable seating, a double venue where two separate stadia co-

habit the same site or an attached arena for basketball and ice hockey.

5.3.3 Financial viability

Multi-purpose use of a stadium does not necessarily have to be based on two sports, a club can sometimes find a compatible partner within the same sport. There are many examples around the world of sports clubs sharing facilities while in Australia ground sharing is supported by the administrators of Australian Rules football.

More commercial developments of the leisure industry can also be compatible. The undercroft of a stand in Bristol, UK, successfully houses an indoor bowling rink and extensions to the stadia at Sheffield Wednesday and Arsenal football

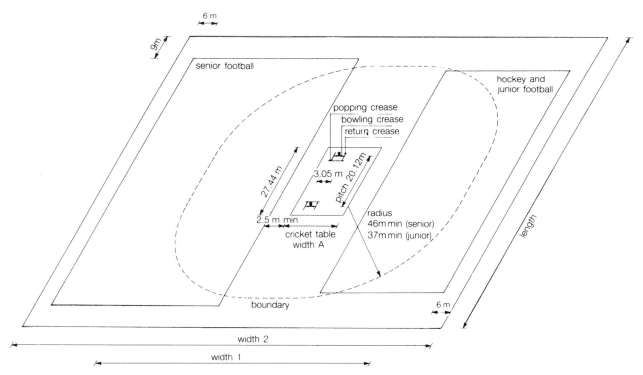

Figure 5.11 Pitch size and layout for cricket.

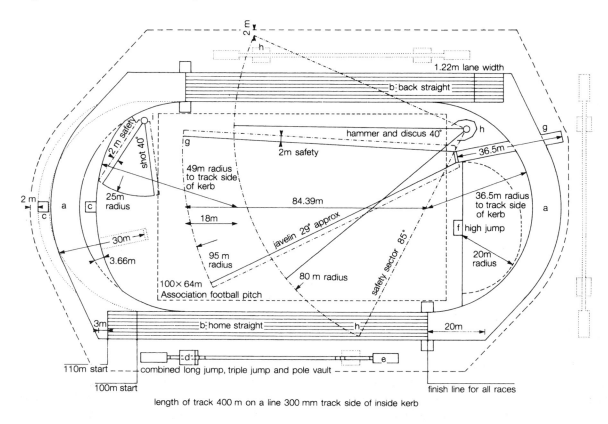

Figure 5.12 Pitch size and layout for athletics track and field.

93

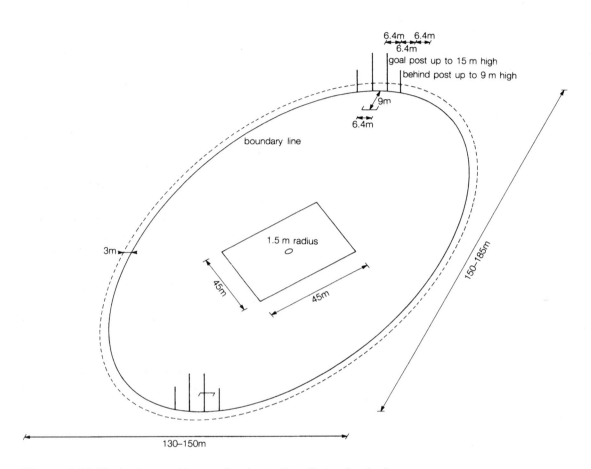

Figure 5.13 Pitch size and layout for Australian Rules football.

clubs have accommodated training halls which double up as function rooms. Other ideas which have been explored are the inclusion of television studios, cinemas, health centres, squash courts, swimming pools, hairdressing salons and children's activity spaces. The unfortunate fact about combining other activities with a stadium is that by its very nature the structure is inflexible with substantial supports at regular points around its perimeter. It is sometimes difficult to insert large spaces into this structure and therefore their inclusion must be planned from the beginning, tending to suggest a certain lack of flexibility. One alternative is to add these facilities on to the stadium as a separate but connected structure. This has been done successfully in a number of places in both Europe and

the USA. Utrecht Stadium in Holland has a substantial office building grafted to its side while the Hoosier Dome and a number of others in the USA have enormous exhibition and convention centres directly attached to the main stadium.

There are very few sports which can make a substantial subsidy to a stadium and if idle stadia are to become well used and profitable it seems that the emphasis in the additional accommodation should be on entertainment and commerce rather than sports.

5.3.4 Maximizing event days

Event days must be maximized while still maintaining the core function of the venue. This multi-use should be designed for at an early stage as every event requires different equipment and support services, some more than others. If these facilities are not designed into the fabric of the building from the start they can be an expensive addition later and may not justify the holding of the event. These specialist 'extras' include such things as the electric power required for pop concerts or the support rings in the roof for a circus. The multi-purpose use of a Stadium is the primary reason for considering covering the entire grounds. For many years sports fans have been prepared to risk the elements and attend an event, but when the financial viability of the development relies on a guarantee of good weather, covered or domed stadia are a valid solution. Most major outdoor events these days are insured against inclement weather, but the premiums paid come out of the profits from the event.

The USA has led the way in maximizing the number of events a stadium may accommodate in one year. New covered venues in Europe are aiming for up to 250 event days per year where only 5 to 10 per cent of these events are football, usually the primary use of European stadia. The use of facilities for more than one purpose is not limited to the pitch, but should include all the support amenities which are contained inside the structure. Private or hospitality boxes can be opened up to be used as banqueting rooms, or with the addition of a small shower and a folding bed could be converted into a hotel bedroom. Players changing rooms and training areas can become health clubs during the week and restaurants and lounges can become convention or conference centres. At the very beginning of a project the list of possible uses for the stadium must be prepared and be selected on a rational order of priorities such as the following.

1 How often will the event occur?
(*frequency*)
2 Amount and cost of specialized equipment required for the event (*establishment cost*)
3 How much money will they generate?
(*revenue*)
4 Are they compatible with preceding or forth-coming events?

(*compatibility*)
5 How long will it take to prepare for and clear up afterwards?
(*set up and knock down time*)
6 Will the event recur on a regular basis?
(*repetition*)

To help in an understanding of how versatile stadia can be and the number of events which are possible, we have listed a typical schedule of events theoretically possible in a modern stadium in the UK (Table 5.4).

Whilst it should be every stadium manager's aim to have as many event days as possible and follow the Toronto Skydome's example of over 200, it is not always possible. It has taken four years for them to achieve this level of use with 107 events days in 1989, 165 in 1990 and 188 in 1991. Wembley Stadium in London is a financially successful stadium, with a seating capacity of 80 000 spectators and one of the most advanced ticket booking systems in the world. However it is limited to around 35 event days a year by the local authority because of the perceived disruption events have on the surrounding area. This is surprising as Wembley has been functioning as a stadium for over 60

Table 5.4 Typical stadium events table

Type of event	Number of days per year
Major football matches	6
Minor football matches	14
Celebrity events	2
Concerts	6
American football	6
Motor sport	4
Sports festival	2
Hockey	1
Schools events	2
Charity events	2
Equestrian dressage and jumping	4
Baseball	2
Boxing	2
Conventions and meetings	4
Exhibitions	10
Athletics	2
Mass dinners	2
Special events	3
Circus	6

years. Wembley Stadium is part of a larger conference, arena and exhibition complex which adds to its viability.

This is another method by which more functions are found for stadia. For this to be done successfully, a covered stadium is ideal such as the Hoosier Dome complex in Indianapolis. It was built on a city centre site next to an existing 12 000 m² convention centre with the stadium's 8000m² planned as an extension to this centre. It used the existing car parking and transport infra-structure and relied on public funding as well as major private sponsorship for its construction. With Europe's regular inclement weather and the catchment population of many large cities, it is not surprising that a number of these multi-purpose covered stadia are being considered.

5.4 Retractable and movable seats

5.4.1 Background

In attempting to provide a truly multi-use stadium as a way of ensuring the financial viability of the development, many ways of altering the structure on a temporary basis have been attempted. In recent years opening roofs and moving pitches have been attempted but the most common and most successful are movable, or at least retractable, seats. The idea evolved in the 1960s from the attempt to house American football, played on a rectangular pitch, and baseball, played on a diamond shaped pitch, in the same building. It was only partially successful – many believe it was an unacceptable compromise for both sports and did not fully satisfy the requirements of either, even though a high standard of venue could be achieved and problems of access could be solved. A reaction against this compromise came in 1972 when the dual stadia complex of Kansas City, Missouri was opened; this included two stadia, one of 78 000-seat capacity to be used for American football, the other of 42 000-seat capacity for baseball.

Nevertheless there have been many subsequent attempts to design stadia which can be reconfigured for the maximum variety of events, particularly in North America. The most ambitious example is the Toronto Skydome which opened in 1989 and can be adapted, by movable seating, to the following uses:

- Auditorium configurations to allow 10 000 to 30 000 seats as desired;
- a hockey or basketball configuration of 30 000 seats;
- a baseball configuration of up to 50 000 seats;
- a football configuration of up to 54 000 seats;
- various configurations allowing up to 68 000 spectators for rock concerts or other entertainments.

The costs of providing an overall space envelope that will accept all the above geometries, and of installation and operation are such that very few stadia could aim for the degree of flexibility outlined above. At more modest levels there is widespread use of movable seating tiers all over the world.

One example helps to satisfy the conflicting demands of football and athletics. In continental European (but not British) stadia spectators do not seem to mind the great distance between spectator and football pitch created by the intervening athletics track, whereas in British football there is a tradition of close viewing which most interested parties wish to preserve. The answer may lie in movable or retractable stands which can be located close to the football playing field for the winter season, covering the athletics track, and then moved back for athletics events in the summer.

The Stade de France in Paris has been designed to allow the seating to move back over the athletics track.

However, such solutions are expensive, and a degree of public funding is usually required to make them viable – either directly or indirectly.

5.4.2 Types

Movable seating can be supplied in any numbers, from a few hundred to several thousand, to suit the types of events anticipated and the configurations required. Generally speaking the greater the variety of events a stadium is required to host, the larger the number of movable or retractable seats to be provided. The most usual types are the following:

- rigid seating tiers mounted on steel tracks;
- rigid seating tiers with large retractable wheels;
- rigid banks of seats moved about on air or water cushions;
- retractable seats on folding or telescopic frames.

The first three types are pushed manually or mechanically from one pre-planned position to another to suit the current event, while the retractable type is compactly stacked or folded into a wall when not in use, and 'concertinaed' out into position when needed. In all cases the ideal is to have prepared storage spaces, usually under the tier above, where temporary seats can be stored out of the way and quickly rolled or folded out into the correct position when required.

5.4.3 The future

The possibilities for movable seating tiers are entering a new era, with better and more easily maintained systems being developed. The stadia of the 21st century may consist of flat concourses at different levels above the playing surface, with retractable seats pulled out as necessary and the remaining levels used for a variety of catering functions. If such ideas are applied it will be necessary to calculate very carefully their effect upon viewing sightlines for the remaining viewing areas.

6

Crowd control

6.1 General

Control of crowds and separation of spectators from participants has been a problem faced by designers since the first time real difficulties were experienced by stadium managers during Roman times. A group of people coming together to enjoy an event is a 'crowd' and must be carefully managed from the moment they enter the zone of influence of the stadium. Sometimes very little encouragement is needed for that crowd to become a 'mob' and eventually that mob to become a 'riot'. The managing of people must be considered from the very beginning of a stadium project if this adverse encouragement is to be minimized. The majority of people place great importance on the way they are treated by staff at a venue with 92 per cent indicating in a survey in the USA that customer service should be the number one priority of management. It is this 'customer service' together with the architecture of the venue which will serve to maintain the goodwill of the spectators.

The Colosseum and similar Roman amphitheatres developed their own type of separation in the form of a surrounding wall – possibly designed more to protect the spectators from the activities taking place in the arena than the other way round. Bullrings in Spain and southern France developed along similar lines with a change in height between the first row of seating and the bullring, essential to ensure the safety of the audience. In the latter part of the twentieth century the roles have been reversed, with the boundary serving to protect the activity area from the spectators.

There are three commonly-used design techniques for separating the activity area from the spectators: perimeter fences, moats and changes of level.

6.2 Perimeter fences

6.2.1 Advantages

There are two good reasons for having a robust fence (Figure 6.1) between spectators and pitch. The first is protection of players and officials from hostile spectators. The second is the protection of a natural grass pitch surface from compaction of the subsoil by spectators' feet.

6.2.2 Disadvantages

A major disadvantage is visual: most fences are an obstruction to proper viewing of the game, and usually are unsightly.

Another disadvantage, paradoxically, is safety. In cases of mass panic on the stands or escape from fire, the playing field is an obvious zone of safety (see Section 2.3.5) and an intervening fence which prevents people from reaching it can create a death trap. Two recent experiences in Britain demonstrate this. The first, more fully described in Section 2.4.1, was at Valley Parade Stadium, Bradford, where an even greater disaster than the one which did happen was prevented only by some spectators being able to escape on to the playing field. The second was at Hillsborough Stadium, Sheffield, where the perimeter fence between the standing terrace

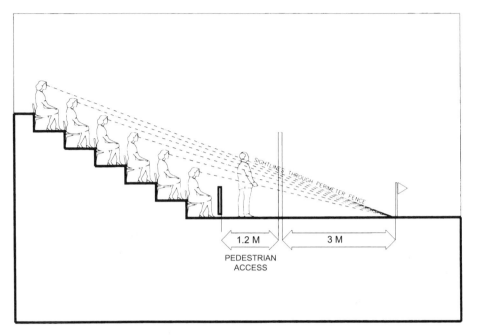

Figure 6.1 Perimeter fences protect the pitch from crowd invasion but also obstruct viewing, are often unsightly and may hinder escape in cases of emergency.

and the pitch was a contributing factor to the death of 95 people in a crowd surge.

6.2.3 Choice

In each case the pros and cons of a fence must be carefully balanced and the case discussed with the governing body concerned and with the local police and safety authorities, whose views will carry great weight. The following factors should be taken into consideration:

• The need for a fence is most likely in the case of soccer, particularly in countries or individual grounds with a history of violent crowd behaviour.

• Some authorities would recommend fencing for top-level international sports generally, but this is a less clear-cut issue.

• The most problematical cases are those where highly valued traditional customs conflict with the latest safety trends – for instance, sports grounds with a tradition of allowing crowds on to the pitch at certain matches. Croke Park in Dublin, the home of the

Gaelic Athletic Association (and where gaelic football and hurling have their roots) has a custom of allowing the crowd on to the pitch to carry off the winning captain on their shoulders (and also allowing lifting small children over the turnstiles to sit on the knees of their parents in the stands). These practices are under threat from the new wave of safety consciousness but are not inherently dangerous if properly controlled. Twickenham had a tradition of spectators coming on to the pitch after rugby matches but this is not now allowed. Customs such as these contribute to the special character of individual stadia and should not be thoughtlessly destroyed by blanket insistence on universally-applied safety techniques. Some modification to take account of individual circumstances should be the aim. Wembley Stadium in London, for instance, has a perimeter fence which can be folded to allow three modes of operation: full height for high-risk events, half height for medium-risk events, and removed altogether for non-risk events. Croke Park has used a device called a 'cat's cradle'. This is a wire cage the height of a low fence which does not obstruct vision but is difficult to climb across.

Premier Division football grounds in the UK have now generally removed perimeter fences altogether.

6.2.4 Design criteria

- A key reference in the UK is the Guide to Safety at Sports Grounds (the so-called 'Green Guide'), in particular chapter 10.16. It recommends, *inter alia*, that perimeter fencing height should be a maximum of 2.2 m. This, it should be noted, is the *minimum* height recommended by FIFA and UEFA for soccer stadia.
- The fence must be robust and if there is not a crash barrier incorporated into the design then the fence should be capable of withstanding crowd pressures equal to those which would normally be expected of a crowd barrier at a height of 1.1 m above the nosing.
- The fence must be as unclimbable as possible.
- The design should allow the fence to be 'unobtrusive' and permit the best vision possible through to the playing area. The use of transparent materials such as glass and polycarbonate are possible but the effect of dirt, weather, unwanted reflections and wear and tear must be considered.
- There must be adequate provision for escape through the fence, either in the form of gates, opening panels or collapsible sections. Whichever method is used for escape it should be recognized that this is a critical element of the design and it should be as 'fool-proof' as possible. The openings should be sized in accordance with the total number of spectators required to gain access on to the playing area in an emergency. These openings should be clearly identified visually. In recent years several versions of an opening or collapsible fence have been developed, particularly in France. If opening or collapsible fences are to be incorporated into a stadium they must be of a design capable of withstanding the significant loads of crowd pressure when in use and it must be ensured that, under these conditions, the opening mechanisms will remain reliable and 'fail-safe'.
- In a multi-purpose stadium the fences should be removable so that they are only used on those occasions when some form of separation is necessary such as for 'high risk' football matches but not for a pop concert. It may be that in the future this type of separation will be required on other sporting occasions.
- Whatever means of access to the field is designed through this perimeter fence it should be under permanent supervision by stewards during an event.

6.3 Moats

6.3.1 Advantages

It is relatively easy to design the pitch side of a moat to be unclimbable and also to police a moat with security staff so that crowd invasion is easily controlled. The moat may serve a further purpose in providing a circulation route around the stadium for three groups of people:

- officials and security staff needing to gain quick and easy access to some part of the viewing stands;
- ambulances and emergency vehicles;
- the media: the Olympic Stadium in Barcelona was modified partly to meet this aim, as mentioned in Section 1.2.5.

The major advantage of the moat is that the crowd control and other functions listed above can be achieved inconspicuously and without impeding the view of spectators to the field. Its aesthetic qualities are therefore far superior to those of a perimeter fence.

6.3.2 Disadvantages

Use of a moat will increase the distance between the playing field and the spectators. For this reason moats may be more appropriate to larger stadia, where an additional 2.5 m or 3 m will be a relatively modest fraction of the overall dimensions involved.

6.3.3 Design criteria

The most precise recommendations are those laid down for football stadia by FIFA and UEFA: a minimum width of 2.5 m and a minimum depth of 3.0 m; sufficiently high barriers on both sides to prevent people falling into the moat; and the provision of safety escape routes across the moat in those stadia where the playing area is a means of escape in an emergency. Moats should not contain water but be constructed in such a way that unlawful intrusion on to the pitch is prevented – for example by climbing obstructions inside them (Figure 6.2).

For stadia generally the following criteria apply:

- It may be important under emergency circumstances to allow access across the moat on to the playing area and therefore a method of bridging the 'gap' should be incorporated, either on a permanent or temporary basis.

- A method of gaining access to the pitch for service vehicles must be found by either a bridge, ramp or adjustable platform so vehicles may drive directly on to the pitch. In some situations heavy vehicles may be necessary, particularly where the stadium is used as a concert venue and large quantities of stage building materials will be used.

- In addition to allowing the spectators to cross the moat on to the pitch in certain circumstances access can also be provided for the spectators into the moat if it is to be used for public circulation. In these circumstances correctly designed stairways must be provided at regular intervals around the circumference of the moat to provide egress into the moat and from the moat to the outside of the stadium. This route can be either underneath the tiers of seating or at the corners (Figure 6.3).

- The dimensions of the moat should be sized so as to prevent spectators attempting to jump across from the front row of the terrace as well as providing a wide enough escape route if it is to be regarded as a means of egress. In addition to the above requirements, if it is to be used for vehicular access around the stadium

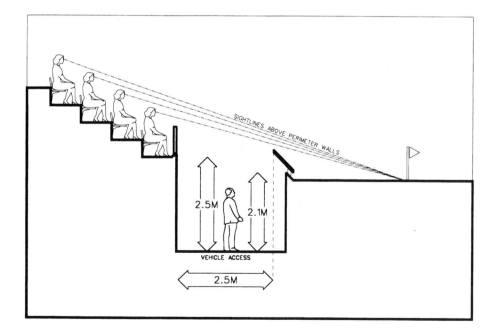

Figure 6.2 An inaccessible moat.

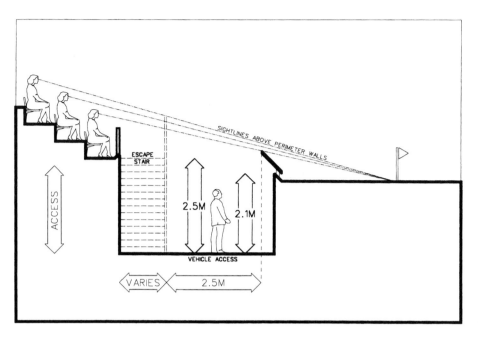

Figure 6.3 A typical accessible moat.

by police, ambulance and other service vehicles, it should have a minimum of 2.5 m clearance.

- The moat may be used to help clean the spectator terraces. Debris and refuse can be air blown or swept forward with the moat containing rubbish skips so that the waste is deposited directly into the container. The front balustrade should have openings or be designed at the base to accommodate this.
- Access for players, performers and police on to the pitch should be provided by way of tunnels or covered crossing points directly into dugouts for the teams, if this is appropriate.
- Kiosks for the sale of refreshments can be provided in the moat under the terrace so that spectators descend into the moat via staircases during the interval.

6.4 Changes of level

The combination of a depression, less deep than the moats described above, and a barrier, not as high as the fences described in Section 6.1.2,

gives quite an effective deterrent to crowd invasion of the pitch while still providing good access around the perimeter of the pitch for official use (Figure 6.4). Alternatively the first row of seats can be lifted sufficiently high above the playing area (Figure 6.5) to make pitch invasion difficult, though not impossible. This is the so-called 'bullring' method often used in the USA.

6.4.1 Advantages

The bullring method has the advantage of being able to accommodate a large number of players, officials and others at the side of the pitch without obstructing the view from the spectator seats, hence its popularity in the USA.

6.4.2 Disadvantages

Both of the methods described above are only moderately effective barriers to pitch invasion, deterring only the less motivated invaders. They are therefore most suitable where crowds are known to be well-behaved or where good stewarding is provided.

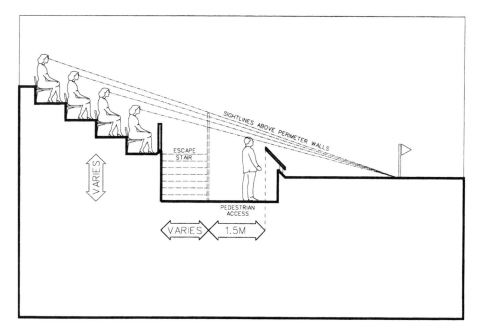

Figure 6.4 A 'half moat' or combination of low fence and shallow moat.

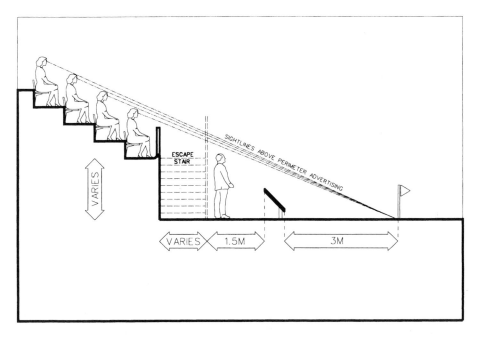

Figure 6.5 The 'bullring' solution, or level change, is widely used in baseball and American football stadia in the USA.

Lifting the height of the first row of seats, as in the bullring method, hampers the design of good sightlines from the seating tier behind, particularly in large stadia.

6.4.3 Design criteria

Typical dimensions of the moat plus barrier method are a 1.5 m deep moat, plus a 1 m high fence on the pitch side. Typical dimensions of the bullring method are to raise the first row of seating 1.5 m or 2 m above pitch level. Figure 6.6 shows a typical handrail detail down gangway, see also Section 13.7.3 (Vertical circulation elements).

Figure 6.6 Handrail along the centre of a gangway, an aid to safety in crowd movement.

7

Spectator viewing

7.1 Introduction

7.1.1 Design aims

The design team's task is to provide seats or standing places for the number of spectators required by the brief, and to do so in such a way that the spectators have a clear view of the event, and are comfortable and safe. This chapter outlines all the viewing design factors.

7.1.2 Sequence of decisions

The starting point for design is the size and orientation of the playing field, both of these being dictated by the sporting functions to be accommodated. See, therefore, Section 2.2 for pitch orientation and Section 5.2 for pitch dimensions.

Next a notional 'envelope' can be drawn for the spectator areas surrounding the pitch. The inner edge will be as close to the pitch as possible, allowing for a safety barrier as described in Chapter 6; while the outer edges will be determined by:

- the required spectator capacity (Section 7.2);
- the maximum acceptable distance from the pitch to the furthest seats (Section 7.3.1), and the preferred viewing locations for that particular sport (Section 7.3.3).

Finally this schematic plan must be converted to a fully developed three-dimensional stadium design taking full account of good viewing angles and sightlines (Section 7.4.2), safety limits on the steepness of rake (Section 7.4.3), and no

unacceptable barriers such as roof supports interfering with the view (Section 7.5).

7.2 Ground capacity

7.2.1 The need for realism

The most important decision in planning a new stadium, or expanding an existing one, is the number of spectators to be accommodated.

When developing a building brief, the design team and client organization often over-estimate this figure. Natural optimism plays a part in this. Sporting clubs always believe their attendance is about to increase dramatically, even though statistical evidence may show that it has been stable for years or even dropping; stadium owners like to believe that if only they had a bigger venue then more people would attend, even though many seats in their existing smaller stadium remain unfilled; and consultants may find it more exciting to get involved in big plans than small ones, which tends to encourage expansive thinking.

There are circumstances in which an attractive, well-planned new facility may attract more spectators. For instance, the club may be able to increase its 'gate' by an organized recruitment campaign or, in the case of European football, if it gains promotion in the league system. Also, the fact that a new stadium is comfortable, safe and well-designed may in itself attract more spectators. But experience shows that attendance will tend to revert to earlier figures, after the novelty has worn off, unless the new crowd can be enticed to stay by means of effective marketing or by the team's performance.

It is therefore a golden rule never to increase stadium capacity beyond that which is known to be necessary, and can be demonstrated to be affordable both in capital cost and running cost. The factors which will lead to a preliminary estimation of ground capacity are the following:

- the sport(s) and other activities to be accommodated;
- the development budget and running costs;
- the size of the catchment area surrounding the development;
- the aspirations of sponsors, public institutions and owners;
- the past history of the site or sports club;
- practical site limitations.

This decision on capacity can only be provisional: it may not be possible to provide the desired number of seats while still giving adequate quality of view, adequate shelter, or fit the stadium successfully on to its site and into its surroundings. The implications of seating numbers must therefore be carefully checked against considerations such as:

- the quality of view and distance from the action;
- the type of roof possible, where relevant, and therefore the extent of shelter;
- the aesthetic character of the development both internally and when viewed from outside the stadium;
- the cost of the structure and support facilities, and its running costs;
- the extent and range of support facilities which are viable.

7.2.2 Official requirements

A minimum seating capacity, and the proportion of standing places to seats, may be set by the types of events to be held at the venue. In some cases the governing bodies will lay down standards which must be met if certain types of matches are to be played there.

Table 7.1 gives recommended seating capacities for various types of football matches. The figures have been extracted from the *Digest of Stadia Criteria* published in 1992 by the Football Stadia Advisory Design Council in the UK. These minima are not rigidly applied because FIFA (the world regulatory body) is anxious not to rule out the possibility of smaller countries staging major matches, but they do give the design team an initial design target. The data in the table are indicative only: the *Digest* itself must be studied for the detailed figures and their correct interpretation. The allowable proportion of standing places in particular should be verified particularly rigorously because regulations are continually tightened, and the general trend is for such accommodation to be phased out.

Standing accommodation versus seats

This question of seating versus standing accommodation has been so hotly debated, particularly in the UK as pointed out in Section 1.3.4, that a few paragraphs of comment are merited. In theory it is possible to accommodate almost twice as many standing spectators per unit area than seated – about two spectators per square metre seated, versus about four standing – which makes standing-room seem economically attractive. In fact this advantage is diminishing, because many amenities must be substantially increased for standing spectators. Once the additional numbers of toilets and catering outlets and the increased circulation, escape and safety barrier space are taken into account the cost per person may actually be greater for standing accommodation than for seated.

Leaving economics aside, the decision will be influenced by two main factors – customer expectations, and regulatory or legal requirements. As regards the customer there are strong traditions in favour of standing provision in some sports. Many sports fans are convinced that standing together on the terraces is essential to the spirit of watching the game; in horse-racing facilities it is traditional for over two-thirds of spectators to stand, and wander around, rather than sit on tiered seats. Establishing what kind of spectator will patronize a given

Table 7.1 Recommended capacities for football stadia

Event type	Total capacity	Number of seats	Number of standing places	Number under roof	Number of seats for officials, VIPs and Directors
World cup					
Opening match, Semi-final, Final	60 000	All	None	Main grandstand, Press box, and VIP seats.	At least 200, up to approx 1100
Group matches	30 000	All	None	Main grandstand, Press box, and VIP seats.	At least 200, up to approx 1100
European championship finals					
Final	45 000	All	None	Two-thirds	At least 200
Opening match, Semi-final	40 000	All	None	Two-thirds	At least 200
Group matches	30 000	All	None	Two-thirds	At least 200
UEFA club competitions					
European Cup final	30 000	All	None	Not stated	Not stated
Cup Winners' Cup final	30 000	All	None	Not stated	Not stated
UEFA Cup final leg	20 000	All	None	Not stated	Not stated
English Football League					
Premier and 1st Division	10 000	No standing		10 per cent	At least 40
2nd and 3rd Division	10 000	No standing after 1999–2000 season		10 per cent	At least 40
Scottish League					
Premier Division	5000 expandable to 10 000	No standing after 1994–5 season		750 in Main Stand + 4000 elsewhere	At least 40
1st and 2nd Division	5000 expandable to 10 000	No standing after 1990–2000 season		750 in Main Stand + 4000 elsewhere	At least 40

Notes:
1 The source of the above information is the *Digest of Stadia Criteria* published by the Football Stadia Advisory Design Council. All the data given are summaries for quick reference; primary sources should be consulted before final design decisions are taken.
2 The table refers to new stadia only. When upgrading existing stadia primary information sources should be consulted.

stadium (in terms of socio-economic group and other relevant characteristics) is crucial to getting the whole philosophy of comfort, shelter and seat price right for that stadium, and no design should go forward until these matters have been fully clarified.

As regards the law, most authorities believe that the greater the proportion of seated spectators, the less likely it will be that there will be crowd problems, and this belief is influencing the regulatory trend. British football authorities have decreed that existing football stadia in the premier league and the first division must be converted to all-seater stadia over a specified period during the 1990s and that no standing terraces be provided in new stadia for these more senior divisions. FIFA and UEFA regulations allow for no standing places in new stadia for national or international matches (see Table 7.1).

If on balance of all the above factors a decision in favour of standing accommodation seems indicated, it must be remembered that these areas may later need to be converted to seating, for instance if a football team gains promotion into a higher division when FIFA or UEFA standards would come into effect, or when national standards are upgraded to demand all-seating stadia.

One way out of the dilemma may be a certain proportion of convertible areas. In Germany, for instance, it is quite common for stadia to be temporarily converted to all-seating for certain matches. While it is technically quite feasible to design stands for such convertibility from standing to seating and vice versa, it increases the capital cost.

One event type where standees are still being tolerated on a large scale is at concerts given in stadia, where the actual playing area is often used for spectators to sit or stand. Fans find their own way and decide for themselves where to take up position, many believing that this spontaneity is essential to the atmosphere of such events. This system is called 'festival seating' in the USA, but it is regarded by the authorities as unacceptable and dangerous because of the lack of control the organizers have over the positioning of the crowd. European practice is beginning to change and several countries now require the playing area to have securely fixed seats in place for a pop concert. The covering of the pitch in these circumstances is discussed in Section 5.1.7.

In conclusion, the present authors believe that instances remain where well-designed standing terraces are acceptable, especially in British football and in horse racing, but they accept that trends worldwide are undeniably towards all-seater stadia, mainly owing to the continual rise in customer expectations of comfort.

7.2.3 Catchment area and past history of the site

In addition to the theoretical numbers laid down by regulation, as in Table 7.1, it is essential to look at the reality of the site itself. While FIFA might require a capacity of (say) 30 000 for certain football matches an analysis of the potential catchment area and, in the case of an existing site, an investigation of past attendances there, may show such a number of spectators to be highly unlikely. Realism must prevail.

7.2.4 Practical site considerations

The ratio between site area and the number of spectators who can be accommodated varies enormously. A few random examples, listed in Table 7.2 indicate the range. Many of these sites also contain other facilities, such as convention or exhibition complexes, and the definitions of 'site area' may well differ from case to case. Therefore no direct comparisons can be made. The purpose of this list is purely to illustrate the impossibility of simple accommodation/site area ratios. Each case must be studied individually.

7.2.5 Cost categories of stadium construction

Stadium capacity may be limited by the required cost of construction. The relationship between construction costs and seating capacities tends to fall into definite categories. If capacity can be kept below the next threshold, and an additional tier and/or structural complication avoided, it may be possible to avoid a disproportionate leap in costs. Table 7.3 summarizes four major categories of this kind.

There are exceptions to this classification of seating capacities and costs. For instance, the Aztec stadium in Mexico (see Figure 7.4) accommodates over 100 000 spectators on a single tier of seats surrounding the pitch; and the McMahon stadium at the University of Calgary in Alberta in Canada accommodates over 38 000 people in two single-tier stands situated only on the sides of the pitch. Because they avoid second or third tiers both of these stadia undoubtedly have lower relative costs than one would expect, but at the expense of quite unreasonably great viewing distances. They are not examples to be followed uncritically.

Table 7.2 Spectator accommodation related to site area

Ground	Accommodation	Site area
Hubert H Humphrey Metrodome, Minneapolis, USA	63 000 spectators and 500 cars	20 acres
Arrowhead and Royals Stadia, Kansas City, USA	112 000 spectators 24 000 cars and 300 buses	500 acres
Atlanta-Fulton County Stadium, Atlanta, USA	60 000 spectators and 6500 cars	95 acres
Houston Astrodome, Houston, USA	66 000 spectators and 28 000 cars	260 acres
Joe Robbie Stadium, Miami, USA	73 000 spectators and 15 000 cars	99 acres
Louisiana Superdome, New Orleans, USA	95 000 spectators and 5000 cars	52 acres
Lord's Cricket Ground, London	27 500 spectators	12 acres
Twickenham Rugby Football Ground, London	75 000 spectators when complete, and	10 acres
Wembley Stadium, London	80 000 spectators 7500 cars and approximately 50 buses	75 acres

Table 7.3 Typical cost categories in stadium construction

Cost category (approx)	Stadium capacity	Typical seating configuration	Typical forms of structure, modes of access, etc.
Low:	Up to 10 000	10 to 15 rows in a single tier	Structure possibly ground bearing. Access direct from front of seating tier or from short stairs/ramps at rear. Support facilities beneath. Roof cantilever only about 10 m, using light steel or concrete sections.
Medium:	10 000 to 20 000	15 to 20 rows in a single tier	
High:	20 000 to 50 000	Up to 50 rows total, disposed in 2 tiers	
Very high:	30 000 to 50 000	Over 50 rows total, in 3 or 4 tiers. 3rd or 4th tiers are usually introduced to overcome site restrictions, or to accommodate a plethora of VIP boxes and similar facilities, and not for increased capacity.	

7.2.6 Staged expansion

Once a minimum and a maximum number of seats for a particular stadium have been established by the above investigations, the client body may opt for a modest initial facility which can grow with the club.

In the case of an open stadium staged expansion is relatively simple. It becomes very difficult if the final stadium is to be entirely roofed (or 'domed' in American terminology). The problem is not the design or construction of the final phase in itself, but the fact that the initial stages, if too modest, may have to bear disproportionately heavy infrastructure, foundation and structure costs to allow for the future additions.

British roofed stadia which have been constructed in a phased manner, and which might be studied if such a development is envisaged, include those at Twickenham Rugby Football Ground in west London, Murrayfield rugby stadium in Edinburgh, the Welsh National Rugby Stadium in Cardiff, and Arsenal football stadium in north London.

7.2.7 Extent of roof

Roofing is expensive and has a significant impact on the aesthetic impact of a stadium, but a percentage of roofed area is essential for spectator comfort in most climates. In some localities the roof must provide shelter against the sun, in others against rain, snow and perhaps wind. In some cases shelter will be needed against both at different times of the year.

For each stadium a careful investigation must therefore be made into the sports to be played, the seasons and time of day they may be played, and the local climate: see Sections 2.2 and 4.8. There may also be official regulations requiring a certain proportion of seats to be under cover (see for example Table 7.1 for new football stadia), and the latest rules should be checked with the relevant governing bodies.

In practice, the seating sections of all new stadia currently being built in Britain and northern Europe are roofed, while the standing terraces are occasionally being left open. It is only in mild climates, such as parts of Australia and the USA, that new stadia are being built with uncovered seats.

7.3 Viewing distances

7.3.1 Optimum viewing distance

Calculation of maximum viewing distance is based on the fact that the human eye finds it difficult to perceive anything clearly that subtends an angle of less than about 0.4 degrees – particularly if the object is moving rapidly. In the case of a rugby ball, which is approximately 250 mm in diameter, or a football, the calculation sets the preferred viewing distance at no more than 150 m between the extreme corner of the field and spectator's eye, with an absolute maximum of 190 m. In the case of a tennis ball, which is only 75 mm in diameter, the preferred maximum distance reduces to around 30 m.

Setting out these distances from the extreme viewing positions, such as the diagonally opposed corners of a playing field, gives a preferred viewing zone and their average configuration suggests a circle struck from the centre spot on the field, generally referred to as the 'optimum viewing circle'. This circle in the case of football and rugby would have a radius of 90 m, and for other sports as in Figure 7.1.

7.3.2 Practical limitations

The simple circular plan areas developed above are only a starting point for laying out the viewing terraces and must be modified in several ways.

First, it must be admitted that some sports (such as hockey and cricket) are played with a small-diameter ball on a field so large that the size of the field makes it impossible to locate spectators within the theoretical viewing distance. In these cases one must face the fact that viewers will have to watch the players rather than the ball.

Second, the spectators are not sitting at ground level but are raised above the ground by as much as 20 or 30 m in a large stadium. In big stadia the effect of this elevation must be taken

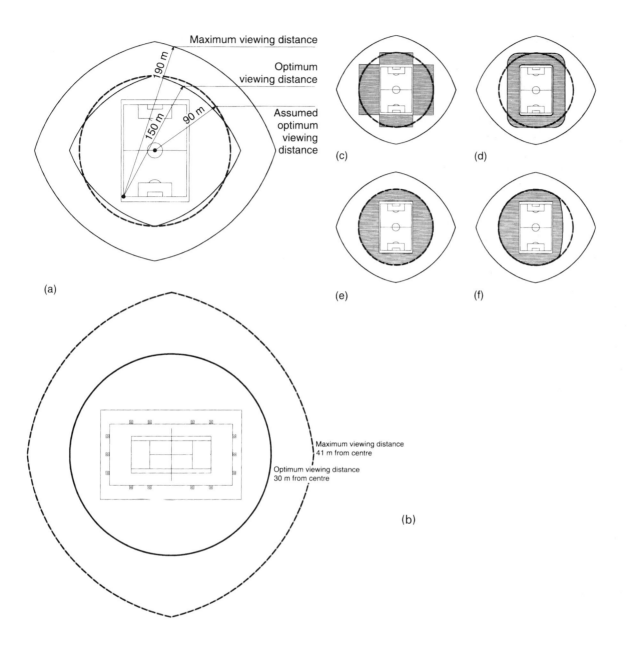

Figure 7.1 Relationship between playing field, optimum and maximum viewing distances and a deduced 'optimum viewing circle'. (a) For football and rugby the optimum viewing circle would have a radius of 90 m from the centre spot. (b) Dimensions for lawn tennis viewing. (c) Separate stands, leaving the potential seating space at the corners unexploited, have traditionally been common. (d) This arrangement brings more spectators within the optimum viewing circle and also offers the possibility of a more attractive stadium design (see Section 4.2.4 of this book). (e) A variation of (c) with the seating areas extending to the limit of the optimum viewing circle, but not beyond it. This type of layout gives an excellent spectator/player relationship. (f) A variation of (d) with only the seating area to the west of the playing field extended back to the limit of the optimum viewing circle. With this layout the majority of spectators have their backs to the sun during an afternoon game.

into account by calculating the direct distances from the elevated spectators to the centre of the field.

Third, spectators have preferred viewing locations for each particular sport, so that seats in some areas of the optimum viewing circle would be less satisfactory than others at the same distance from the game. This is discussed in the next section.

7.3.3 Preferred viewing locations

It is not always self-evident where viewers like to sit for particular sports. In the case of football, conventional wisdom holds that the best seats are on the long sides of the field, which give a good view of the ebb and flow of the game between the two opposing goalposts. But there is also a tradition for highly motivated team supporters to view the game from the short ends, behind the goal posts, where they get a good view of the side movements and line openings which present themselves to the opposing teams. To designers who do not understand these traditions it may seem ludicrous that a football supporter may insist on watching from behind the netting of the goal posts in crowded

conditions when there is ample space available on the long sides. But such preferences exist, and the design team must identify them for the stadium under consideration, and suitably modify the 'optimum viewing circle' to locate the maximum density of spectators in their preferred positions.

Figure 7.2 shows preferred viewing positions for various sports; and Figures 7.3 to 7.10 analyse some well-known existing stadia.

7.3.4 Exploiting the corners

A decision must be made whether to place four rectangular stands on the four sides of the field with open corners (Figure 7.1c) or whether to surround the pitch with a continuous 'bowl' stadium (Figure 7.1d).

Leaving the corners open is cheaper in construction costs and may in some cases benefit a natural grass pitch by promoting better circulation of air and quicker drying of the grass. But it also sacrifices valuable viewing space, and the trend is towards fully exploiting the area within the maximum viewing distance as shown in Figure 7.1e. A continuous 'bowl' stadium may offer more comfortable conditions

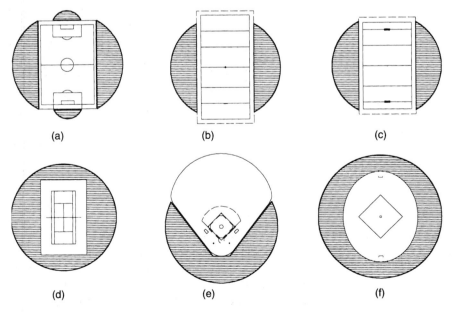

(a)   (b)   (c)

(d)   (e)   (f)

Figure 7.2 Preferred viewing positions for some principal sports. (a) Football; (b) American football; (c) rugby league; (d) lawn tennis; (e) baseball; (f) Australian Rules football.

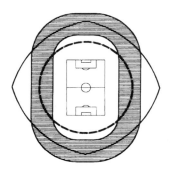

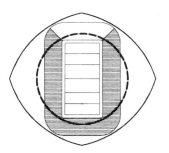

Figure 7.3 Wembley Stadium, London, first built in 1924, modernized for the Olympics in 1948, and renovated again in 1985 to become a major multi-use venue. For viewing quality (for football) the arena is too large, the three concentric terraces pushing most of the 80 000 seats outside the optimum viewing circle, some of them being even beyond the maximum viewing distance. Overlapping multi-tier terraces would bring spectators closer to the action. It will be replaced by a new stadium: see page 254.

Figure 7.5 The former Welsh National Rugby Stadium, Cardiff. The overlapping two-tier terraces (which are straight, not curved) placed most of the current 57 000 spectators within the optimum viewing circle.

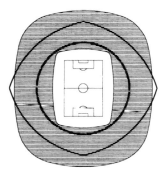

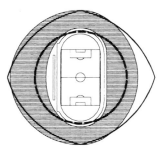

Figure 7.4 Aztec Stadium, Mexico City, built in 1966 exclusively for football. The layout is of the type shown in Figure 7.1d but far too large for satisfactory viewing: most of the 105 000 seats on the single-tier terrace are outside the optimum viewing circle and very many are beyond the maximum viewing distance.

Figure 7.6 The Olympic Stadium built for the 1972 Olympics at Munich and designed primarily for athletic events. The seating geometry is closer to a circle than those above, and is asymmetrical to accommodate most of the 80 000 spectators to the south of the playing field. The arena is so large that virtually all spectators are pushed beyond the optimum viewing circle, but the outer perimeter of the seating areas is kept mostly within the maximum viewing distance. The depth of seating is at a maximum along the sprint lines and finish line.

for spectators and players than an open-corner layout, as mentioned in Section 4.8, and may look better than four separate stands meeting awkwardly at the corners (see Section 4.2.4).

7.3.5 Designing for multi-use stadia

Multi-use stadia make sense financially, but they do not necessarily offer the spectator the quality of viewing he would like. Each particular sporting type has its own ideal viewing distances and seat positions, and while it may be possible to satisfy these in a stadium dedicated to one particular kind of sport it becomes much more difficult in a facility that must accommodate different sports with different characteristics. Examples of compatibility and incompatibility include the following:

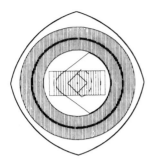

Figure 7.7 A completely circular stadium in the District of Columbia, USA, for American football and baseball. Spectator distances for football are acceptable but those for baseball too great, demonstrating the difficulty of providing for both sports in the same facility.

Three further examples of stadium layouts, all in Britain, for the sake of comparison:

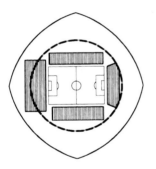

Figure 7.8 Arsenal football stadium in London, UK.

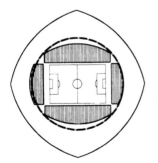

Figure 7.9 The Sir Alfred McAlpine football and rugby stadium at Huddersfield, UK.

- Football and rugby are broadly compatible. The playing fields are somewhat different in size but both are rectangular, and while preferred spectator locations are not identical (Figure 7.2) the differences are quite small.

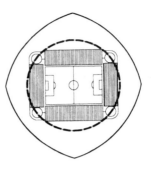

Figure 7.10 Watford football stadium.

- Football and athletics are much less compatible. Even though these sports are frequently accommodated in the same stadium, especially on the continent of Europe, this is at great cost to viewing quality. Placing an athletics track around the perimeter of a football field has the effect of pushing football fans so far away from the pitch that their sense of involvement with the game suffers.
- American football and baseball (the two great national spectator sports in the USA) are not happily compatible. For reasons of cost they have sometimes been accommodated in the same stadium, but the shapes of the football rectangle and the baseball diamond are so different that viewing conditions for many spectators must be disappointing.

7.3.6 Conclusion

It must be clearly decided at briefing stage which sports are to be accommodated, at what seating capacities, and the precise degree to which optimum viewing standards may be compromised in pursuit of these aims. Failure to settle these issues at an early stage could lead to a very unsatisfactory stadium.

7.4 Viewing angles and sightlines

We have now evolved a schematic diagram of the proposed viewing areas which hopefuly satisfies three criteria:

- The spectator areas are large enough to accommodate the required number of viewers.

- All spectators are as close to the action as possible, and maximum viewing distances have been kept within defined limits.
- Most spectators are located in their preferred viewing positions in relation to the playing field.

The next step is to convert these diagrammatic plans into three-dimensional stand designs with satisfactory 'sightlines'.

The term 'sightline' does not refer to the distance between spectator and pitch (though non-technical commentators may loosely use it in this way): it refers to the spectator's ability to see the nearest point of interest on the playing field (the 'point of focus') comfortably over the heads of the people in front. In other words it refers to a height (Figure 7.11), not a distance. A worked example showing the calculation of N, the riser height is given below:

$$N = \frac{(R + C) \times (D + T)}{D} - R$$

where: N = riser height;
R = height between eye on 'point of focus' on the playing field;
D = distance from eye to 'point of focus' on the playing field;
C = 'C' value,[1]
T = depth of seating row.

If we analyse a spectator position where $R = 6.5\,\text{m}$, $D = 18\,\text{m}$, $T = 0.8\,\text{m}$ and we want a 'C' value of 120 mm, then the height of the riser must be:

$$N = \frac{(6.5 + 0.012) \times (18 + 0.8)}{18} - 6.5$$
$$N = \frac{6.512 \times 18.8}{18} - 6.5$$
$$N = 6.8014 - 6.5$$
$$N = 0.3014\,\text{m}.$$

[1] 'C' value = 150 mm spectators with hats
120 mm reasonable viewing standard
90 mm head tilted backwards
60 mm between heads in front

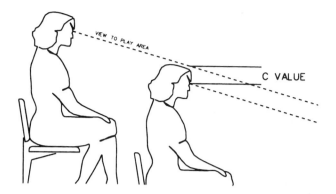

Figure 7.11 The term 'sightline' refers to a spectator's ability to see a critical point on the playing field over the head of the spectator below, and is measured by the '*C*' value.

In principle the calculation method is simple, but in real design it becomes cumbersome because the angle must be calculated many times over for each individual row in a stadium (Figure 7.12). This is because the optimum viewing angle varies with both the height of the spectator's eye above pitch level and its distance from the pitch; and every time either of these factors changes for a particular row of seats the computation shown in Figure 7.12 must be repeated.

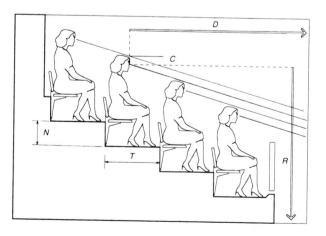

Figure 7.12 Viewing angle. *D* = distance to focus, *C* = '*C*' value, *T* = tread width, *N* = riser height and *R* = riser height from focus.

7.4.1 Use of computer calculations

Possibly because the calculations are so complex, or because some designers are reluctant to have the clean geometry of their architectural concepts degraded by real-life considerations, several recently-built stadia have failed in this respect. One of the Italian venues for the World Cup in 1990 was found after construction to have such inadequate sightlines that remedial action had to be undertaken immediately, with only partial success. The designers of a Bristol stand were sued by the sports club because of inadequate sightlines for the new facility.

Given the vital importance of getting these sightlines right, it is strongly recommended that computer analysis, using tried and tested programs, be applied to the task. No software is commercially available, but professional practices specializing in sports stadium design have generally developed their own computer programs which not only carry out all the necessary calculations, but can also generate drawings of the result. Many options can therefore be tried out, with a precise stand profile produced within a matter of seconds. It is possible then to project a three-dimensional image of the playing area as seen from any individual spectator position – an operation so demanding that its use is still exceptional at time of writing. One of the earliest applications of this technology was the design for the Arsenal North Bank stand in London by LOBB Sports Architecture.

7.4.2 Calculation method

The method for carrying out such a calculation is shown in the box of Figure 7.12; the vital steps in the decision-process are set out below:

1 *Decide the 'point of focus' on the playing field.*
In deciding the 'point of focus', choose the part of the playing field actually in use by the players that is closest to the spectators, as this will be the most onerous condition for the design.

2 *Decide a suitable 'C' value.*
'C' value is the assumed distance between the sightline to the pitch, and the centre of the eye of the spectator below (Figure 7.12). In general 150 mm would be an excellent design value, 120 mm very good, and 90 mm reasonable. 60 mm is generally regarded as an absolute minimum for most situations, with spectators able to see mostly between the heads of the people in front or by craning their necks. For new design a 'C' value of 90 mm is an ideal minimum.

But choice of a suitable figure is affected by several factors. For instance, when the 'C' value is too small for good viewing spectators can improve their line of sight over the heads of those in front simply by tilting their heads back, thus raising their eye level. If this needs to be done only occasionally spectators may be happy; but they would resist having to do it all the time, especially for events of long duration (see Table 8.1), and especially in the more expensive seats.

Choosing a low value such as 90 mm or even 60 mm makes for easier stand design (Figure 7.13), and in the case of large stadia these may be the maximum feasible values if an excessively steep seating angle is to be avoided; but in the case of sports where the action moves widely across the field, or where the spectators in front are regularly expected to wear hats, such a value would make for unsatisfactory viewing.

Conversely, choosing a high value such as 120 mm would give excellent viewing, but make for steeply raked stands and create great design difficulties in large-capacity or multi-tier stadia, particularly in the more distant rows.

Choosing the 'C' value is therefore a matter of judgement rather than incontrovertible fact, and judging it right is absolutely vital to the success of the stadium.

3 *Decide the distance between the front row of seats and the point of focus.*
The greater this distance, the shallower can be the rake of the stand, and the lower the back rows, all of which are advantageous factors (Figure 7.14). However, site restrictions may well dictate a tight spacing, in which case a steeply raked stadium becomes inevitable.

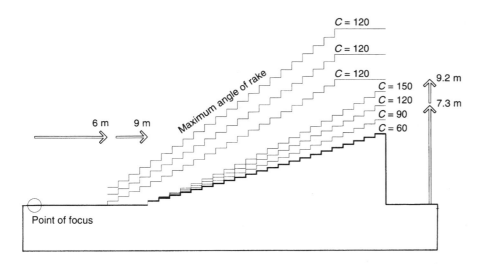

Figure 7.13 Quality of vision is improved by increasing the heights of seats above pitch level; and for any given height of seat above pitch level, the closer the seat to the critical point on the pitch (the 'point of focus') the better will be the '*C*' value.

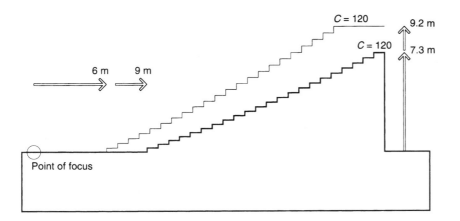

Figure 7.14 The closer the first row of seats is to the point of focus, the steeper the rake will be, and the higher the back of the stand for a given '*C*' value.

4   *Decide the level of the front row of seats relative to the playing field.*
The higher these seats are raised above playing field level, the better viewing standards will be, but the steeper the rake will be (Figure 7.15). The chosen method of separating the crowd from the playing field (fence, moat or change of level, as discussed in Chapter 6) will influence this decision. It is recommended that eye height above the pitch should not be less than 800 mm, with 700 mm as an absolute minimum.

7.4.3 Final design

By juggling all the above factors against each other (Figures 7.16 and 7.17), and against site constraints and construction costs, a theoretical stadium geometry will emerge. Some tests that must be carried out on the hypothetical profile are the following.

Angle of rake
Choosing a stadium profile that minimizes the distance between spectators and playing field

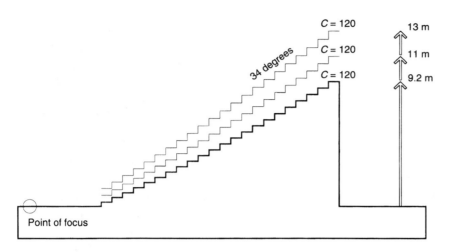

Figure 7.15 The higher the first row of seats above pitch level, the better viewing standards will be, but also the back of the stand will be higher. This may cause problems of building cost and of appearance, and may obstruct access of sunlight to a grass pitch.

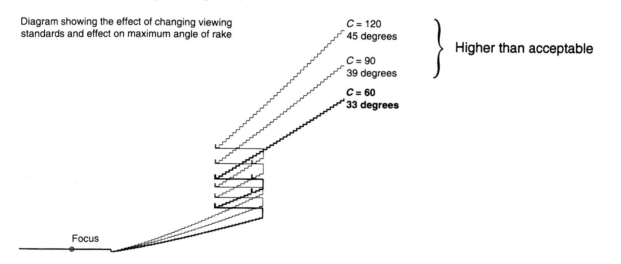

Figure 7.16 One example of the varying results obtained by juggling the factors identified in the foregoing figures.

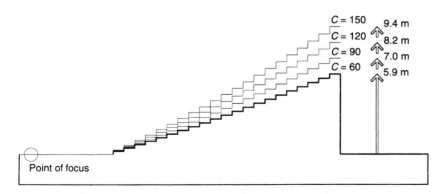

Figure 7.17 The effect of changing '*C*' values on the angle of rake.

may give a rake that is too steep for comfort or safety. It is generally accepted that an angle of rake steeper than 34 degrees (approximately the angle of a stair) is uncomfortable and induces a sense of vertigo in some people as they descend the gangways, even if regulations in some countries do allow steeper angles. In Britain the *Guide to Safety at Sports Grounds* (published by HMSO) and also known as the Green Guide, recommends a maximum angle of 34 degrees. In Italy up to 41 degrees is allowed, but this extremely steep rake is usually found only towards the backs of the upper tiers. Handrails are then provided in front of each row of seats for safety and to counteract the sense of vertigo.

Not all countries have specific regulations, but in all cases the local codes of practice and legislation must be checked. Where no specific regulations exist the angle of rake will normally be determined by staircase regulations.

Varying riser heights

The calculated rake for a deep stadium will not be a constant angle, but a curve (Figure 7.18), with each successive riser one or two millimetres greater than the one in front. The building process tends to favour standardization, and constructing a stand in this way could be more expensive than straight tiers. Therefore it is customary to divide tiers into facets which provide optimum viewing angles while reducing the variety of riser heights. In Europe and North America, where precision in pre-cast concrete work is relatively easily obtained, the changes in stepping heights could be as little as 10 to 15 mm. In regions with less sophisticated technologies it would be wise to increase the stepping differences to 20 or 25 mm.

When varying seating tier heights cause stair risers also to vary, there might be a conflict with the local building regulations, which sometimes prohibit variations in stair riser heights. This should be checked. In England and Wales the most recent regulations take note of the situation, and waivers are usually obtainable.

7.5 Obstructions to viewing

This factor is more critical for some sports than others. In motor or horse racing, a few columns in front of the spectators may be acceptable because the cars or horses are large objects whose movement past the columns is easily tracked. In tennis, by contrast, the repeated invisibility of a small-diameter ball as it speeds to and fro behind an obstructive column would be intolerable. The structural aspects of column-free roof design are discussed in Section 4.8. The Ulleval Stadium in Norway is shown in Figure 7.19.

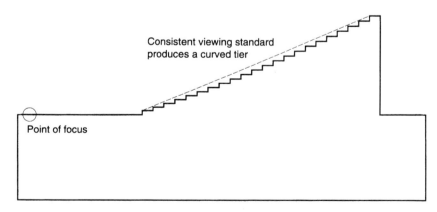

Consistent viewing standard produces a curved tier

Point of focus

Figure 7.18 The riser heights required to maintain a specified '*C*' value in each row of a tier will not be constant, but will vary from each row to the next. In practice such a curved profile will be built as a series of facets which strike a balance between optimum viewing angles and standardization of construction.

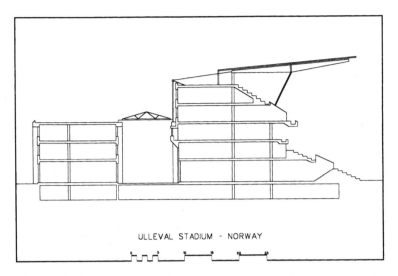

ULLEVAL STADIUM - NORWAY

Figure 7.19 Important as the foregoing calculations are, viewing standards form only part of the requirements which determine the layout of a modern stadium – as may be seen in this cross-section of Ulleval stadium in Norway.

8

Spectator seating

8.1 Basic decisions

Having arrived at a geometry which relates the spectator areas to the playing field so that the spectators can see the action clearly and without having to crane their necks, the next design task is the seats themselves. Seating design is a matter of reconciling four major factors: comfort, safety, robustness and economy.

8.1.1 Comfort

The degree of comfort required depends partly on the seating time for that particular sport, as shown in Table 8.1. The longer the spectator must sit in one position the more comfortable the seats must be. Comfort costs money, but it also helps attract the customers without whose support the stadium cannot succeed. No easy rules can be given for the trade-off between comfort and cost that must be undertaken in each stadium design, except to say that the worldwide trend is towards higher comfort rather than lower cost.

8.1.2 Safety

From the point of crowd behaviour there are opposing arguments concerning the safety of seating types.

The common view is that tip-up seats make for greatest safety because they provide a wider 'seatway' or 'clearway' (Figure 8.1) than other types, thus making it easier for the public, police or first-aid personnel to pass along the rows during an emergency. Against this, some critics argue that bench (i.e. backless) seats are safer

because spectators can step over them during an emergency, but this argument seems lost.

Seats with backs provide greater comfort and we have no doubt that they will become the norm for the future. But in view of the preceding comments, design teams should investigate carefully the kinds of events and the types of crowds involved before finally deciding seat types.

For fire safety (i.e. the combustibility of the seat material) see Section 8.4.3 below.

8.1.3 Robustness

Two principal questions will help decide how robust seats need to be:

- Are the spectators in the particular stadium likely to behave destructively, for example stand on seats, climb over them, or jam their boots against the seat in front while watching a game?
- Are the seats to be under cover and protected from sun and rain, and will they be regularly maintained and cleaned?

A careful evaluation of these factors will influence choice of seat, frame and fixings as described in Section 8.5 below.

8.1.4 Cost

The very cheapest seating type, usually wood or aluminium slats on a concrete plinth, will seldom be acceptable in major new stadia (Figure 8.1). Apart from customer unwillingness to sit on such an uncomfortable surface for any length of time, this primitive arrangement will probably be

Table 8.1   Seating times for various types of events

Event	Seating time
American football	3 to 4 hours
Athletics	3 to 5 hours; sometimes all day (e.g. Olympic events)
Australian Rules football	1.5 to 2 hours
Baseball	3 to 4 hours
Cricket	8 hours a day, perhaps for several days in a row
Football	1.5 to 2 hours
Gaelic football	2 hours
Lawn tennis	2 to 3 hours
Pop concerts	3 hours or more
Rugby	1.5 to 2 hours
Rugby 7-a-side	8 hours

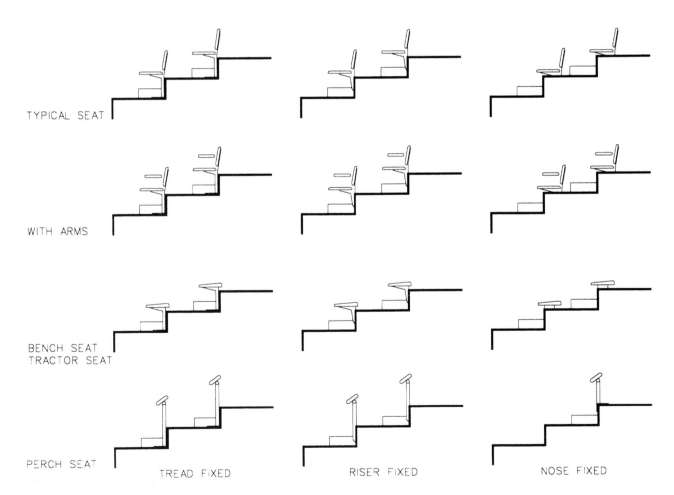

TYPICAL SEAT

WITH ARMS

BENCH SEAT
TRACTOR SEAT

PERCH SEAT

TREAD FIXED   RISER FIXED   NOSE FIXED

Figure 8.1 There are many seating variations but the plastic tip-up type, either riser-fixed or tread-fixed, is the most common.

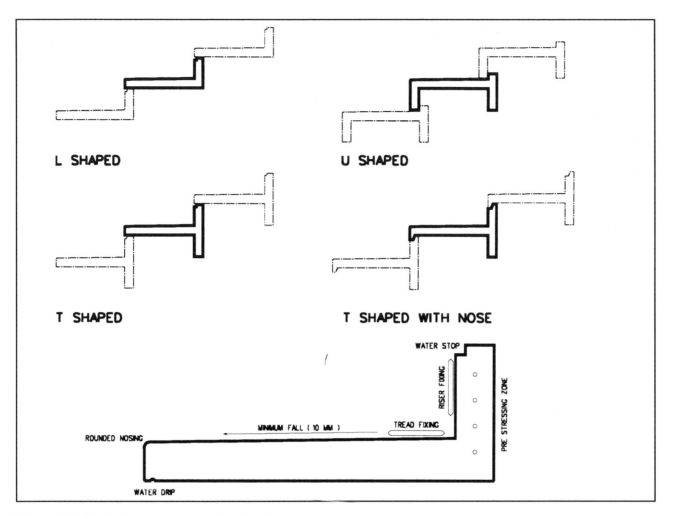

Figure 8.2 Typical precast concrete steppings.

unacceptable to regulators. In the case of British football grounds, grants are not available from the Football Trust unless bench seats have indents to mark individual positions.

So the cheapest realistic option will be moulded metal or plastic 'multiple seats' fixed directly on to the concrete terraces, and the most expensive will be upholstered tip-up seats with armrests.

8.2 Seat types

The following examination starts at the cheapest end of the market and describes the various types of seat in rising order of cost and comfort.

8.2.1 Bench seats

Modern bench seats consist of lengths of moulded metal or plastic with individual seat indents, and are usually fixed to the concrete terrace by means of a metal underframe to give the correct height (Figure 8.3). They are cheap and robust and take up less space than any other kind, the minimum 'seating row depth' as recommended by the British Association of Spectator Equipment Suppliers (BASES) being 700 mm, but see also Table 8.2. However these seats are not comfortable and should be used only in the cheapest admission areas, if at all. If they are used corrosion and decay prevention must be very carefully considered.

Figure 8.3 Bench seats with small backs.

8.2.2 One-piece seats without backs

These are much like the type above, but supplied as individual seats. They are also known as 'tractor' seats (Figure 8.4).

8.2.3 Bucket seats with backs

These are generally similar to tractor seats, sharing the advantages of low cost and easy

cleaning, but they are more comfortable. However, they have the disadvantage of requiring much more space than any other seat type except for fixed seats with backs. Minimum 'seating row depth' is recommended by BASES at 900 mm, compared with 700 mm for bench or backless seats, and 760 mm for tip-up seats, these figures to be read in conjunction with Table 8.2.

8.2.4 Tip-up seats

These cost more than any of the above types, and are less robust, but they are rapidly becoming the most widely-used seating type in stadia (Figure 8.5). They are comfortable, and even if non-upholstered when first installed they can be upgraded later. Tipping up the seat allows easy passage of spectators, police or first-aid assistants, making for greater safety, and it also facilitates cleaning around and beneath the seat.

It is recommended that the seat should be counterweighted (or perhaps sprung) to tip up automatically when not in use; and that moving parts should not have metal-to-metal contact, so that the pivoting action is not degraded by corrosion.

Minimum seat width is recommended by the 1997 British *Guide to Safety at Sports Grounds* (the so-called Green Guide) at 460 mm without arms, 500 mm with arms. However, the Guide

Figure 8.4 One-piece seats without backs.

Figure 8.5 Tip-up seats cost more than the previous types and are less robust, but they are becoming the norm.

Table 8.2 Dimensional standards for seats and standing areas

Country	Seats		Seating areas	Standing areas
	Maximum number of seats per row	Minimum seat dimensions: width (mm) depth (mm)	People per m² (maximum)	People per m² (maximum)
England*	28 seats	460 700 minimum 500 760 with recom- armrests mended 500 recom- mended	3	4.7 (current standard)
(FSADC Guidelines)	28 seats	450 760		
USA	22 seats	450 762 (with back) 450 559 (seat only)		
Germany	72 seats	500 800	2.5	5
Austria	30 m bench length	450 750	3	5
Italy	40 seats	450 600	3.7	
Switzerland	40 seats	450 750	3	5
Norway/Sweden	40 seats	500 800	2.5	5
Netherlands	15 m bench length	500 800		

Note: The above figures must be verified before use, as standards are constantly being revised.
* Data from *Guide to Safety at Sports Grounds* (Green Guide).

recommends 500 mm width for all seats. The present authors believe that 465 mm is a reasonable minimum seat width without arms, and 500 mm an acceptable minimum with arms. Minimum 'seating row depth' is recommended by the BASES at 760 mm; but see also Table 8.2. The authors endorse this 760 mm as a minimum, with a recommended 800 mm.

8.2.5 Retractable and movable seats

Retractable or temporary demountable seats are quite widely used in North America to allow stadia to be adapted to a variety of purposes.

Details are given in Section 5.4 of this book, but it should be noted here that if such seats are used they should not interfere with the sightlines or otherwise reduce the viewing standards of the fixed seating tiers.

8.2.6 New trends in seat design

In addition to a trend towards greater comfort we believe there will also be a tendency for stadium seats to accommodate new technologies both in manufacturing techniques and in communications. Each seat will become the centre of a range of personal services to the spectator as is the case with airline seats. There will be pockets in the seats in front for programmes and brochures, there will be sockets for audio systems, and there may be heating elements which can be adjusted for personal comfort. Seats may be also fitted with rentable binoculars.

8.3 Seat materials, finishes and colours

8.3.1 Materials

Seating materials must be weather-resistant, robust and comfortable. They may include aluminium and certain timbers, but the most popular materials nowadays are plastics – polypropylene (the most widely used), polyethylene, nylon, PVC or glass reinforced plastic. These are easily mouldable to comfortable shapes, and many colours are available (Table 8.3).

Support framing is usually metal (fabricated mild steel or, at a higher price, cast aluminium) but moulded plastic frames are beginning to

appear, and combined all-plastic seats and frames. It is too early to comment on the performance of the latter.

8.3.2 Finishes

The plastic seats themselves are self-finished, but their metal frames must receive an applied finish to give adequate life expectancy. We believe that the useful life of a seat assembly should be expected to be approximately 20 years in most cases, though some forms will last longer than others.

As to specific types of finish, an electrostatically coated nylon powder finish is acceptable only where seats are sheltered from the elements; hot dip galvanizing (in the UK to British Standard 729) is suitable for seat frames exposed to the weather; while the best protection of all is probably given by electrostatically coated nylon powder on grit-blasted, hot-dip galvanizing. This is more expensive than the other types mentioned but provided it is applied effectively, with the nylon not peeling off should its surface be broken, the nylon coating gives added

Table 8.3 Properties of the major plastics used for seat manufacture

	UV Polypropylene	UV/Fire Retardancy Polypropylene	UV High Density Polyethylene	Polyamide (Nylon)	PVC Compound	G.R.P.
Raw material cost factor	1.0	1.4	1.2	3.2	1.8	Approx. 7.0
Availability	Readily available	Limited	Readily available	Limited	Limited	Limited
Colour range	Very good	Good	Very good	Limited	Limited	Very good
Volume manufacture	Very good	Good	Very good	Good	Good	Very poor
Flame retardancy to BS 5852	Ignition Source 0	Ignition Source 7	Ignition Source 0	Self-extinguishes	Self-extinguishes	Self-extinguishes
Reaction to low temperatures (−5° C)	Brittle	Brittle	Very good	Very good	Very good	Very good
Reaction to high temperatures (+50° C)	Very good	Very good	Good	Very good	Very good	Very good
Reclamation and recyling	Easy	Moderate	Easy	Moderate	Specialized	None
Weatherability	Good	Good	Good	Very good	Very good	Very good
Deformation	Recovers	Recovers	Poor	N/A	N/A	N/A
Number of years in production	27	04	20+	19	01	25+

Note: The 'raw material cost factor' does not necessarily reflect the unit cost to the buyer and is given only as background information. This table is published with permission of the Football Stadia Advisory Council.

protection against acid rain, salt and heavy impact.

8.3.3 Flammability

Fire retardance is a vital factor in stadium safety, and the latest legislation or regulations must be consulted before specifying seats.

In the UK the minimum standard of fire retardancy at time of writing is Ignition Source 0 of British Standard 5852 Part 1. Seats are available to the higher standard of Ignition Source 5, of Part 2, but currently in fewer colours, and at a higher price, than the less resistant materials. The use of additives in the plastic to give greater fire retardance is in any case controversial, because when the material ultimately does burn it may produce toxic fumes.

Some authorities argue that the design of the seat is as important in fire safety as the material, and that factors such as the use of double-skin forms which avoid thin, easily ignitable edges should be taken into account when specifying seats.

8.3.4 Colours

Colours are important and can assist the management of the stadium to build colour coded blocks into the seating pattern and match that pattern to the ticketing system. The colour of the seat is also a major factor in the ambience of the stadium when it is partially empty. An alternative approach is to use a varied pattern of colours giving the effect of a number of seated people. This helps to reduce the feeling of emptiness when there are only a few spectators. Some colours perform better by maintaining their colour thus reducing the effects of brittleness caused by ultra violet rays and other environmental pollution, such as acid rain. This can be significant over the expected life of a seat of around 20 years. Additives to plastics can affect this colour quality as well as the actual colour pigment used in manufacture. These additives will also affect the presence of static electricity, which can adversely affect the comfort of spectators.

Colour fastness is measured in the UK according to the British Standard 1006:B01C 'Blue Wool Standard' and it is recommended that this, or a similar standard, be used when specifying the colour of seats. Extent of exposure to the elements dictates how long the seats selected will look well and hold their colour, but that level of exposure is difficult to define as it will even vary within the stadium bowl itself. UV stabilizers and absorbers will help to retain the seat's appearance. The general rule is that intense colours such as black, blue, red and green are more light fast than softer pastel colours such as sky blues and pinks. Although different seating manufacturers tend to have their own colour range, this selection is really only relevant if the order is for a small number of seats. If sufficient quantities are required almost any colour is possible, depending only on the product chosen.

8.3.5 Cleanability

The seat must be designed to drain easily and not hold water. This is often achieved by designing a drain hole in the centre of the base. It should be capable of accepting a seat number, being easy to clean, and deterring vandalism. Users will give it more respect if it is clean and well maintained. Cleaning around and under the seat should also be easy, and fixing should be designed with this in mind. In general the fewer the floor or tread fixings, the easier it is to clean the stadium. Riser fixings are therefore preferable.

8.3.6 Fixings

The seat frame should be bolted to the concrete steppings with rustproof fixings – preferably stainless steel, which does not add much to the overall cost of seating, but greatly enhances appearance and durability. Fixings must be very robust: spectators will occasionally stand on seats, or rest their feet on the seats from behind, exerting considerable force. Designers tend to under-estimate the extent of wear and tear received by stadium seats, but one useful standard test is the Furniture Industry Research Association (FIRA) test in the UK. This test is based on British Standard 4875, Part 1, rating 5.

The alternative forms of fixing from which the designer must choose are given in Section 8.7 below.

8.3.7 Refurbishment of existing stadia

In the refurbishment or upgrading of existing terraces the construction of the steppings will limit the forms of fixing which will be feasible – particularly in older facilities. This can be an important factor in re-equipping an existing stadium with a large number of seats, simply because of the number of fixing points which will be required. Complete units of several seats, perhaps even including floors, can be super-imposed over an existing construction. The construction materials for such units can include steel, aluminium, pre-cast concrete or even glass-reinforced plastic.

8.3.8 Other factors

'Riser' type of fixing tends to be preferable to the 'tread' type – see Section 8.7 below. Each seat should be capable of accepting a seat number, and perhaps a sponsor or name plate.

There is also a growing requirement for seats to accept holders for drinks, fixed to the seat frames for stability. These can generally be fitted where a tread width of not less than 700 mm is used.

8.4 Choice

In most stadia, and certainly in larger ones, the above considerations will probably lead to the provision of a variety of seating types, at a variety of prices, for different types of customer.

Areas of cheaper, less comfortable seating may be provided in the form of benches or backless seats (Figures 8.2 and 8.3). These may allow closer spacing between seats, accommodating more spectators in a given area, in addition to being cheaper to install. But they have the disadvantages described in Sections 8.3.1 and 8.3.2.

The majority of seating will almost certainly be in the form of individual seats with backs – very probably the tip-up kind (Figure 8.5). They are the most comfortable type, giving the greatest width of seatway (see next section) thus providing greater convenience and safety than backless seats. In the case of football stadia

FIFA is clear in its recommendation that in major stadia all seats should have backs.

At the top end of the range VIP and other special areas, which will be under cover from weather and not exposed to the worst excesses of crowd misbehaviour, will require comfortably proportioned upholstered seats with backs and arms. The whole subject of private viewing areas is covered in more detail in Chapter 9.

8.5 Dimensions

Seating dimensions must be such as to allow enough space, both side-to-side and from front to back, for comfort and must allow easy passage for police or other personnel during emergencies.

8.5.1 Safety

The absolutely essential requirement is to maintain a clear seatway to allow the movement of spectators along the seat row (Figure 8.6). The minimum recommended dimension is 400 mm (the UK Green Guide states that this may be reduced to 305 mm where there are only 7 seats in a row served by a gangway on one side, or 14 seats where there is a gangway on both sides). The bigger the seatway the better, and there are many factors to be considered before coming to a decision. These include:

- The maximum numbers of seats in a row allowed by national regulations. In the UK the maximum is 28.
- Police and stewards may be required to physically remove a spectator. The greater the likelihood of unruliness in the crowd, the more important a wide seatway becomes.
- First-aid personnel may be required to carry out a spectator who is unwell.
- During winter spectators wear large over-coats. Stadia likely to be in use during very cold weather may therefore need larger seatways than those in localities where the weather is always warm.
- Cleaners may have to move along the rows, often with large garbage sacks.
- Wider seatways allow spectators to get out and buy from the concessions more easily.

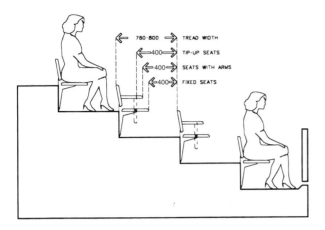

Figure 8.6 Minimum seat dimensions.

8.5.2 Comfort

A minimum width of 450 mm is widely accepted around the world; but given the fact that around 95 per cent of men and women are within 480 mm across the shoulders (not including the thickness of clothing, which will be bulky for winter sports) it seems inadequate. 500 mm would give spectators more scope for adjusting their position without disturbing their neighbours. The authors would recommend an absolute minimum of 465 mm without arms, and a minimum width of 500 mm with arms.

8.5.3 Recommendations

Table 8.2 and Figure 8.6 give recommended seat dimensions taking into account the above factors. These dimensions must be checked against any relevant local or national codes which may apply, though the latter rarely exist and are often inadequate.

Seat height also affects comfort, and a range of between 430 mm and 450 mm is recommended.

8.6 Seat fixings

8.6.1 Fixing types

There are four basic types of fixing, as shown in Figure 8.1. They are:

Tread fixing
The frame rests on, and is bolted to, the terrace floor.

Nose fixing
The frame or seat rests on, and is bolted to, the front edge of the terrace tread. This may be an easy modification to an existing terrace where the spectators sat directly on the concrete.

Riser fixing
The frame is bolted to the front face of the terrace riser, leaving the tread clear.

Combined tread and riser fixing
This may be used where the risers are very shallow – say, less than 200 mm.

8.6.2 Fixing choice

Choice of seat and choice of fixing method are related. Matters to be considered include:

- Seats can be fixed either on lengths of linked framing, or on individual frames. The former is cheaper, but a combination of linked frames and individual frames may be needed to cope with stadium geometry.
- If an existing stadium is being upgraded, a frame type which requires the least modification to the existing supporting terraces will save money. In this connection see Section 8.4.7.
- Frames resting on the tread tend to gather litter around the fixings, and make cleaning more difficult.
- Frames resting on the tread or floor are more likely to rust or corrode in rainy climates.
- Frames fixed to the vertical surface and keeping clear of the floor or tread are easier to clean around, and less prone to corrosion, but they need a minimum riser height of around 200 mm for concrete risers, which may not always be available.

In summary we can say that riser fixing is generally the preference – being easier to clean and less likely to corrode – particularly for tip-up seats, but it is subject to the riser-height limitation mentioned above.

8.6.3 Frame finishes

The three principal types of frame finish – electrostatically coated nylon powder, hot-dip galvanizing, or a combination of the two – were discussed in Section 8.3.2 above.

Figure 8.7 shows a future seat design.

8.7 Seating for spectators with disabilities

Much of the detail relating to the provision of spectator seating is set out in Section 13.8, including scales of provision.

A valuable guide on this subject is the FSADC publication *Designing for Spectators with Disabilities*, published by the Sports Council, which gives information on viewing areas and sight-lines. It is not possible in this publication to go into detail on the various solutions offered.

However, regarding the location and dispersal of viewing areas, the following recommendations are made. The FSADC advises that areas for disabled spectators should, where possible, be dispersed throughout the stadium to provide a range of locations at various levels and various prices. *For practical and safety management reasons, however, it will normally be necessary to retain some grouping of wheelchair-using spectators.*

When siting viewing areas the FSADC recommmends that:

● Viewing areas should be accessible to spectators with disabilities with the minimum of assistance.

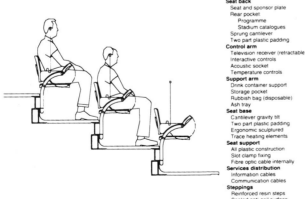

Figure 8.7 Future possibilities in seat design.

Figure 8.8 Individual seats designed with a club motif, Oriole Park, USA. Architects: HOK. Photo: Jeff Goldberg/Esto.

● Designed viewing areas should be provided for both home and away supporters. Many supporters with disabilities suffer isolation and intimidation when situated among or close to able-bodied supporters of the opposing team.
● Spectators who use wheelchairs should not feel cut off from spectators in the main body of the stand.
● Access should be available to different areas of a seating deck for semi-ambulant and ambulant disabled.
● Smaller groups of disabled spectators dispersed throughout a stand are a more manageable proposition for safe evacuation than larger groups.

9

Private viewing and facilities

9.1 Introduction

Whether private viewing facilities are required, and if so on what scale, is an aspect of the brief that must be carefully thought out for each stadium. These areas often subsidize the seat prices elsewhere in the stadium. The underlying principle is that of differential provision and pricing in order to cater for as many market segments as possible, as explained below.

9.1.1 Range of seating standards

Demand for superior standards of comfort and refreshment facilities, and the willingness or ability to pay for these benefits, varies from person to person. A successful stadium will positively exploit these differences by providing the widest feasible range of seating quality (in terms of viewing position, seat comfort and environmental quality), an equally wide range of catering and other support facilities, and a choice of prices geared to what individual customers are prepared to pay for such differing levels of service.

Table 9.1 lists ten basic categories of seating/ standing accommodation in descending order of luxury and price. These are not the only possibilities: other variations such as upper and lower tier, or front and rear positioning, will add to the possible range of viewing standards and ticket prices. The third column of the table indicates the approximate percentage of spectators who may be expected to fall into each category in a given stadium, the basis on which tickets are likely to be sold, and the probable space standards. All of this data is indicative only.

9.1.2 Private facilities

If Andy Warhol was right in suggesting that everyone nowadays is famous for fifteen minutes then it might follow that we will all require VIP facilities at some stage in our lives. Whatever the validity of this theory, private viewing accommodation will be needed in virtually all future stadium developments which need to be financially self-supporting. As sporting events must compete more intensively with the many alternative leisure pursuits available, the provision of comfort instead of spartan simplicity becomes essential for a growing sector of the market. Also these exclusive seats make a large contribution to stadium profitability. An individual attending a private box may pay many times the price of an average seat and is usually committed to spending handsomely on food and drink bought on stadium premises (or, alternatively, have it bought for him).

The income generated from such services is generally quite disproportionate to the cost of provision. Many new developments could not viably proceed without these more exclusive facilities, and for some clubs they are a lifeline of financial success. Many of the older stadia are therefore being retrofitted to capture new markets and maximize revenues in this way.

Because private and club facilities can be exploited for a variety of social and other functions, a stadium containing such facilities is generally better suited to multi-purpose uses than a stadium without. To allow such exploitation

Table 9.1   Range of viewing standards that might be provided in a stadium

1 Private boxes	Self-contained private dining and bar facilities	8 to 12 person boxes 1–2% spectators 3 year contract Tread 850 mm padded and arms
2 Executive suites	Group private dining and shared bar	4–20 person suites 1–2% spectators 1–3 year contract Tread 850 mm padded and arms
3 Club seating and dining	Group seating and group dining with shared bar and lounge	Tables of 2–6 in restaurant 1–2% spectators 1–3 year contract Tread 800 mm padded and arms
4 Club seating	Group seating with shared bar and lounge facilities	Lounge self-contained 2–4% spectators 1–3 year contract Tread 800 mm padded and arms
5 Members seating and dining	Group seating with shared dining and bar facilities	Dining and bar self-contained 1–2% spectators season ticket plus dining Tread 760 mm with arm rests
6 Members seating	Group seating with shared bar facilities	Bar part of 5 above 2–5% spectators season ticket plus Tread 760 mm with arm rests
7 Public seating (several standards)	Seating with public bars and concession areas	Wide range of concessions 50% spectators match or season ticket Tread 760 mm with backs
8 General seating	Bench seating with public bars and concession areas	Range of concessions 5–15% spectators match or season ticket Tread 700 mm no backs
9 Perch seating (optional)	Perched positions with public facilities	Range of facilities 5–15% spectators match or season ticket Tread 610 mm wide
10 Standing terrace (some stadia)	Standing areas with public facilities	Range of facilities 5–15% spectators match or season ticket Tread 380 mm

these facilities should always be designed for flexible use and adaptation.

9.2 Trends

9.2.1 North America

In the USA, stadium managements work hard at maximizing the number of VIP seats. They try equally hard to maximize the number of revenue-generating facilities added on to these areas, thus enticing customers to spend as much time as possible on the premises before, during and after sporting events. In this way managements hope to extract the maximum amount of money from their captive patrons as a simple necessity at a time of soaring costs.

Patrons with exclusive accommodation rights are encouraged to arrive well before the event and to use the stadium facilities for meals before or after matches, for entertaining business colleagues, and for carrying on business transactions by means of telephones, fax machines and computer facilities provided in a 'business centre' in the VIP area. In the more advanced stadia customers may spend most of the day enjoying themselves (and possibly doing some business) in the VIP area on match days, instead of merely attending for two or three hours. Texas Stadium in Dallas provides a good demonstration of the above possibilities.

9.2.2 The UK

Stadium management in the UK is generally not as commercialized as in the USA, but all the trends outlined above are at work in Britain. Wembley Stadium in London is a leading existing example, and the general nature of future sports stadia may be foreshadowed by the Sir Alfred McAlpine football and rugby stadium in Huddersfield, Yorkshire. Designed by HOK + LOBB, it contains a range of facilities:

- 25 000 spectator seats in total;
- 50 executive boxes;
- 400-seat banqueting hall;
- bars and restaurants, shops and offices;
- 30-bay floodlit golf driving range, dry ski slope;
- pop concert venue;
- 800 car parking spaces;
- football and rugby museums;
- crèche;
- concessions
- indoor swimming pool, dance studio and gymnasium.

9.2.3 Other countries

Trends in private facilities vary throughout the world. With due allowance for exceptions it can be said that managements in Japan are following roughly the same course as those in the USA; that those in France and Spain are also taking an increasingly commercialized approach; but that those in Germany tend to oppose anything that smacks of 'privilege', preferring to provide customers throughout the stadium with seats that are as equal as designers and managers can

make them. In the Middle East and the Far East stadia are mostly large utilitarian bowls, with no frills, where most people come for the single purpose of watching a game of sport. The main exceptions to this general rule are race courses, which are most elaborate in Asia.

9.3 Design

9.3.1 Degree of detachment from the pitch

An important early decision with private viewing facilities of all kinds is whether the people in these areas should see the match from behind a fixed glass wall. This is quite common practice in the USA (Figure 9.1) but less so in the UK. British examples include Tottenham Football Club and Queens Park Rangers stadium in Loftus Road, London.

Choice must be left with the stadium owner, but the authors believe that an atmosphere of full involvement with the game is vital, and that 'piping' crowd noise into a sound-proof enclosure behind a fixed glass wall is not an adequate substitute. The preferred solution is to locate private enclosures or boxes with seats in the well of the stadium, outside the building enclosure, and to locate the hospitality and other facilities behind these, shielded by glass (Figure 9.2).

Once this basic decision is taken the detailed design of the various types of private facility can commence, as outlined below.

9.3.2 Private boxes and executive suites

As indicated in Table 9.1 these are the most exclusive and highest priced facilities. Each box (Figure 9.3) commonly accommodates 10 to 20 people but there is no rule about this: the determining factor may simply be the number of seats that can be fitted in without compromising comfort or viewing standards. Each box is usually provided with its own food servery, bar and perhaps toilet (or, if this is too expensive, access to group toilets). The notes below should be read in conjunction with Figure 9.2 which shows three typical configurations.

Figure 9.1 Stadium suites behind glass at the Jordan-Hare Stadium, Auburn University in Alabama, USA.

Kitchens and serveries

These should be at the back of the box, possibly with separate access from the box users so that catering staff can come and go without disturbing customers. Depending on the standard of catering provided the servery can be as simple as a single straight bench without drainage, or as luxurious as a well-fitted U-shaped bench arrangement with integral bar, ice-making machine, coffee maker, and water supply/drainage facilities for washing-up.

If the boxes are planned as pairs their utility services can be combined in one duct, and one door may give access to both serveries.

Toilets

Each box could have its private toilet but this will be expensive and a more usual solution is for toilets to serve a group of boxes. Toilets should have private and secure access and be to 4-star hotel standard. If toilets are provided in groups, there should be a higher proportion of female toilets than for the rest of the stadium.

Private box lounge

This is a common lounge where box-holders can meet other holders for socializing or business. It should have a food servery, bar and access to private toilets.

9.3.3 Executive suites

These suites are similar in principle to club enclosures (see below) but they provide higher standards of comfort and style, and probably a higher degree of privacy to cater for more demanding customers willing to pay higher prices. There are examples in the USA which offer patrons a prime view of the playing field from theatre-type seats in an air-conditioned club room with a range of superior catering services available exclusively to members.

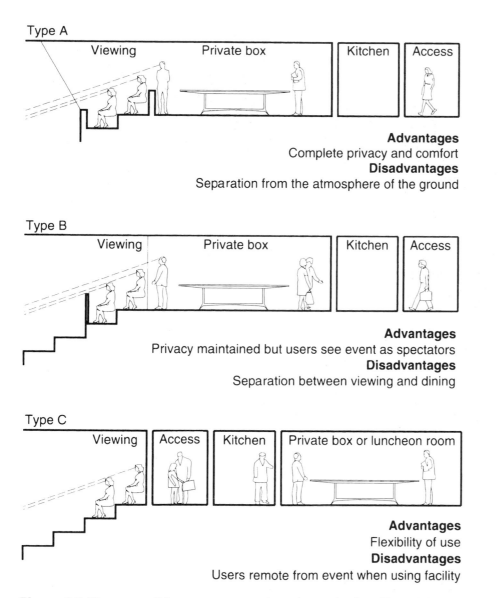

Figure 9.2 Three possible arrangements for private viewing: Type A behind glass (as shown in Figure 9.1), Type B in the well of the stadium, with the private box immediately behind; and Type C in the well of the stadium with an access corridor immediately behind. Each option has its advantages and disadvantages as noted.

9.3.4 Club enclosures

Club enclosures are 'exclusive' sections or levels of the general stadium with their own restaurants, bars and toilets, and very comfortable seating, catering for affluent patrons who are willing to pay a premium for superior facilities but not prepared to commit themselves to 10 or 20 individual places as expected of a private box-

holder. They are likely to be found mainly in larger stadia.

Since the use of such facilities will vary from one match to another these areas should be designed so that they can fulfil other functions on non-event days, or when they are not being used for a particular event.

Each club area will have its own bar and perhaps kitchen facilities, depending on the

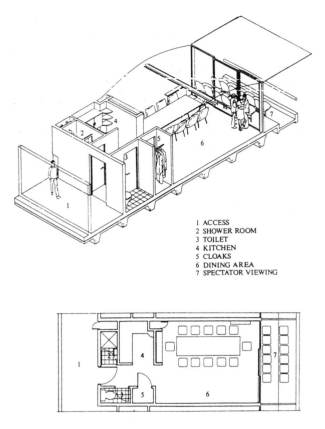

1 ACCESS
2 SHOWER ROOM
3 TOILET
4 KITCHEN
5 CLOAKS
6 DINING AREA
7 SPECTATOR VIEWING

Figure 9.3 Typical layout of a private box of Type B in Figure 9.2.

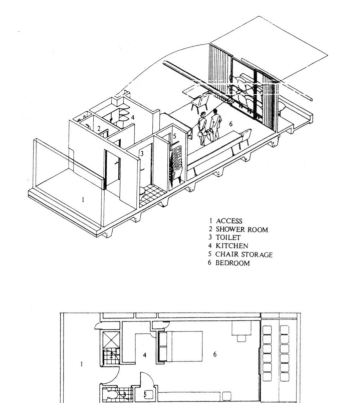

1 ACCESS
2 SHOWER ROOM
3 TOILET
4 KITCHEN
5 CHAIR STORAGE
6 BEDROOM

Figure 9.4 A private box that can be converted into a bedroom.

catering organization of the particular stadium. It may have its own individual toilets, which should not be combined or shared with other users. Accommodation may be needed for three types of users.

Guest room

This is used for entertaining invited guests of the host club, and the area of the room is usually of the order of 60 to 100m². The space needs to be directly linked to the directors' facilities of the host club and preferably have direct access to the directors' viewing area, but need not overlook the pitch.

Visitors' room

This area is for use by the directors and guests of the visiting club. Again, the room area should be about 60 to 100 m² and be directly linked to the directors' facilities of the host club with direct access to the directors' viewing area. It need not overlook the pitch.

Sponsors' lounge

This is a space used by the sponsors of the club or individual event to entertain their invited guests. It can consist of one or more private hospitality boxes (see above) or be provided as a completely independent space which, when not being used by the sponsor, is let out for general entertainment purposes. The approximate area might be 50 to 150 m² and it need not overlook the pitch.

9.3.5 Members' enclosures

These are similar in nature to the club enclosure above but less luxurious, as suggested by the provisions in Table 9.1.

9.4 Multi-use

If carefully designed, private facilities such as club enclosures or boxes can serve many purposes other than being used for the actual event. The use of movable walls between boxes, for example, would allow the area to be opened up into a larger dining room at times when the boxes are not in use, and perhaps as a public restaurant on non-event days.

Private boxes are quite similar in size to hotel bedrooms and in theory they could, with a modest increase in capital cost to include a full bathroom, be designed for such dual use from the outset (Figure 9.4). The Skydome in Toronto has come closest to this ideal. Huddersfield Alfred McAlpine Stadium has furthered this concept by designing private boxes which can be converted into hotel rooms.

10

Food and beverage catering

10.1 Introduction

Attractive and efficient catering facilities will increase customer satisfaction and can also make a vital contribution to stadium profitability and spectator safety.

More people attending an event now expect to buy a reasonable quality and range of food and drink on the premises, and their expectations are constantly rising as a result of the great improvement in catering standards generally. The challenge to stadium owners and managers is therefore to provide the widest possible range of eating and drinking facilities, from quick-serve outlets at one extreme to luxurious private dining rooms at the other. If they can get the scales of provision, the locations, the quality of service and the price levels for all their customer types they stand to earn valuable additional revenue.

Generally the spend per head on food and beverages at an event is higher in the USA than elsewhere, partly no doubt because US spectators have more money to spend, but also because American managements have gone to great lengths to please the customer by the scale, quality and attractiveness of the catering outlets. Other countries, including the UK, are beginning to follow the north American example.

A balance must be struck between the capital and running costs of extensive kitchen and serving facilities, and the return they generate in terms of direct sales.

10.1.1 Maximizing revenues

An obvious way of improving the 'revenue to cost' ratio is to make the maximum use of catering facilities once they have been installed. Wherever possible these should be designed to cater not only for regular stadium spectators but also for receptions, banquets, dinners and other functions throughout the year. Restaurants ought to be open not only on match days, but on as many other occasions as customers can be encouraged on to the premises; private box-holders should be encouraged to use their facilities not only during matches, but for general social relaxation or corporate entertainment on event days and at other times as discussed in Chapter 9.

If spectators are to be encouraged to make full use of restaurants and catering concessions, other aspects of stadium design and management need to be addressed. Spectators should be encouraged to arrive at the stadium early and stay late – a use-pattern which would also ease the problems of crowd circulation and traffic movement.

In the UK and Australia part of the problem lies in changing strong existing traditions whereby spectators attend a local pub before a sporting event, particularly football and rugby, the pub acting both as a meeting point and a suitable beverage outlet. This results in late arrival at the stadium and an unnecessary crush, creating crowd control problems. Indeed, pre-match drinking was one of the suggested contributory factors to the Sheffield Hillsborough disaster in the UK in 1989. In addition, having fans spend their money off the premises does nothing for stadium profitability.

Some of the methods for extending customer time at the stadium lie in marketing and management, for instance providing warm-up events before the match, or showing highlights of the event on a video screen afterwards.

But design too must play its part: there must be adequate circulation routes to seats, and treads of sufficient width to make spectators feel comfortable about carrying their purchases back to their seats without disturbing others. The provision of accessories such as carrier bags, trays and frames for carrying several drinks safely and drink holders fixed to seats also help to encourage increased purchasing.

Long-established habits will change only if people learn to expect a good standard of product and service, with an enticing range of foods and beverages available. There should, within reason, be something for everyone – the customer who wants to enjoy a leisurely sit-down meal in prestige surroundings; the customer with less to spend, who will be satisfied with a self-service cafeteria; and the customer in a hurry, who wants a variety of fast-food or take-away outlets to choose from in a concourse near him. And it is important to realize that these categories no longer reflect the stratifications of society: the take-away kiosk may be patronized by the holder of a high-price ticket who happens to be in a hurry, and the sit-down restaurant by a less affluent family giving themselves a treat. All facilities should be accessible to everyone (Figure 10.1).

10.1.2 Sharing capital costs

It is now common for the stadium owner to enlist the support of an established catering organization, thus sharing the burden of capital costs, and bringing in the wealth of marketing and managerial expertise which exists within such specialized organizations. Catering firms in turn are starting to appreciate the opportunities which exist at sporting venues where tens of thousands of people come to spend their day in an atmosphere of relaxed leisure. This is precisely the mood in which the public parts with its hard-earned money, and catering specialists know how to capitalize on this mood.

The viability of using a catering firm is directly related to the number of events held per annum. The fewer the events, the greater the attractions of using outside catering (with once-a-year events as described in Section 10.1.4 below as

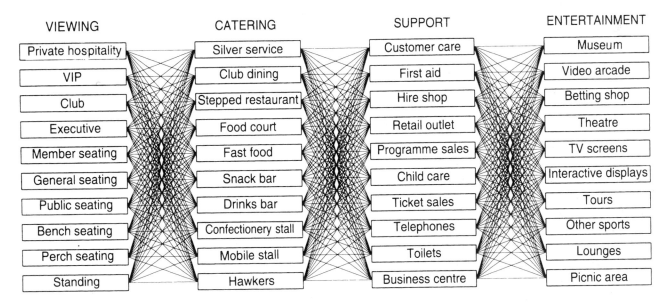

Figure 10.1 The trend in stadium design is away from fixed relationships between customer class and service type, towards freedom of choice between wide range of services. The diagram shows the rich network of potential cross-connections that is desirable.

the extreme example). Conversely, the greater the number of events the greater the opportunity for the stadium organization to set up its own internal catering operation using permanently employed staff.

Leased concessions

It is now common for a named franchise such as MacDonalds or Burger King to take a concession space for the sale of its products, and in larger stadia there may well be several independent franchise outlets in a single concourse.

Leased concessions can operate in several different ways. One arrangement is for the catering firm to finance the construction of certain catering outlets in a stadium in return for a period of exclusive sales at that venue. The stadium will usually take a percentage of the sales in this situation. Such a partnership needs careful control. From a design point of view the caterer will understandably want to dictate much of the planning and layout of the stadium catering facilities as it affects his income, and he will have essential knowledge on the provision of cabled and piped services to feed these areas. The stadium owners and management must heed these views, especially as the caterer might well invest millions as part of the arrangement; yet it is essential they remain in overall control of functional and aesthetic design matters if the stadium design is to be consistent.

10.1.3 Self-managed operations

Self-managed operations are owned and managed by the stadium administration, though usually operated by a separate department to the one running the grounds. They can in theory include the same wide range of operations as specialist contractors, but in practice are often limited to the large fixed catering facilities such as restaurants, bars and private boxes, leaving the fast-food sales to concession holders.

The advantage of a stadium operating its own catering organization is that it may then have better control of revenue and also of customer service, with more power to vary the catering 'mix' at any desired time.

Rangers Football Club in Glasgow, whose home is the Ibrox Stadium, is a British example of stadium owners managing all aspects of the catering operation themselves.

10.1.4 Temporary catering facilities

There are many examples of enormous catering operations undertaken with very little in the way of permanent infrastructure. Although this mobile method of catering is used throughout the world the British seem to be particularly adept at it, probably because so few major sporting events in the UK possess adequate permanent facilities.

At the Silverstone Grand Prix the total catering facility consists of only one restaurant serving about 200 people, and a small kitchen. On the day of the Grand Prix, however, thousands of hot meals are sold to the 185 000 spectators who attend over the three days. Around 95 000 people attend on the day of the final and more than 12 000 hot sit-down meals are served in the one and a half hours before the race. Around 95 per cent of these meals are served 'under canvas' from temporary kitchens and dining areas set up inside tents and other temporary buildings.

Even more impressive are the figures for the Wimbledon Championships. Because of its two-week duration it is the largest sporting catering organization in the world. In addition to snacks and drinks, 1500 catering staff serve 100 000 lunches in private marquees erected on the grounds. The amount of food and drink consumed during this brief period each year includes 12 tons of smoked salmon, 23 tons of strawberries, 190 000 sandwiches, 110 000 ice-creams, 285 000 teas and coffees, 150 000 scones and buns, 12 500 bottles of champagne and 90 000 pints of beer.

The help of temporary caterers is regularly enlisted at the Henley Regatta and at virtually every British racecourse which has a major meeting, most notably Cheltenham, the home of national hunt racing. In March each year around 55 000 spectators in 11 000 cars and 360 coaches converge on Cheltenham Racecourse for the three days of the Gold Cup. During that period 8000 sit-down meals are served every day in temporary accommodation, 6000 of them in a vast tented village erected specially for the occasion and taken down immediately after the event is finished. In addition to temporary catering accommodation there are also temporary private boxes, betting outlets, bars and an entire precinct of shops. This is the largest temporary 'tented village' at any annual sporting occasion in Britain, perhaps the world, except for the Ryder Cup which is held in the UK once every four years.

A major disadvantage of this form of catering is that it relies on temporary staff who are enlisted for the duration of the event and then return home hoping to work again on the next occasion, which could be weeks away. Such a pattern of employment tends to suit housewives and retired men and women who can be flexible with their time and income, but are not in the highest skill category for the job. The large operators employ a core group of permanent and well-trained supervisors and take on casual serving staff under their direction, particularly for the larger events.

Environmental health requirements are becoming more stringent and may have an effect on temporary catering layouts, costs and efficiency. The maximum temperature at which refrigerated food must be kept is tending downwards (in Britain, 5 deg C rather than 8 deg C), there are increasingly strict standards for floor surfaces, and so on. The latest requirements should be checked with local health authorities.

10.1.5 Design of catering facilities

In stadium design a choice must be made between three broad patterns of catering operation:

- a central kitchen serving all eating areas;
- dispersed kitchens serving individual eating areas;
- a central kitchen with smaller satellite kitchens between the main kitchen and various individual serveries, each such servery possibly covering a group of private boxes or one large function area. It is typical, for example,

for a central kitchen to have a satellite kitchen on each of the upper decks of a multi-tiered stand, serving the outlets on that level.

Each particular case must be analysed on its merits and the most appropriate options chosen. Such strategic analysis, and the design of the kitchens themselves (which must have adequate storage, preparation and delivery spaces), are highly specialized matters which cannot be adequately covered in a book dealing primarily with stadium design. Before commencing detailed design all decisions should be checked with experts in the field. Technology and practice constantly advance and even the best published information sources quickly become outdated.

Good communication and distribution between the various kitchen and serving areas is critical and an independent service elevator (preferably about 2.4 m by 3.0 m) and internal telephone system are essential between different levels of operation. If carefully planned the service elevator can also be used to service the concession area and other functions such as rubbish removal, equipment transportation and general maintenance operations. In smaller venues it may be possible to use the service elevator for passengers as well but then the elevator would only be available for use by the caterers before the spectators arrive and after they leave. This would place constraints on the caterers' operations.

10.1.6 Scale of provision

The size and number of eating and drinking facilities in a stadium will depend on market conditions, the needs of users and the needs of management. It would be rare for a sit-down restaurant of say one cover per 100 spectators not to be viable on the day of an event at any stadium, simply because of the number of spectators in attendance; but how realistically this size could be maintained and operated on non-event days would depend on management. The trend now is to use the restaurant for conference functions on days with no sporting events.

Whatever areas are provided for dining should, wherever possible, be linked with movable walls so that a range of spaces can be created to serve one large group, or a series of smaller groups, depending on need. This flexibility is crucial since nobody knows what tomorrow's demands might be, and how the building will be expected to cope.

10.2 Automatic vending machines

Vending machines are the simplest and fastest form of catering service, requiring no personnel and very little space. Units are available for dispensing cold beverages, hot drinks (tea, coffee and chocolate), confectionery, various types of snacks and even mini-meals. The simple fare offered, impersonality of service and cost of provision means that they cannot be a substitute for conventional catering methods. But they do have advantages as a supplementary service:

- They can help cope with peak demand when the restaurants and concessions are overloaded.
- They offer faster service (as little as 5 seconds for a snack and 12 seconds for a carton of tea or coffee).
- They can be located throughout the stadium, thus allowing customers from all seating areas to get a quick snack or drink without going far from their seats.
- They can offer a service 24 hours a day.

Their disadvantages are the cost of provision, their vulnerability to vandalism and the need for maintenance. Perhaps it is for these reasons that vending machines are not particularly widely used in sports stadia.

10.2.1 Types and dimensions

Automatic vending machines are available as floor-standing or wall-mounted types. Freestanding or surface-fixed units are easiest to install or (when no longer wanted) to remove. But they are more vulnerable to vandalism than recessed types and more likely to create untidy,

cluttered public areas. Management must exercise constant vigilance if tidy stadium concourses are not to degenerate into a mess as obtrusive dispensing machines, etc. are placed in every convenient space, perhaps by concessionaires, without adequate control.

The larger machines are floor-mounted (up to 2 m high by 0.9 m deep by 1.2 m wide), and may be with or without legs. Refrigerated models must be mounted about 0.2 m from the wall for adequate ventilation. Service access for most models is from the front. The smaller machines are wall-mounted (up to 0.9 m high by 0.6 m deep by 0.7 m wide), and should be positioned at approximately chest-height so that users can operate them without having to bend over.

All the foregoing generalized comments and dimensions are for preliminary space estimation only, and precise data must be obtained from manufacturers, suppliers or proposed concession holders.

10.2.2 Shell and service requirements

Though the vending machines may be owned and installed by concession holders the stadium management will have to make adequate provision to receive them. Most machines will require some or all of the following services, with isolating switches and valves, depending on the types of product they dispense:

- an electrical supply (probably single-phase) for illumination, power, beverage making, microwave heating and chilling;
- mains water supply, possibly to a specified pressure, for beverage making;
- hot water supply nearby for cleaning;
- drainage outlet for overflow and cleaning.

To cope with spillages and deliberate vandalism all surfaces surrounding food and beverage machines must be durable and impervious, and detailed for easy cleaning. Lighting must be excellent to attract customers, to allow instructions to be easily read and to deter vandalism.

Management should provide disposal bins with self-closing flaps and leakproof inner linings adjacent to all machines. These are to receive discarded wrappings, waste food, and the half-emptied beverage cartons which so quickly turn any area into a sordid situation if proper provision is not made.

10.2.3 Locations and scales of provision

Automatic vending machines are usually provided in areas where space does not allow for a concession kiosk. The latter will always be more popular than machines where there is a free choice. The number of machines to be installed may be calculated from the number of snacks to be served in a given period such as ten minutes. Specialist contractors will be able to give expert advice.

10.2.4 Ownership and leasing arrangements

Automatic vending machines may be purchased by the stadium owner, or installed by a vending company who will then provide services such as regular re-stocking, cleaning and maintenance under contract. If a contract arrangement is envisaged, the information given above must be checked with proposed contractors to ensure that the stadium design allows for their requirements.

10.3 Concessions

These are the next simplest form of catering. Like automatic vending machines they are economical on space, but being staffed they offer a more people-friendly service and are less likely to be immobilized by mechanical breakdown. There are three basic types of concession kiosk, each dependent on food type.

Confectionery kiosks

All the products are wrapped and non-perishable, therefore no equipment is required and the stand is very simple. Its essential components are storage, display space and a servery; it may be little more than a counter. Choice of food is necessarily limited, but there is the possibility of the stadium selling its 'own-brand' products.

Gifts and memorabilia may also be sold at these outlets.

Snack bar kiosks

These sell heated food (such as pies and rolls) and hot drinks and therefore need some basic equipment, such as heat/hold cupboards. The kiosk normally consists of a front servery counter and a back storage/preparation counter (Figure 10.2), with the staff acting both as 'servers' and 'collectors'.

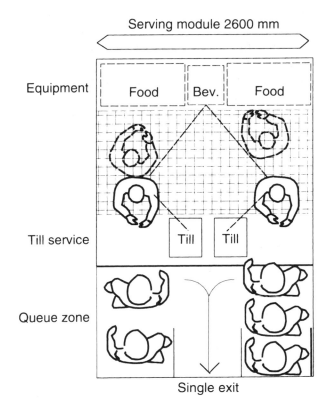

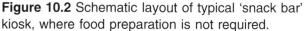

Figure 10.2 Schematic layout of typical 'snack bar' kiosk, where food preparation is not required.

Fast-food kiosks

Cooking and preparation takes place in these kiosks, which sell items such as burgers, steaks, chicken or chips. The kiosk therefore has a complete island 'feed-through' bench with separate counter staff (who serve) and support staff (who cook the food and load the shelves).

A major decision to be taken when there are multiple kiosks throughout the stadium is whether they should be serviced from a central cooking kitchen, or do their own cooking.

The advantages of a central kitchen are that more food varieties can be made available; that equipment duplication is minimized; that food storage conditions are better controlled; that kiosk staff do not need to be as skilled; that pre-cooking can be done at the most effective times; and that cooking can be combined with restaurant cooking.

The advantages of kiosk cooking are that output and demand can be more closely matched; that the cooked food may be fresher than if brought in from a distant kitchen; that 'good food smells' in a concourse can be a marketing advantage; and that kiosk staff are offered more responsibility and opportunities.

10.3.1 Layout and dimensions

Subject to the comments above on various kiosk types, the essential elements of any take-away stand except the simplest are a serving counter, storage space and preparation space. The basic principles are to design the counter so that the person serving needs only to turn to the right or left to reach the majority of items on sale, and to avoid cross-overs with other staff. The counter may need a security screen to the concourse, and this must be designed for aesthetic compatibility with the stadium as a whole, not be fitted by the caterer as an afterthought.

Precise layout and dimensions will vary with the type of food and beverage on sale and the scale of operation. If there are multiple kiosks in the stadium their design should be standardized throughout. Initially, this should mean economies in equipment purchases, and it will also make it easier for staff to transfer from one kiosk to another without retraining.

If people are likely to congregate near the stand to consume their purchases, the area they will take up may be estimated at $0.5\,m^2$ to $0.6\,m^2$ per person. There should be plenty of wall-shelves and free-standing shelf units for the use of people with food and drinks.

10.3.2 Locations and scales of provision

The primary locations for concession kiosks are as close as possible to the access vomitories and concourses, planned so that queues do not obstruct circulation. A total allowance of $1.5\,m$ of counter length per 300 spectators is a figure used in some football stadia, but it may need to be increased where intervals are shorter and the crush for service greater. The principal factors involved are match quality, weather and how easy it is to get service, all of which have an impact on spectator demand.

10.3.3 Shell and service requirements

Except for the most basic stands, selling only packets of confectionery and the like, the preparation space should be provided with the following services (incorporating isolating switches and valves):

- hot and cold water supply and drainage outlet;
- electrical supply and lighting, with three-phase outlets for cooking;
- mechanical ventilation, and an extracting system above the cooking and food preparation apparatus;
- general space heating or cooling for staff comfort, depending on the extremes of temperature likely to be encountered.

10.4 Bars

Even if it is decided that alcohol will not be served during certain sporting events, the provision of bar facilities may still be necessary because the stadium will be used at other times for purposes where such a service will be demanded. Bars of various types may have to be provided.

- At one extreme, intensively used crush bars in public concourses, where large numbers of customers must be quickly served during half-time. These will be highly functional in design, with multiple serving points, and designed for a high proportion of standees.

- At the other extreme, intimate bars in club lounges or luxury dining facilities, where the emphasis will be on a luxurious setting and high-quality service, with comfortable seating for customers who are in no hurry.

There may well be several intermediate grades of bar facility, and portable bars may be necessary for some functions.

10.4.1 Layouts and dimensions

For preliminary space planning purposes it is advisable to allow a customer area of roughly $0.5\,m^2$ per person if everyone stands or $1.1\,m^2$ plus per person if half are seated.

The bar itself consists of a counter, backed by a serving space, and behind that a shelf for drinks display and preparation, and drinks/glasses storage below or above the counter. If it is compatible with the stadium policy on concessions, part of the counter, perhaps 3 m to 5 m in length, may be devoted to serving snacks heated in a microwave oven, and probably coffee.

It makes for economy and efficiency if a central serving area is accessible to several bars, saloons or lounges, with bar tenders able to go to the counter where they are needed. The servery should always have direct access to the storage area and possibly a small kitchen.

10.4.2 Locations and scales of provision

There are no particular rules regarding location, and bars should be located where space is available.

At any one time one metre of counter length could accommodate between five standing customers (crowded) and three (more comfortable). For customers seated on stools counter length is 0.6 m per person.

10.4.3 Shell and service requirements

The bar area should be set back from the circulation route to reduce congestion, and must be fitted with a roll-down grille or shutter to provide security when the bar is not in use. The grille arrangement should be aesthetically compatible with the stadium design and not a later addition.

If the provision of bar services are to be contracted out to specialists who will be fitting out the spaces to their own specifications, the shell should be provided with the following services (incorporating isolating switches and valves):

- hot and cold water supply and drainage outlet;
- electrical supply and lighting, possibly with three-phase outlets for cooking;
- mechanical ventilation, and an extract system above the cooking and food preparation apparatus;
- general space heating or cooling for staff comfort, depending on the extremes of temperature likely to be encountered.

10.4.4 Ancillary accommodation

There must be storage facilities for drinks (and, in large premises, perhaps also for kitchen supplies).

WCs and washbasins must be provided adjacent to bars, and such facilities should be easily accessible and clearly signposted. The provision of toilets is covered in Chapter 11. In most countries this matter is governed by law, and the scales of provision must be checked with the authorities in each case. In the UK the relevant statutes are:

- The Licensing Acts – for all premises where alcohol is to be served.
- The Public Health Act of 1936, Section 89 and the Food Hygiene [General] Regulations – for all refreshment houses where food and drink are sold.
- The Offices Shops and Railway Premises Act – for employee facilities.

It is most economical if toilets, which are very costly, are located to serve a variety of nearby facilities; and the whole stadium should be planned with this in mind (see Chapter 11).

10.5 Self-service cafeterias, food courts and restaurants

Self-service eateries require fewer staff than restaurants with table service (see Section 9.6) and are designed and managed for a faster rate of customer through-put. This is a vital factor in sports stadia, with their concentrated demand peaks.

The arrangement is familiar to all: food is displayed in a line of refrigerated or heated glass-lidded cabinets, and customers move past with trays, helping themselves to what they want and paying at the end. Part of the counter may be devoted to a carvery and/or hot meal servery where staff assist the customers by carving the meat for them, and serving them with meat, fish and vegetable dishes from heated containers.

The food court is an elaboration of the above principle with several serveries, devoted to a variety of food types and price ranges, surrounding a single seating area. Customers collect their food and drink from their chosen counter, and then find a table in the central area.

10.5.1 Layout and dimensions

Because of the specialized nature of such an operation the restaurant will probably be leased to a specialist operator, who will design and fit out the space himself. Layout and dimensions should be discussed with such firms before the stadium design is finalized.

10.5.2 Locations and scales of provision

Self-service restaurants or cafeterias are usually located at the lower levels of the stadium, near the main kitchens and service roads. They require large spaces.

There are no reliable figures on scales of provision, but a ratio of one seat to 50 or a 100 spectators may be used as a starting range. The precise ratio will depend on the nature of the stadium, the character of its clientele, and the degree to which its catering facilities might also be used for non-sports events.

10.5.3 Shell and service requirements

The stadium management may be required only to provide a simple serviced shell ready to be fitted out by a specialist tenant, in which case the latter should state his requirements. They will almost certainly include the following:

- hot and cold water supply with isolating valves;
- drainage outlet;
- electrical supply and lighting, including three-phase supply for cooking, with isolating switches;
- mechanical ventilation and an effective extraction system for the cooking and food preparation apparatus (in case of mechanical breakdown or malfunction natural ventilation should also be available);
- heating or cooling for staff and customer comfort, depending on the extremes of temperature likely to be encountered;
- security screens between the restaurant and the concourse.

It is possible that additional fitting out would be appropriate, depending on the leasing arrangement, and this might include:

- cooking equipment such as cookers and fryers, depending on the type of food sales;
- warmers, beverage storage, cold storage and freezers (these to be large enough for a full day's use);
- washing-up equipment including sinks and perhaps dishwashers.

10.5.4 Ancillary accommodation

There should be direct entry for service access and bulk deliveries, and easy exit for waste disposal. Restaurants generate a great quantity of refuse of a kind which quickly becomes offensive if not removed.

WCs and washbasins must be provided adjacent to restaurants, and such facilities should be easily accessible and clearly sign-posted (see also the notes under Bars, Section 10.4.4).

10.6 Luxury restaurants

High-class restaurants will attract customers willing to spend more money in return for better food and service in more spacious surroundings, probably taking more time over their meal. Because of the mark-up such facilities could be particularly lucrative for the stadium management.

10.6.1 Layouts and dimensions

These matters are too specialized to be covered in detail in the present book, and layout should be discussed with specialist firms before the stadium design is finalized.

Ready access will be required for bulk deliveries and waste removal.

10.6.2 Locations and scales of provision

Prestige restaurants are usually located near to the club areas and private boxes.

No generalized guidance can be given on the scale of provision, which will depend on the nature of the stadium, the character of its clientele, and the degree to which its catering facilities might also be used for non-sporting events.

10.6.3 Shell and service requirements and ancillary accommodation

The same notes apply as under Sections 10.5.3 and 10.5.4 above. Figure 10.3 shows a hand-held device for personal ordering.

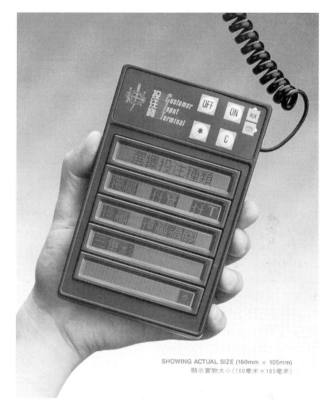

SHOWING ACTUAL SIZE (160mm × 105mm)
顯示實物大小（160毫米×105毫米）

Figure 10.3 In the future ordering may be done from a personal hand-held control and catering service points will be reduced.

11

Toilet provision

11.1 Toilet provision generally

Toilets and/or ablutionary facilities may be
needed for several individual types of stadium
user in addition to those for the mass of
spectators. These include:

- private box holders and other VIPs: see
  Chapter 9;
- television crews, press reporters and radio
  commentators: see Sections 14.2.2 and 14.6.2;
- management and staff: see Section 15.7;
- match stewards and police: see Section 15.7;
- players and referees: see Section 16.2;
- medical examination teams: see Section 16.6.

These facilities should be thought of in conjunction with spectator toilets so as to minimize the
number of sanitary appliances and drainage
stacks in the stadium while still making adequate
provision for all types of users.

In smaller stadia it would be uneconomic and
quite unnecessary to provide separate toilets for
all the groups listed above: common facilities
could serve several categories of users provided
only that everyone is within easy reach of a
usable and suitable toilet. In the largest stadia it
may be necessary to provide completely separate facilities. For each particular case the
design team must find the right balance
between:

- the cost advantages of having only a few
  centralized drainage stacks in a stadium (these
  being a particularly high-cost element, especially at the upper levels of multi-tiered
  stands), and

- the user convenience of maximal dispersal of
  toilets throughout the stadium, with short
  distances (preferably no more than 60 m) and
  the minimum of changes of level between
  users and the nearest facility.

11.2 Toilets for spectators

The bulk of these will of course be inside the
stadium but there should also be toilets outside
the perimeter fence (Zone 4, as defined in
Section 2.3) for the benefit of those queuing
for an event.

11.2.1 Scales of provision

Good toilet provision is intrinsic to a venue's
image while inadequate provision, uneven distribution and poor quality are major sources of
complaint from spectators. Insufficient toilets or
urinals to meet the needs of large crowds of fans
can also lead to misuse of the facilities, offending
and driving away potential visitors and club
members, thus reducing stadium revenue.

There are two separate design problems to be
addressed:

- the proportion of male to female spectators
  who will be using the toilets;
- The intensive use of toilets in very short
  periods of time.

Male to female ratio

Every type of event, or club membership, will have its own ratio of male to female spectators. For instance:

● If a stadium is designed for multi-purpose use, including concerts, then the male:female ratio will approach 1:1.
● Tennis or athletics clubs or events will have higher proportions of women than will soccer or rugby.
● Clubs with high family memberships will usually have above-average proportions of females.
● Higher status clubs, and clubs in pleasant parts of town, will tend to have a higher proportion of women than those with a 'basic' image or environment.

At a particular event there may also be different gender mixes in different parts of the stadium:

● There will be a higher proportion of women in the private or family enclosures of British football stadia than in the standing terraces.
● There will be a higher proportion of women among the home supporters at a European football match than among the 'away' supporters.

On the basis of the above data the gender mix should be reflected in the proportions of toilets provided for that event. Organized clubs keep a record of the male/female split for particular occasions, and such club records are the only reliable source of briefing information for a new stadium design. Figure 11.1 shows a pair of units based on an 80:20 male:female ratio which would be suitable for many current stadia, and which could be distributed evenly throughout the building.

In view of the variation of the male/female ratio from event to event some flexibility should be built into toilet provision. Movable partitions, or defined sections which can be labelled either 'male' or 'female' for a particular event, are two possibilities. These solutions may seem an extravagance, but the problems of inadequate provision and customer dissatisfaction are so great in stadium design that all possible solutions must be considered in the interests of attracting more spectators.

Numbers of appliances

The fact that demand comes in extreme peaks (for brief periods toilet facilities can barely cope with the number of users, while for most of the time they are completely unused) creates a serious problem for the design team. The cost of providing enough WCs and urinals to avoid all queuing would be extravagant, while the problems caused by saving money and not providing enough facilities affronts customers.

In the absence of more specific guidance from the client or from local regulatory bodies the

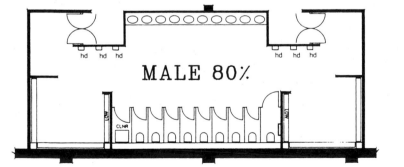
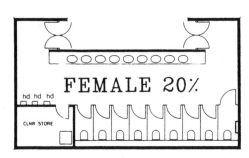

Figure 11.1 Moderately sized toilet units such as the two illustrated above, evenly distributed throughout the stand, are preferable to highly centralized provision. The correct male:female ratio should be researched for each individual case but the 80:20 ratio shown here is a widely recognized 'club' standard. Note the plan layout for fast throughput. Toilets for spectators who are disabled are kept separate, see Section 11.3.

recommendations in Table 11.1 should be used. They are from the Football Stadia Development Committee published by the GB Sports Council. These figures should, if possible, be improved upon, particularly in stadia where spectators will be exposed to winter weather (which causes more frequent use of toilets) or where events are staged with long stretches of time between intervals or where large amounts of beer may be consumed.

Temporary facilities

Owing to the high cost of providing permanent toilets we suggest that only the normal anticipated use of the stadium be catered for in this way, but that provision be made for adding portable facilities (for example 'portaloos' in the UK) for special events, such as pop concerts, which may attract vastly greater numbers of spectators than normal, or continue for longer periods. Preferred locations for such additional facilities need to be planned in advance, so that they can be easily slotted in and serviced.

11.2.2 Location of toilets

The aim should always be a large number of smaller toilets (such as the units shown in Figure 11.1) dispersed throughout the stadium rather than a small number of big units – though this must be balanced against the cost advantages of a centralized drainage system, and a reasonable compromise struck between cost and convenience.

Such units should be distributed as evenly as possible, including all levels of a multi-tiered stand, with no seat more than 60 m from a usable toilet and preferably on the same level. Toilets should lead off concourse areas, be easily and safely accessible, and be on the same level as the concourse. They must never lead directly off stairs: if a change of level is essential at that point it should be in the form of a ramp. The location should allow for plenty of circulation space around the entrance and exit areas, wide entrance and exit doors, and through circulation, with spectators able to enter by one door and leave by another with single-direction flow. Stadium toilets should always be located against an outer wall to allow for natural light and natural ventilation (see below).

Finally, as already mentioned, there should also be toilets outside the perimeter fence (Zone 4) for the benefit of those queuing for an event; and if temporary toilets are to be used for infrequent events then their locations must be designed into the complex at the beginning to allow for easy installation and servicing.

11.2.3 Detailed design

All surfaces should be hardwearing, impervious and easily cleanable, with coved corners and angles. They should be capable of being hosed down, with a trapped outlet to drain away water. Providing urinals flush with the finished floor helps in this regard.

Sanitary appliances should be specified from 'vandal resistant' ranges, with cisterns and pipe-

Table 11.1   BS 6465: Part 1. Minimum recommendations for cinemas, concert halls and similar buildings

	Urinals	*WCs*	*Wash basins*
Male	Minimum of 2 for up to 100, plus 1 for every other 80 males or part thereof	Minimum of 1 for up to 250, plus 1 for every other 500 males or part thereof	1 per WC and 1 per 5 urinals or part thereof
Female	No recommendations	Minimum of 2 for up to 50, 3 for 51 to 100, plus 1 for every other 40 females or part thereof	Minimum of 1, plus 1 per 2 WCs

Note: There are no official UK recommendations specifically for sports stadia, and the above figures for places of entertainment are the closest approximation. If applied to sports stadia the balance of provision is unlikely to be right, and Table 11.2 should be followed. But if the stadium is to be used also for non-sporting events, then WC and wash basin provision should satisfy the above formula rather than the lower figures in Table 11.2.

Table 11.2 The UK Football Stadia Design Advisory Council's minimum recommendations for newly constructed or refurbished sports stadia and stands. These figures apply to each individual accessible area

	Urinals	*WCs*	*Wash basins*
Male	1 per 70 males	1 for every 600 males, but not less than 2 per toilet area, however small	1 for every 300 males, but not less than 2 per toilet area, however small
Female	No recommendations	1 for every 35 females, but not less than 2 per toilet area, however small	1 for every 70 females, but not less than 2 per toilet area, however small

Note: Slab or trough-type urinals should be calculated on the basis of not less than 600 mm per person. All suitable wall areas not needed for other purposes should be exploited for additional urinal provision over and above the minimum recommendations.

work concealed in independently accessible ducts. In the case of urinals, flushing troughs should be used rather than independent cisterns as the former require less maintenance and are quickly recharged.

Hot and cold water should be provided from impact taps which turn themselves off automatically after a specified period. There should also be hand dryers.

In climates where frost may occur it is essential to provide reliable trace heating to the pipework and cisterns, or reliable background heating to the toilet space, throughout the winter – even when the stadium is not in use. If this is not done the system must be drained down after each match in winter to avoid the danger of burst pipework.

Toilets should have natural lighting and generous natural ventilation. Mechanical systems are expensive and prone to malfunction or complete breakdown, leading to very unpleasant conditions in an intensively used toilet.

11.3 Provision for spectators with disabilities

A certain percentage of the toilets provided should be suitable for use by disabled people, both in terms of their location and their design. This percentage may be laid down by local regulations, which should always be consulted. *Toilet Facilities at Stadia* recommends that wherever there is provision for 10 or such spectators, there should be at least 2 toilets. A typical provision is one special WC per 12–15 spectators with disabilities whichever of these figures is the greater. They should be distributed throughout the stadium, but accessible to the appropriate areas. They will frequently be unisex.

12

Retail sales

12.1 Introduction

People attending a sporting or other event are a natural captive market: they have come to enjoy themselves, are in a leisurely (possibly euphoric) state of mind, and may well want to take away some memento of the occasion.

As every unit of currency spent within the stadium perimeter will contribute to the financial viability of the stadium as a whole, it is in the interest of management to exploit this profit-making opportunity to the full: an enticing variety of retail outlets in and around the stadium should be a vital part of every design or management brief.

Some owners and managers have been very energetic in exploiting these opportunities. In the UK, for instance, Wembley Stadium has aggressively pursued several different uses of its facilities (sport, entertainment, exhibitions and conferences) and has in each case exploited the merchandising opportunities offered by the huge captive markets. The results are impressive, with retail sales at its pop concerts measured in hundreds of thousands of pounds per annum. Or, to take a very different example, at the Cheltenham Gold Cup a veritable 'village' of shops is set up around the course for two or three days every year, very successfully selling everything from key-rings to Rolls-Royce cars.

12.2 Advance ticket sales

Spectators who have enjoyed their day are in an ideal frame of mind to buy tickets for future events, and they must be given every opportunity to do so. Advance tickets should therefore be sold before, during and after each sporting event from booths strategically located for maximum sales.

12.2.1 Locations and scales of provision

In addition to the main ticket offices in the central ticket sales area at least four advance-ticket booths should be provided between Zones 3 and Zone 4 (see Section 2.3), with a number of windows accessible from Zone 4 and one window accessible from Zone 3 (i.e. inside the perimeter fence) depending on stadium size.

The total number of windows should be one window per 1000 spectators serving Zone 4, plus one window per 5000 spectators serving Zone 3. On this basis a 20 000 seat stadium would have four advance-ticket booths, each with five serving windows facing Zone 4 and one window facing Zone 3.

The booths should be evenly distributed around the grounds, but in such a way that the windows serving Zone 3 are clearly seen by the crowds leaving the stadium after a match. The windows should be at least 10 m away from the turnstiles so that normal circulation is not obstructed by queues of ticket-buyers congregating around the ticket booths.

12.2.2 Design

Each kiosk should be provided with the following fittings:

- counters fitted with money trays;
- lockable cash drawers;

- signs with interchangeable panels for seat prices;
- heating or cooling as required;
- general power outlets and lighting;
- queuing rails for crowd control.

The booths should be designed to be eye-catching, both in terms of its form and its signs, the latter possibly including imaginative neon signs – as for instance in the Toronto Skydome in Canada.

12.3 Programme sales

The sale of programmes is vital to any stadium, and there should be plentiful selling points in all spectator areas.

12.3.1 Locations and scales of provision

Programme kiosks must be provided in all subdivisions of the spectator area, both inside the perimeter (Zone 2 and Zone 3) and outside (Zone 4). Serving positions should be provided in the ratio of one position for every 2000 to 3000 spectators in the surrounding zone. Additionally, mobile vendor or 'hawker' sales should be considered in the ratio of one per 500 spectators.

12.3.2 Design

Each kiosk should have from two to eight serving positions, depending on the type of sales and the number of spectators to be served, and be fitted with a roller shutter, pin boards for a display of current events, and light and power points. Each kiosk should have direct access to a secure store room of about $6\,m^2$, and a storage area for restocking of approximately $15\,m^2$ to $20\,m^2$, both fitted with shelves.

12.4 Gift and souvenir shops

An enterprising large stadium may have the following range of gift shops and related facilities:

Permanent souvenir shop

This is a gift shop selling stadium or club-related sports equipment, books, tapes and other souvenirs. It may be combined with the following facility.

Stadium museum/exhibition space

This is a showcase for the history of the grounds (and the sports played there) displaying equipment, trophies and films. The latest ideas in interactive video displays are ideal for this location and have been used extensively at theme parks around the world. A good example is the Noucamp Stadium in Barcelona.

Detached shop

A good example is the club shop at Arsenal Stadium in Finsbury Park, London.

12.4.1 Locations and scales of provision

The Souvenir Shop should be located so that it can be approached from both inside the grounds (Zone 2 and Zone 3) and outside (Zone 4). Accessibility from Zone 4 is important to allow the shop to operate even when the stadium is not in use. As ease of parking would assist such off-period sales, a nearby short-stay parking area should be provided.

From all points of view an ideal location for the souvenir shop would be adjoining the administration offices and central ticket sales office. This allows for ease of operation and staffing, plus dual use of a small parking area by both administrative staff and shop customers. The same remarks apply to the Stadium Museum and the Exhibition Space.

12.4.2 Design

Retail sales outlets in stadia are usually provided to concessionaires as serviced shells, possibly fitted out by the stadium management. There must be adequate storage space, either as a room of about $10\,m^2$ near each individual concession, or as a centralized area of perhaps $200\,m^2$. These must be securely lockable.

Each shell should be provided with the following services:

- heating or cooling as required;
- general power outlets and lighting;
- security grille;
- pinboards for posters;
- audio and video system;
- display cases and shelving – clothes are the biggest selling items and suitable racks must be provided.

12.5 Museums and visitor centres

Museums and visitor centres can be very important additions, ensuring a large number of visitors to the stadium. The Barcelona Noucamp Stadium, for example, repeatedly has more visitors per annum to the museum than spectators to see games in the stadium itself. It is possibly the most attractive museum in the city, rivalled only by the Picasso Museum, and is obviously a major source of income. The museum is fitted with extensive photographic displays, trophy cases, models of the stadium and moving image displays. Outside there is a well-used shop selling clothing, souvenirs and memorabilia, together with parking for a large number of coaches and refreshment facilities both inside and outside.

Similar successes include Wembley Stadium in London, which runs visitor tours of the stadium with crowd sound effects to thrill the visitors, and Manchester United's stadium which also has an impressive museum. England's national 75 000 seat rugby stadium at Twickenham in London has a very large shop and a museum of rugby, which has interactive displays and items of memorabilia, together with an audio-visual theatre showing footage and matches from early days to the present. Visitors are invited to explore behind the scenes, the changing areas and experience the players' tunnel.

See also Chapter 21 on Tourism.

13

Circulation

13.1 Basic principles

Circulation planning in stadium design has two main objects: the comfort and the safety of occupants.

Comfort

People should be able to find their way to their seats (or to toilets or catering facilities, or back to the exits) easily, without getting lost or confused. In addition, they should be able to move about with pleasure, not being jostled in overcrowded spaces, having to climb excessively steep stairs, or risk losing their footing as they negotiate the many changes of level which are inevitable in large stadia.

Safety

Safety requires maintenance of all the above desirable characteristics in panic conditions – when, for example, hundreds (perhaps thousands) of spectators are fleeing in fear of a fire, an outbreak of violence in the crowd, or some other real or imagined danger. Even better, preventive measures should minimize the risk of such situations arising in the first place. This should preferably be achieved by skilful design, so that people *want* to go where they have to be in the stadium and are not *made* to go there.

In the following sections we show how these requirements can be catered for in practical terms:

- First, in Section 13.2, we examine the implications of circulation requirements upon stadium layout as a whole.

- Then, in Sections 13.3 and 13.4, we give planning guidelines for the circulation routes themselves.
- Finally, in Sections 13.5 to 13.7, we augment the above planning principles with detailed design data – dimensions, types of equipment and the like.

13.2 Stadium layout

Circulation planning has two major influences on the overall stadium layout – zoning the stadium for safe escape from fire, and subdividing the stadium for crowd management.

13.2.1 Zoning

As already described in Section 2.3 the modern stadium is designed as four concentric zones:

- Zone 1 is the *playing field* and central area of the stadium.
- Zone 2 consists of the *viewing areas* and the *internal circulation area*, i.e. the seating/standing tiers and terraces and their gangways and vomitories.
- Zone 3 is the *external circulation area* surrounding the stadium building but within the perimeter fence.
- Zone 4 is the area *outside the perimeter fence*. It will contain the car parks and the bus and coach off-loading areas.

The purpose of the zones is to enable spectators to escape in case of emergency – first from Zone 2 to either Zone 1 or Zone 3 (the 'temporary safety zones'), and thence to the 'permanent safety zone' of Zone 4 and the outside world. Such escape must be possible in specified times, which then determine the distances and widths of the relevant escape routes: see Section 13.6.2.

In stadia accommodating more than 15 000 or 20 000 spectators all four of the zones should be present but in smaller stadia, where spectators exit directly to the exterior from the spectator viewing and internal circulation areas, Zones 3 and 4 can be combined. Such small stadia will not justify a perimeter fence, but to compensate for that they will require particularly diligent stewarding at the exits.

13.2.2 Sub-division

Subdividing the total ground capacity into smaller units or sectors of about 2500 to 3000 spectators each allows for easier crowd control and for a more even distribution of toilets, bars and restaurants. Each of these sectors should have its own independent circulation routes as well as its share of ancillary facilities.

Separation of different categories of spectator should form part of this division system. For example:

- separation of seated and standing areas; and
- segregation of fans from opposing clubs.

The actual division between areas can sometimes be achieved simply by barriers or changes of height.

In the case of separating rival fans each sector should be completely independent. This independence may go as far as to require protected routes leading all the way from the nearby transport services to the turnstiles (secured by police), and from the turnstiles to the seating areas.

Because of the decisive effect of the subdivision pattern on circulation route planning, management must be consulted at an early stage on how the seating areas in the stadium are to be split up.

In single-tier stands the division lines may run from top to bottom, with policed 'sterile zones' separating the two blocks of 'home' and 'away' fans. This pattern has the advantage of flexibility (the sterile zone can easily be shifted from side to side to allow for a greater or smaller number of fans in a particular area) but the sterile zones represent a loss of revenue, and the problem of ensuring access to exits, toilets and catering facilities for everyone needs careful planning.

In two-tier stands the top-to-bottom division is again a possibility; alternatively one group of fans can be put in the upper tier and the other in the lower tier. If the 'away' fans are in the upper tier there is no risk of pitch invasion, but there is a real possibility of missiles being hurled on to the 'home' fans below, and any kind of trouble is difficult to deal with because of the relative inaccessibility of the upper levels. If the 'away' fans are put in the lower tier trouble is easier to deal with, but there is a risk of pitch invasion, thus calling for larger police numbers or more intensive stewarding.

13.3 Access between Zone 4 and Zone 3

Ideally, and if space allows, a modern stadium should be surrounded by an outer perimeter wall or fence some distance from the stadium, separating Zones 4 and 3. Such a perimeter barrier should ideally be at least 20 m from the stadium, strong enough to withstand crowd pressures, high enough to prevent people climbing over, and containing several types of entrance and exit gates:

- public entrances leading to the main seating terraces;
- private entrances giving players, concession holders and VIP ticket holders separate access to their particular areas;
- emergency service access for ambulances, etc.;
- flood exits for emergency emptying of the grounds.

These are now dealt with in turn.

13.3.1 Public entrances

In some stadia, checking of tickets coming into the grounds is made at this perimeter point; in others it is made at the stadium entrances between Zones 3 and 2; in yet others by some combination of the two.

Circumnavigation between gates

If control is exercised at the perimeter, and if each entrance gives access only to some parts of the stadium (either by physical design, or by subsequent management policy) then circulation routes should be provided in Zone 4, outside the perimeter barrier. People who have come to the wrong entrance gate should be able to circumnavigate to the correct one while still remaining in the same Zone. Conversely, if there will be no control on seating positions at the perimeter then there is no need for such circulation routes, as spectators may enter the stadium via any turnstile. These matters should be clarified beyond doubt with management at briefing stage if faulty design is to be avoided.

Congregation space outside gates

Outside all perimeter access points in Zone 4 there should be sufficient space provided to allow the congregation of spectators before entering through gates or turnstiles. This congregation space should be sized and positioned so as to avoid congestion and allow a free flow of spectators when the gates or turnstiles are opened. See also the notes on crowd control barriers under Section 13.7.1.

Other safety measures

In all cases public entry doors should be used only for the purposes of entry, and all public exit doors only for the purposes of exit. The simultaneous use of any gateway for both entry and exit can create risk. If such two-directional gates are used they must be *additional* to the exit gates required for emergency outflow as calculated in Section 13.6.2 ('timed exit analysis').

Amenities such as ticket offices, toilets, bars or restaurants should always be located a safe distance away from the nearest entrance or exit to allow a congregation of people without risk of a crush.

Number of gates

There are several ways of allowing spectators into the stadium, but most fall into the two broad categories of gates and turnstiles. Gates are cheap, and an open gate can allow approximately 2000 spectators to pass through per hour whereas turnstiles are expensive and will only pass through 500 to 750 spectators per hour. Detailed design notes are given in Section 13.7.1.

Location of gates

The location of entrance gates in the perimeter barrier will depend on three factors which may to some degree conflict with each other, requiring an early decision on priorities:

- To avoid congestion entrances should be spaced at regular intervals around the circumference.
- If mutually hostile fans must be kept apart it is again desirable for entrances to be widely separated.
- But management may want entrances to be grouped closely together for convenience of staffing and security.

Any conflicts between the above requirements must be resolved before design commences, by obtaining a very clear statement of design priorities from management at the briefing stage.

Segregation of fans

It is necessary here to say more about the second factor mentioned above – whether to allow for the enforced segregation of certain groups of spectators before they enter the stadium.

Where the anticipated spectators are known to be 'game-orientated' rather that 'team-orientated', and to behave peacefully, there is no need for special provisions. Spectators at tennis, rugby or athletic events tend to fall into this class. So, perhaps for different reasons, do American football and baseball crowds: because distances between competing clubs in the USA are so great, there are seldom large numbers of 'away' fans present at matches.

The case is generally different with football crowds in Britain and Europe (principally the

Netherlands, Italy and Germany) and in South America. These fans tend to be strongly partisan and attend matches primarily to support their home teams. Supporters of competing sides may be hostile and aggressive, in which case they cannot be allowed to mix freely and must be separated all the way from their arrival in Zone 4 to their seats.

Provision must then be made for systems of barriers (preferably movable) in Zone 4 which will funnel groups of spectators to widely separated entrances, which in turn lead to separate parts of the stadium. This causes two problems for designers:

- Separate turnstiles and horizontal and vertical circulation spaces, perhaps also with separate toilets etc., could lead to expensive duplication of facilities.
- It will be necessary to visualize at this stage how the stadium may be divided between seating areas for 'home' and 'away' supporters, and the entrances and routes must be so designed that rigid separation can be maintained at some matches, while freedom of movement is possible at others.

13.3.2 Private entrances

These entrances are for players, VIPs, directors, sponsors and the media. They should be close to a special VIP parking area, with a sheltered connecting route, and should be well separated from the public entrances.

Access should be by open gate rather than turnstile, with a higher level of security staff present, and lead to a secure route all the way to the seat. Quality of design and finishes must be markedly superior to the rest of the stadium, with the ambience of a superior hotel.

13.3.3 Emergency service access

Provision should be made in the perimeter barrier for emergency service access between Zones 4 and 3. These access points must be stewarded constantly and will be opened only in exceptional circumstances. They should connect directly between the stadium interior (Zone 1)

and the public road network (Zone 4) for fast and unimpeded ingress and egress by ambulances, fire engines or other emergency service vehicles. Widths and gradients must allow for this.

13.3.4 Flood exits

Apart from the gates and turnstiles described under *Public Entrances* above there must be separate and additional flood exits, allowing a stadium that may have taken three hours to fill, to empty within a matter of minutes.

These exits should be located at regular intervals around the perimeter so that every seat is within a reasonable distance from an escape, and preferably in a direct line with the vomitories and staircases in Zone 2 to allow spectators a clear, direct and continuous line of egress from the building (though this is not always possible). The gates must open outwards and have a sufficient clear width to allow the prescribed number of people to pass through safely. A width of 1100 mm is acceptable in the UK but the authors recommend 1200 mm.

13.4 Access between Zone 3 and Zone 2

13.4.1 Stand entrances

First ticket checks and, if necessary, body searches will probably have been made at the outer entrances (see Section 13.3.1 above). Second ticket checks are made at the stand entrances, which may be either gates or turnstiles. These checks are more informal than those at the outer entrances, and more of a customer service than a stringently applied safety measure.

The same basic rules apply as for outer entrances: there must be enough space to avoid all risk of a crush developing and public facilities such as ticket offices, toilets (except those for people queueing to get in), bars and restaurants must be located a safe distance away.

13.5 Overall design for inward movement

13.5.1 Clarity of routes

People enter the stadium from the area outside (Zone 4) and must then thread their way through a succession of turnstiles, corridors, circulation passages and doorways to the individual seating or standing position (Zone 2). But a large multi-level stadium can be a very confusing place and a spectator may rapidly become exasperated if he cannot, for example, find his way from the entrance gate to block 12, row K, seat 275 and must repeatedly double back to try another route. There are four methods for minimizing or avoiding this problem:

- keeping choices simple (so that people are never faced with complex or difficult decisions);
- ensuring clear visibility of the whole stadium (so that people always know where they are in relation to exits);
- clear signs;
- good stewarding.

Good stewarding is a matter for management rather than design and will not be pursued here; but detailed notes follow on the three design measures listed above.

Simple choices

As far as possible the visitor should never be faced with an interchange where many routes are open to him, only one of which is right. It is easy to make a mistake at the best of times and moving along in a crowd, perhaps under pressure or in conditions of haste, almost guarantees getting it wrong.

The ideal is to provide the spectator with a series of simple Y or T junctions as he moves from the entrance gate to his seat, facing him in each case with an elementary choice of 'yes' or 'no'. He must be confronted with one (and only one) decision at a time, in such a way that when he has taken the final decision he has arrived at his seat. Six typical decisions are:

1. Am I a 'home' or 'away' supporter? At stadia where intergroup conflict is possible (e.g. football) these two groups should be segregated before they have even entered the stadium (see Section 13.3.1).
2. Am I a seated or standing ticket holder?
3. Am I seated in the upper or lower tier?
4. Am I in the blue or red section?
5. Is my seat in rows 1 to 10, or 11 to 20?
6. Where is my seat in the row?

The flow diagram (Figure 13.1) shows in schematic form a typical circulation pattern where choices have been reduced to 'yes' and 'no' decisions both when entering the stadium and when leaving. In this example there are several main entrances, each giving access to a different part of the stadium, thus making it possible for management to segregate 'home' and 'away' fans even before they have entered the stadium simply by allocating separate entrance gates to each.

The above straightforward principles are complicated by two practical requirements. First, there may be a need (already mentioned in Section 13.3.1) to separate the entrances used by 'home' and 'away' supporters. If so, this will tend to conflict with the desirability of keeping all entrances close to the administration centre, and therefore close to each other.

Second, while the primary circulation route should lead the spectator in the correct direction in deterministic fashion as described above, there should also be a secondary route allowing the spectator who has ended up in the wrong place to find his way back. This secondary 'correcting route' is almost as important as the primary circulation routes.

Clear visibility

Sports stadia are not the place for clever architectural games relying on tight, disorienting passageways opening into great public spaces to create a sense of spatial drama (as do some highly acclaimed theatres, concert halls and cinemas). Clarity is the first priority at every stage of entering or leaving the stadium, and designers should try to make the stadium as open as possible, so that crowds are visually

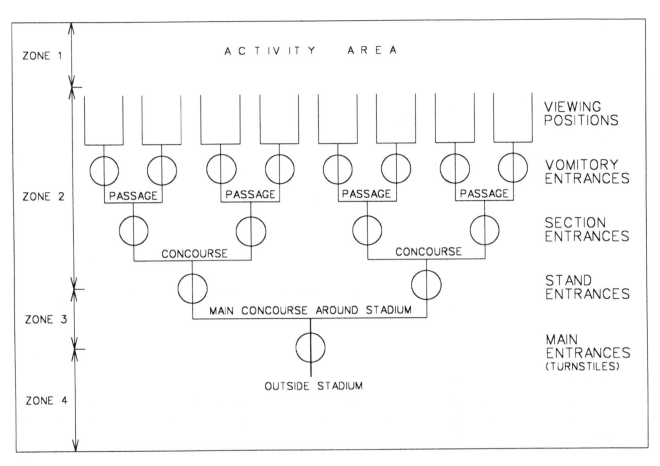

Figure 13.1 Spectator flow from gate to seat. Movement will be smoothest and safest if the spectator is faced with a sequence of simple choices, as shown.

aware at all times of where they are, and that alternative means of escape are open to them if needed.

It is desirable that spectators should be able to see from one exit stair to another and be aware that there is an alternative route. This helps prevent them panicking.

The need for maximum visibility is especially important in the case of sudden changes in direction, in width of corridor, in surface level, or in lightness and darkness. Such abrupt changes can be dangerous and should in general be avoided; but if that is impossible then the stadium-user should see them clearly in advance so that he does not stumble upon the transition unprepared.

An awareness of the layout of the stadium may be enhanced by carefully-judged changes in level. For instance, spectators can be made aware that they are about to enter a different area, and must adjust their pace, by a short upward ramp. Or their sense of where they are and what lies ahead can be improved by enabling them to see over the heads of those in front, by means of a downward ramp or stair.

Figure 13.2 shows a beneficial change of level of this kind, through a vomitory. Entering the seating tier via a ramp or a short flight of stairs serves two purposes: on entry, forward pushing by the spectators into the relatively narrow seatways is reduced by the preceding rise in level; and on leaving, spectators can see over the heads of those in front of them and are therefore much more aware of the circumstances ahead. This 'awareness' is important as

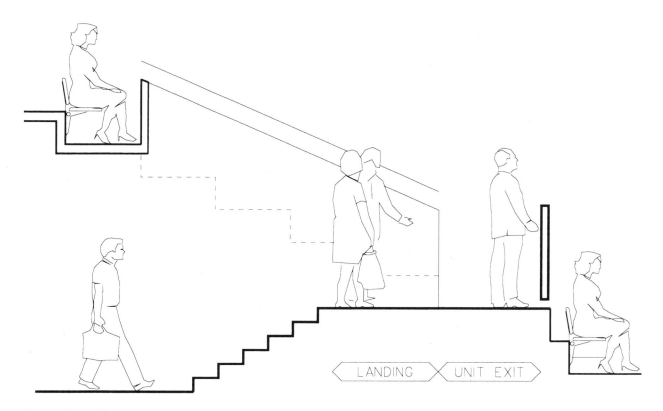

LANDING   UNIT EXIT

Figure 13.2 Changes of level can be beneficial if carefully designed. The short stair helps slow down incoming spectators, and enables those leaving to see over the heads of the people in front. Provision for people in wheelchairs has to be handled separately.

it is the unknown which creates anxiety in a crowd and can lead to panic.

Clear systems of signs

Clarity of stadium layout should be reinforced by an equally logical system of signs if spectators are to find their way about easily, dependably and safely.

A comprehensive sequence of signs should begin off the site, directing traffic and pedestrians first to the correct part of the ground, then to their particular entrance, and then stage by stage to every individual part of the building. The 'direction' signs leading people along their route must be supplemented at regular intervals by 'information' signs which give information on the location of different seating areas, catering outlets, toilets and other amenities. All signs should be designed for ease of reading; placed high enough to be seen over people's heads and located in a consistent way so that people know

where to look as they hurry through the building. Control should be exercised during the entire lifetime of the stadium to ensure that signs remain compatible with the overall design of the stadium and its landscaping. The needs of people in wheelchairs must constantly be borne in mind.

To make things easy for the customer, signs should be colour-coordinated with the areas to which they lead, and with the tickets for those areas (for example red signs and tickets for the red seating area) and they should provide information in easy stages. For example, a spectator heading for seat K27 in block 12, section 7 would find the following sequence of 'staged' signs easy to understand and follow:

SEATING BLOCKS 6 to 12

followed by:

SEATING BLOCK 12, SECTIONS 6 to 10

followed by:

SEATING SECTION 7 ROWS 13 to 27

The alternative combined sign shown below would be much more difficult to grasp, leading to dangerous hesitations and contra-flows in the traffic:

SEATING BLOCK 6 to 12, SECTIONS 6 to 10, ROWS 1 to 36

In addition to signs, large clear maps, above head level, are vital at all key points, particularly to help people who have difficulty with the local language. They should be oriented so that 'up' on the map points in the same direction as the reader's view of the stadium (otherwise the viewer must go through mental contortions correlating directions on the map with those in the stadium) and each map should have a *You are here* arrow.

13.5.2 Safe areas

While clarity and simplicity of circulation routes will do much to promote safe, comfor-table spectator movement, it should be recognized that on entering or leaving an area some people will inevitably change their minds and decide to head for the opposite direction instead. This happens for many reasons, from forgetting a coat to wanting to visit the toilets or wishing to see friends. Such changes of direction can have a disrupting effect on the natural flow of the remainder of the crowd.

We recommend that indecision of this kind be planned for, in as much as it is impossible to change human nature. Quiet or safe areas should be provided off the sides of the circulation routes much as lay-bys are provided beside motorways. These lay-bys enable people to stop and take stock of the situation without obstructing others, and then head off in the opposite direction if they wish.

Lay-by areas of this kind can be used as a method of stepping out the sides of the circulation route, to widen it towards the exits (Figure 13.3). This has the advantage of increasing the flowspace outwards, while at the same time providing safe areas for people who want to stop and think, or turn round.

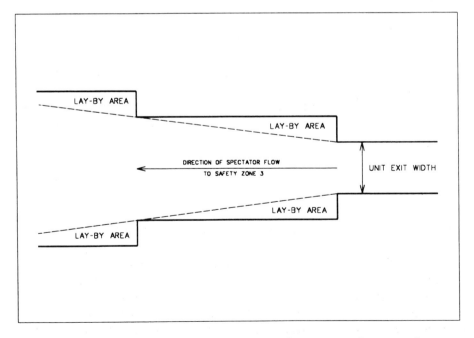

Figure 13.3 Lay-by areas on the main circulation routes allow people to stop and think without blocking the traffic flow.

13.5.3 Distancing of facilities from circulation routes

Many ancillary facilities must be provided in a stadium if spectators are to fully enjoy an event: programme sales kiosks, bars, cafeterias, child care centres and the like. These should be eye-catching and pleasing, but off the main circulation routes so that queues of people do not disrupt the primary circulation flow. Such facilities should always be located at least 6 m away from entrances or exits.

13.6 Overall design for outward movement

13.6.1 Normal egress from stadium

This layout should follow the same pattern as the branching of a tree. Tracing the route back from the individual seat to the exit gate, one may say that the individual twigs lead to small branches, which lead to larger branches, which lead ultimately to the trunk which is the public road. The twigs or smaller branches should never be connected directly to the trunk as this may cause the flow on the branchline to hesitate, causing congestion and aggravation and (if the stadium is being emptied in conditions of emergency) serious risk.

Signs and maps should work both ways – for incoming spectators trying to find their way to their seats, and also for spectators trying to find their way back to the exits. Exit signs must be particularly clearly visible, possibly illuminated, and will be governed by safety legislation in most countries, which means that the design team should check with the local fire and safety authorities.

13.6.2 Emergency egress from stadium

In the UK the *UK Guide to Safety at Sports Grounds* (the so-called Green Guide) recommends that the escape time from any seat, in all new stadia constructed of concrete and steel, must be no more than eight minutes. Unfortunately it does not specify where the escapee should be after eight minutes.

The requirement in Italy is that it must be possible to clear the seating areas of all spectators in five minutes, and then to clear the entire building structure of spectators in a further five minutes.

The above examples serve to indicate the kind of rules which may apply, and are illustrative only. Each country will have its own national and/or local regulations, and all regulations change over time, therefore the current situation should always be checked with the local fire and safety authorities before design commences.

In many cases such rules will specify evacuation of a stadium simply in terms of a number of minutes, but this is not a completely adequate yardstick for safety. The true requirement is that spectators must be able to move from their seats to a temporary safety zone, and thence to the permanent safety zone (see Section 13.2) in a specified time. From this requirement may be calculated both the maximum allowable *distances* from spectator seats to intermediate places of safety, and thence to exits, and the minimum allowable *widths* of all the passageways and doorways along those routes. The calculation that should be made is that known as 'timed exit analysis' (TEA).

Timed exit analysis
This is a step-by-step computation of the time it takes spectators to move from their nearest vomitory (the journey from seat to vomitory being ignored for the purposes of this calculation) to a place of permanent safety. It proceeds as follows:

1 Take the 'worst case' in each subdivision of the stadium. This will be the vomitory furthest from the exit in the section under review.
2 Calculate the distance in metres from that vomitory to the 'temporary' safety zone (see Section 13.2.2), and thence to the 'permanent' safety zone. Level areas and ramps must be measured separately from staircases.
3 Assume that spectators move along the level floors and ramps at 100 m per minute, and down stairways at 30 m per minute. Further assume that 40 people per minute can pass

through one 'exit width' (600 mm for corridors and also for doorways, gates, etc.).

4 Add up the walking times for the 'worst case' spectator selected above, all the way from his vomitory to Zone 4.

5 Subtract this time from the 'escape period' required by regulation, or in case of doubt from eight minutes.

6 Calculate widths of all passages and doorways or gateways along these routes in units of 600 mm (i.e. a passage that is 600 mm wide is 'one unit exit width', one that is 1200 mm wide is 'two exit unit widths'. Now check that the total number of spectators seated or standing

in a particular section can actually exit in the time calculated above, and if they cannot then widths must be increased.

7 Repeat the above 'distance' and 'width' calculations for each subdivision of the stadium, so that no spectator seating or standing area has been missed out, and revise the stadium layout if necessary until the entire stadium complies with safety requirements.

An example is given in the box (Figure 13.4).

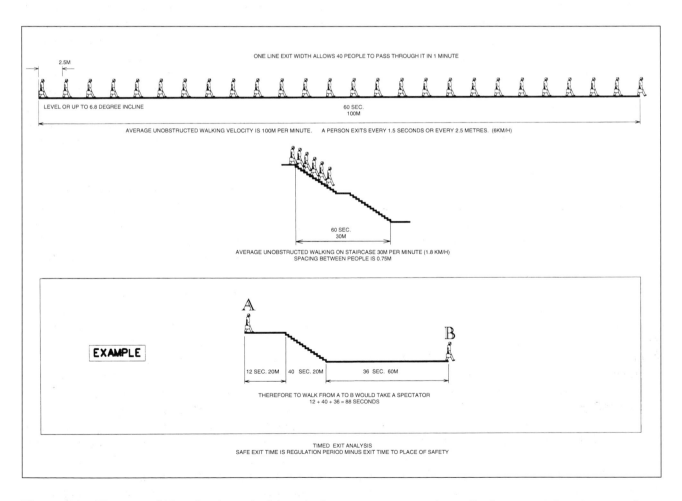

Figure 13.4 The use of 'timed exit analysis' to design escape routes that will allow spectators to move from their seat to a place of safety within a specified time. Minimum evacuation times will increasingly be laid down by law as societies become more safety conscious.

13.7 Elements

13.7.1 Entrances and exits

Gates and turnstiles

Gates are cheap, and an open gate can permit the passage of approximately 2000 spectators per hour; but they are a relatively unsophisticated form of control apparatus. Turnstiles are expensive and will allow only 500 to 750 spectators per hour to pass, but they offer the stadium management several advantages:

- They automatically count the number of spectators.
- They check tickets more precisely and more reliably than a human attendant could do, and can automatically exclude ticket-holders from areas they should not enter.
- With computer bar-coding technology becoming more accessible, tickets will soon be able to be individually coded or even individually named. A simple 'swipe' of the ticket at the entrance will be instantly recorded on the stadium computer, which could result in a steward being alerted to a problem with the ticket or the customer, the gate refusing to open, or the customer being advised that a message awaits him at the office. This technology will become increasingly widely exploited as it offers management a full and detailed record of event attendance, a record of individual customer characteristics, and the possibility of more precisely targeted marketing.
- Turnstiles can be used for the paying of money – but this should be discouraged as it leads to problems of security and financial control. Ticket purchase on the day should be handled in separate ticket sales areas at least 10 m away from the turnstiles (see Section 12.2.1).

Turnstiles also have disadvantages:

- Although some machines can be folded back in the 'open' position – to allow exiting through the same opening as entry – they are not usually a good method for clearing the grounds.

- Really high-volume, reliable, sophisticated systems such as those seen in metro stations currently cost more than stadium managements are willing to spend, while those which are affordable to stadium managements may not be good enough or secure enough.

Turnstiles are gradually being improved and responding to new computer technology, and will increasingly revolutionize customer throughput at stadium entrances.

Scales of provision

Registering reversible turnstiles, and space for ticket takers, should be provided on a basis of one turnstile for every 500 to 750 spectators depending on the type of event (see below). In addition to these, one exit turnstile should be provided for each group of turnstiles to allow for the ejection of spectators when required.

Subject to the requirements of local safety regulations or authorities, which must always be checked, the following data offers useful guidance. These figures should be verified before use in case of subsequent amendment after publication of this book.

- In the UK the Green Guide (the UK Guide to Safety at Sports Grounds) recommends a maximum entry rate of 660 persons per hour passing through each gate or turnstile. This allows an easy calculation to be made. If the brief states that a particular section of the stadium must be filled in one hour, then one entry turnstile must be provided for every 660 spectators. If a section must be filled in forty-five minutes, then one entry turnstile must be provided for every 495 spectators – and so on.
- For football grounds in Scotland, the Scottish League requires at least one entrance turnstile of the automatic revolving type per 500 of capacity, with a total minimum in all cases of ten turnstiles, not including entrances for season ticket holders or special passes.
- For football grounds in England and Wales the Football League (the senior league for clubs belonging to the English Football Association) gives no specific figures; but the GM Vauxhall Conference (the senior league

for non-league English Football Association clubs) requires that each segregated area must have at least one entrance turnstile of the automatic revolving type per 500 of capacity, with a total minimum of six.

Ancillary spaces and equipment

There should be fixed crowd control barriers and the possibility of additional temporary barriers in front of turnstiles to control queues. For long queues these should be arranged in a serpentine pattern. Such barriers, especially temporary movable ones, are likely to develop a messy appearance after the stadium is no longer under the designers' control. The design team should take particular care to specify a system which can be adapted to changing circumstances by managers for many years to come, without degrading the stadium image. It may be necessary to design a special area in advance of the gates or turnstiles where spectators can be searched to prevent prohibited items being brought into the stadium.

Storage space should in all cases be provided at each entrance gate or turnstile to store items confiscated during entry. A cashier's and/or controller's booth should also be provided adjacent to each entrance gate or turnstile. Requirements will depend on the way management intends to handle control and money-taking, therefore this must be checked at the briefing stage.

In severe climates, heating or cooling may be needed at the entrance area for inclement seasons.

13.7.2 Horizontal circulation elements

Dimensions

Spectators should be able to move from the entrances to their seats fast enough to allow the stadium to be filled in a reasonable period (say, two hours), and in the reverse direction they must be allowed to escape in a very much shorter period in case of emergency.

For egress great care must be taken to design a pedestrian 'pipeline' that will maintain its required feed-through capacity all the way between the perimeter gate and the individual seat, without risk of congestion at any point along the way.

An evaluation must be made of each stage of the journey:

1 *Entrances.* For convenience, the number of people passing through the gates or turnstiles per unit of time should be limited to a certain maximum, otherwise problems of dispersal and the risk of bottlenecks may occur. Scales of provision were given in Section 13.7.1 above.

2 *Exits.* Outward-opening flood exit gates must be provided to allow the high-volume flows of people described in step 6 of Section 13.6.2. Their clear widths must be based on 40 to 60 people per minute passing through one 'unit exit width' of 600 mm.

3 *Concourses, corridors and other passageways.* Minimum widths will be set by the TEA calculation outlined in step 6 of section 13.6.2.

4 *Areas of particular congestion.* There must be generous additional space to the minimum calculated widths at all entrances to (or exits from) toilets, eating/drinking facilities, and ticket windows – the latter to be spaced at least 10 m away from entrances and exits. It is particularly important to allow ample circulation space at the head and foot of each stair flight or ramp, where people get slowed down by the change of gradient. These points may in effect become funnels, with a mass of fast-moving people behind pushing against those in front who have been slowed down. If there is not enough space for the pressure to be dispersed, very dangerous situations can develop.

13.7.3 Vertical circulation elements

There are a limited number of methods to provide vertical circulation which will link the various levels of the stadium and give access to the concourses. The alternative options are taken in turn below.

Stairs

Stairs have the advantage of being the most compact vertical circulation method, in plan, and consequently the easiest to design into a scheme. But they have the disadvantage of being arguably more dangerous than ramps in an emergency situation. They should be planned in pairs if at all possible, the two stairs preferably sharing a common landing so that there is always an alternative route available should one of the stairs become blocked (Figure 13.5).

Maximum gradients will depend on the local building regulations, which must be consulted, but would normally be around 33 degrees.

Figure 13.5 Stairs sharing a common landing so that there is an alternative exit route should one of the stairs be blocked. Computer image by Lobb Partnership.

Within the prescribed limits a steep angle is actually an advantage as it allows a fast descent and rapid emptying of the stadium. Clear widths will be determined by the emergency egress requirements outlined in Section 13.6.2.

Finishes, provision of handrails and lighting design may be influenced by the local building regulations, which should be checked.

Ramps

Ramps have become popular recently and are used extensively in Italy and the USA (Figure 13.6). They have several advantages:

- Spectators are less likely to lose their footing on a ramp than on a stair, and if they do stumble or fall the consequences will be less serious than on a stair.
- Ramps are an ideal method of allowing service vehicles to move from level to level. This eases the problems of large-scale stock, catering or retailing provision, and of refuse removal. Ramps also allow easy passage for wheelchairs, and for transporting sick or injured spectators to the exits during events.

Circular ramps have particular advantages:

- Because the slope down a circular ramp will vary according to the line of descent taken, pedestrians are given a certain amount of freedom to select either a steeper, faster route near the centre, or a shallower, easier route near the perimeter.
- The view walking along a circular ramp is less forbidding than a long straight ramp.
- Whilst a straight ramp must have landings at intervals, a circular ramp need not – though this needs to be carefully checked against national and local regulations. The latter often do require mid-landings for reasons of safety and convenience for disabled people and wheelchair users.

For all the above reasons ramps are a safe, convenient and increasingly popular way of moving large numbers of people to different levels of the stadium, and circular ramps are the most common form.

The disadvantage of ramps is their size. Since the maximum gradient is 1:12 their internal circumference works out at no less than 35 to 45 m. This makes a ramp a very awkward element to absorb into the site area, and difficult to handle elegantly from the architectural point of view. The corners of the stadium are the most usual position (Figure 13.6) and visually successful examples include the Joe Robbie Stadium in the USA and the San Siro Stadium in Milan.

Maximum gradient will be determined by the local building regulations, but should in the authors' view not exceed 1:12. Minimum width will be determined by the calculation described

Figure 13.6 The use of circulation ramps is common in the USA, as seen here in the Joe Robbie stadium in Miami. Architects: Hellmuth, Obata & Kassabaum (HOK).

in Section 13.6.2, subject to local building regulations.

Finishes, provision of handrails and lighting design may be influenced by the local building regulations, which should be checked.

Escalators

Relatively few escalators have been installed in sports stadia because of their high capital cost and the fact that their capacity cannot usually be taken into account when calculating the exit widths required.

There have however been some exceptions to this, particularly in racecourse stadia, where escalators have been used in many different countries. Here they give fast access to the higher

viewing levels and can of course be reversed, operating upwards before the race and downwards afterwards.

Examples of use include the Arrowhead and Royals stadia in Kansas City, Missouri, the Giants Stadium in New York, the Selangor Turf Club in Kuala Lumpur and Twickenham (UK).

Elevators

Elevators (lifts) are too small and slow to account for the movement of any significant number of people. Their most appropriate role in sports stadia is to transport relatively small numbers of people to the upper levels of the stadium with speed and comfort. Such users may include:

- VIPs. Their private hospitality boxes tend to be at the upper levels of the stadium, and their comfort must be catered for even if this is expensive.
- The media. Radio, TV and newspaper rooms, too, are likely to be at the upper levels and could possibly be associated with the private hospitality facilities. The same elevators might then be used by both groups.
- Staff and service operations. Providing special elevators for service staff would be expensive, and it would be best to locate a small number of elevators in such a way that various usage could be made of them, including staff. Management must then ensure that there are no clashes of use, for example elevators conveying refuse at a time when VIPs are likely to be using them.
- Disabled and wheelchair users. Elevators can provide otherwise impossible access to upper levels for people in wheelchairs (see below).

13.8 Facilities for people with disabilities

The UK Building Regulations (1986) state that there should be 20 places for wheelchair-bound disabled people or 1 in 100 of the total number of seats available to the public, whichever is the greater. This is equivalent to 10 places per 1000. In Italy they use a standard of 1 in 400 or 2.5 places per 1000 spectators and recently an IAKS working party on stadia decided upon 1 in 300 or 3.3 places per 1000 spectators, while at the Skydome they provide 1 in 100 or 10 places per 1000. Where possible these places should be

covered or at least have some protection from the elements.

For indoor arenas, the UK Building Regulations state that there should be a minimum of six places for wheelchairs or more based on 1 in 100 of the total seats available to the public. This figure is double the provision required in stadia. The Sports Council and the British Sports Association for the Disabled (BSAD) published a guide to the minimum number of wheelchair places which should be provided for indoor arenas, on the basis of a sliding scale and this requirement is set out in Table 13.1.

Dimensions and detail

A wheelchair space should be a clear open area with a width of 900 mm and a depth of 1400 mm, accessible to a wheelchair user and providing a clear view of the event. The eye level of people with disabilities must be taken into account when designing rails and glazed screens. Each area should also provide for a friend's seat and ideally measure 1400 mm by 1400 mm. The spaces should not be together but dispersed among the spectators. Where a person leaves a wheelchair in order to occupy a normal seat provision should be made in the design to accommodate the wheelchair out of the circulation system but close enough to be readily accessible by the individual. Those who must remain in a wheelchair during the event should be accommodated in a position which does not obstruct the movement or clear vision of others.

Table 13.1 Recommended provision in indoor arenas for wheelchairs (source: Sports Council)

Stadium capacity	Minimum number of wheelchair spaces
0 to 1000	6 spaces
1001 to 2000	8 spaces
2001 to 5000	10 spaces
5001 to 10 000	10 spaces plus 1 for each 1000 over 5000*
10 001 to 20 000	15 spaces plus 1 for each 2000 over 10 000*
21 001 to 50 000	20 spaces plus 1 for each 3000 over 21 000*

* For example 15 spaces for 10 000 capacity, 20 spaces for 20 000 capacity and 30 spaces for 50 000 capacity.

Access and other design factors

Entrance routes should be obvious and not arduous for people with disabilities and, where possible, they should use the same entrances as the general public. Changes in level should be kept to a minimum and designed to blend into the design of the landscape and the building. Other factors which need to be taken into account are set out in Table 13.2.

Generally an appreciation of the difficulties experienced by disabled people should be reflected in the design of all facilities including circulation spaces. Entrance routes should be laid out to assist the mobility of everybody including people in wheelchairs or using walking aids. All changes in level should be avoided if possible but where they do occur, inclines should be gentle. The partially sighted can also be assisted by coloured or textured surfaces and special attention should be paid to the heights and positioning of signs and street furniture so as to be obvious and not to cause an obstruction. If kerbs are unavoidable their cross-overs, and other ramps and paths, should conform to recommended design data and permit wheelchair access.

There must be adequate parking conveniently situated for the main public entrance and box office and separate provision at the competitors entrance, bearing in mind that sporting competition between disabled people is growing in popularity. There also need to be easy arrival points with clear signs to direct disabled people into the building with a 'press for assistance' button conveniently positioned adjacent to the entrance. Main entrances and approaches should be clearly recognizable from a seated position and sheltered from the elements.

Because of the risk of breakage safety glazing should be clearly visible with markings at low level. Special attention should be paid to lobby and corridor widths, configuration of doors, door furniture, surface finishes and reception desk heights, all of which will aid safe and comfortable passage into and around the building.

It should go without saying that disabled people should have ready access to all parts of the stadium where amenities are provided, although in some circumstances it may not be safe to permit wheelchair access at certain times such as peak circulation periods. To aid mobility there should be readily accessible lifts to all levels which satisfy the relevant mandatory requirements. To assist the partially sighted, information signs should be based on symbols rather than words wherever possible. Signs should be clearly legible and easily distinguishable from backgrounds. Strong intensity and contrasting colours are preferred. Restricted access or 'no entry' signs should be very prominent; audible warnings which are movement sensitive can be used very effectively in these areas.

Facilities such as lifts, unisex toilets and information centres should be located near entrances and main amenities, avoiding long distances and arduous routes. Approach ramps should not be steeper than 1:20 and have a clear width of at least 1200 mm. Short lengths of ramp may have to be steeper but should never be above a slope of 1:12. If this steepness of incline is necessary the ramp must have landings as detailed in the British Standard BS 5810: this is a good standard which sets out clear guidance on landing railings.

Table 13.2 Recommended design factors for people with disabilities

Access	Wide doors, gates and corridors
Parking	Located adjacent to main entrances and box office and marked 'For Disabled People Only'
Information	Signs low enough to be easily read from wheelchairs
Toilets	Located near to entrances and main amenities, and easily accessible without having to negotiate steps or steep ramps
Refreshments	Accessible and at low level for customers in wheelchairs

Escape

The main publications in the UK on escape for disabled people during emergency evacuations of stadia are the British Standard BS 5588, Fire Precautions in the Design and Construction of Buildings Part 8: 1988 and the Code of Practice for Means of Escape for Disabled People and also *Designing for Spectators with Disabilities,* an FSADC publication. These documents recognize the problems encountered with stepped seating and the importance of emergency evacuation of people having a disability without causing disruption to the majority of spectators exiting the facility. It advocates giving particular attention to the escape routes available from integrated viewing areas for disabled spectators. The principles of evacuation are based on initial movement to a place of refuge within a protected route and then exit to a place of safety. Refuges should be enclosed areas with a construction having a half hour standard of fire resistance. Complementary to a carefully planned escape route is a well rehearsed management procedure in an emergency. Specific arrangements should be made with management for stewards to marshal disabled spectators and to supervise their safe exit. In an emergency they need more attention than able-bodied people and the stadium management should take this into account in their plans. British Standard BS 5588 and the Guide to Safety at Sports Grounds stresses the importance of staff training and programmed fire drills.

Access by the disabled to any floor which does not have direct egress to outdoors is likely to remain controversial. There is real concern over escape for disabled people from upper floors in an emergency, particularly for those in wheelchairs. Application of the new UK Building Regulations is also likely to vary. Consultation with fire prevention and licensing officers is advisable to clarify the position from the outset of any stadium project. The reality of the situation is that stadium designers and managers should ensure that, during an emergency escape, the able-bodied are not put at a higher risk from discarded wheelchairs. In addition to the design criteria above there are other factors which need to be considered:

- good communication between security and emergency services and the club or stadium management;
- good communication from all services in the stadium with the stadium control room;
- efficient public address system for addressing the crowd in an emergency;
- well-established emergency procedures;
- separate, detached areas for the disabled should be avoided where possible;
- stadium facilities must be designed to recognize that employees might also be disabled. The stadium administration facilities must cater for this provision and meet national codes and standards.

14

The media

14.1 Basic planning

14.1.1 General

Facilities for the media are an integral part of stadium design. These facilities involve the three main categories of public information and entertainment services – the press (including newspapers and magazines), radio and television.

The support facilities described below will be needed in full in the case of major new stadia. In smaller venues some may be scaled down or omitted or combined with others, subject to briefing advice from the client or from the media themselves. Because of the importance of these services we recommend consultation with radio and television companies at the earliest design stages.

14.1.2 Locating media facilities in the stadium layout

Detailed advice for specific facilities is given in the sections below, but we start with four basic planning considerations which will influence the stadium layout as a whole.

First, all media facilities should be grouped together on the same side of the stand as the team dressing rooms. It is extremely inconvenient for media representatives to have to cross to the other side of the stadium to attend interviews.

Second, this cluster of facilities should be close to, and easily accessible from, the parking zone for television and radio broadcast vehicles, and perhaps for outside catering and toilet vehicles, as described in Sections 14.2.1 and 14.2.2 below.

Third, these facilities should also be relatively close to a section of the parking area set aside specifically for media representatives' cars.

A final overall planning factor is that one section of ordinary spectator seating should be adjacent to the Press area, and accessible from it, so that it may be converted to Press usage when demand for Press seats outstrips provision, as will happen when exceptionally newsworthy events are covered. Making proper provision for such dual use while conforming with the specific requirements given in Section 14.3.1 will need careful planning.

14.1.3 Types of media facilities required

Up to three separate types of media activity take place in a stadium and each one must be catered for.

Direct coverage of the event
This activity happens while the match is in progress and requires:

- Press seats for the use of newspaper and magazine reporters. The seats must have an excellent view of the pitch and the central area of the stadium. See Section 14.3 below.
- Cabins for radio commentators, again with an excellent view of the pitch and central area. See Section 14.4 below.
- Cabins for television commentators, obviously with an excellent view of the pitch and central area. See Section 14.5 below.

● Platforms for television cameras. See Section 14.5 below.

Interviews with players and others

This activity happens inside the stadium before and after the match, away from the pitch, and requires interview rooms and support facilities inside the stadium, preferably but not necessarily overlooking the pitch and central area. See Section 14.6 below, for large stadia.

Preparation and transmission of copy

This activity requires a press working area and associated telecommunications facilities, with no need at all to overlook the pitch. See Sections 14.6 and 14.7 below.

14.1.4 Scales of provision

Because broadcasting technology changes so rapidly it is essential to consult media representives before taking any firm decisions. But

Tables 14.1 to 14.4 give provisional advice for the early stages of planning. All these tables are taken from the Digest of Stadia Criteria with the kind permission of Britain's Football Stadia Advisory Design Council. They apply specifically to football, but figures for other sports can, to some degree, be deduced from them. It should be noted that Olympic stadia require a minimum of 1800 seats for the media.

14.2 Outside facilities

Increasing numbers of technical and staff support vehicles are nowadays brought on to site during radio or television broadcasts, and parking space must be provided for these fairly near to the media entrance. This area should be fenced in and secure, with controlled access during events. It should be provided with electrical and water supplies, telecommunications and drainage services.

Table 14.1 Press facilities for World Cup, European Championship and other major international and national football games, as recommended by FIFA and UEFA

Competition	Press seats – total	Seats with desks and telephones	Seats with desks only	Seats without desks or telephones	Places for photographers in stands	Interview room – capacity or room size*
World Cup finals						
Group match	500	300			50	125
Opening and semi-final	1000	500			100	175
Final	1750	1000			100	175
European Championships						
Group match	400	60	190	150	40	125
Opening and semi-final	600	100	300	200	50	200
Final	800	125	475	200	60	250
FIFA/UEFA recommendations for new stadia						
Major internationals	400	250			30	200 m²
Other internationals	200	120			30	150 m²
Major national games	200	120			30	100 m²
Other national games	30–100	10–50				50 m²

* FIFA/UEFA recommend that for World Cup and European Championships the interview room should be equipped with CCTV and with interpreter services such as 3 interpreter cabins and facilities for consecutive translators.

Table 14.2 Radio and television facilities for World Cup, European Championship and other major international and national football games, as recommended by FIFA and UEFA

Competition	Positions for TV and Radio commentators (3 seats each)	Television control centre – room size (m^2)	Television interview studio – room size (m^2)	Radio control centre – room size (m^2)	Television interview studio – room size (m^2)
World Cup finals					
Group match	125	ns[†]	50	ns[†]	ns[†]
Opening and semi-final	150	ns	50	ns	ns
Final	150	ns	50	ns	ns
European Championships					
Group match	60	30	50	20	20
Opening and semi-final	70	30	50	20	20
Final	80	30	50	20	20
FIFA/UEFA recommendations for new stadia					
Major internationals	50	30	30	ns[†]	ns[†]
Other internationals	20	30	30	ns	ns
Major national games	20	30	30	ns	ns
Other national games	5	30	30	ns	ns

[†] Not specified.

Table 14.3 Press, radio and television facilities for UK domestic football leagues, as recommended by the various leagues identified below. All figures are minima

Competition	Minimum press seats with writing facility	Minimum telephone requirements	Other media provision
Football League	12	4 exclusive lines	
Scottish League	20	3 exclusive lines	TV: platform + 2 commentary positions Radio: 3 commentary position
GM Vauxhall Conference	6	2 exclusive lines + home club needs	
Beazer Homes League	Grade C – 4 Grade D – 2	Grades C and D – 1 exclusive line	Not compulsory to have separate press box in Grade D
Diadora League	Grade A – 4 Grade B – 3 Grade C – 2	1 exclusive line	
HFS Loans League	Grades A and B – 4	1 exclusive line	

14.2.1 Parking area for technical support vehicles

Radio and television technical support vehicles will require heavy cabling runs into the stadium for each particular event, and it would make sense to provide permanent cable ducts from their parking zone to the relevant parts of the stadium for this purpose. There should be early consultation with the relevant radio and television companies to determine the required duct routes and dimensions.

Table 14.4 Working areas for press, radio and television representatives as recommended by FIFA and UEFA. These areas should be part of the stadium or be adjacent to the press box

Competition	Press centre capacity or room size (m^2)	Private telephone cabins	Public telephones	Telefax	Telex	Wire photo facilities	Dark rooms*	Office for press officers – room size (m^2)
World Cup finals								
Group match	250	20	10	12	4	4	8	ns†
Opening and semi-final	500	50	10	15	6	6	10	ns
Final	1000	50	10	15	6	6	10	ns
European Championships								
Group match	200	20	10	5	3	4	4	10
Opening and semi-final	300	30	10	5	3	6	6	10
Final	400	40	10	5	3	6	8	10
FIFA/UEFA recommendations for new stadia								
Major internationals	200	set by	set by	4	advisable	advisable	advisable	20
Other internationals	150	local	local	3	nc ††	advisable	advisable	20
Major national games	100	needs	needs	2	nc	nc ††	nc ††	20
Other national games	50			1	nc	nc	nc	nc

* Dark rooms to be equipped with electricity and running water.
† Not specified.
†† Not compulsory.

14.2.2 Parking area for temporary catering and toilet vehicles

Mobile canteens and toilets for media personnel may be required for matches attracting particularly heavy radio or television attention. Special parking areas should be set aside for these, clearly designated, and provided with drainage, water and electrical services. The canteens and toilets should be separated. The canteen location should be relatively pleasant and clean, not a corner of the parking area reeking of diesel fumes.

14.2.3 Media parking

There should be a reserved parking area fairly near the media entrance for the cars of visiting media personnel.

14.3 Press facilities

14.3.1 Location and design

Newspapers and magazines are the oldest form of news and entertainment dissemination. They remain of great importance and must be properly catered for.

The press seating area must be located along one side of the stadium (a side not facing the sun during daytime matches) with excellent views over the pitch area. This side should be on the same side as the dressing rooms. It must be under cover and must be separated from the public seating area by a well-defined barrier. Access should be via a separate protected entrance route that is well supervised; this entry route could be combined with VIP access: see Section 13.3.2.

The press seats themselves should have either a folding or fixed desk top (Figure 14.1). Seat

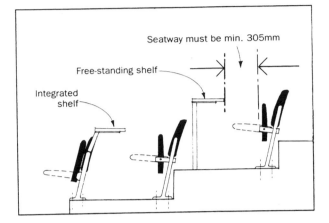

Figure 14.1 Press box seating options.

width should be at least 500 mm, and to allow comfortable working conditions, which may involve writing, making telephone calls and using a fax machine, there should be ample space between seats. Each desk top should be provided with a fax and telephone point and lighting, to allow coverage of night-time events.

As already mentioned, it may be necessary on occasion to re-allocate some of the public seats to the press and one section of public seating must be located and designed so as to allow this. The location of this section of spectator seating must afford an excellent view of the field, and must be under cover. These seats need to be directly accessible from the main media working area; separable from the rest of the spectator area by temporary barriers; and the seating design should allow for writing surfaces to be fitted. There must be provision for telephone and fax outlets to virtually each position.

14.4 Radio broadcast facilities

Facilities are needed not just for national or international broadcasting, but also for local broadcasting, which includes transmissions to local community areas and hospitals. These services are increasing in popularity.

14.4.1 Commentators' cabins

Commentators' cabins should be provided in a central location to the side of the pitch, with excellent viewing and openable windows. They should be located so as not to face the sun. All commentators must be able to comfortably see all parts of the central area and pitch, and preferably also the players' entrance to the field, while seated comfortably at their desks.

Cabins should open off a secure and protected lobby area. Each cabin must have a continuous worktop against the window overlooking the pitch, comfortable movable seats and monitor screens let into the worktop, all designed in accordance with advice from the relevant radio stations. Normally there will be three commentators per cabin, sitting at least 1.5 m to 1.8 m apart at individually serviced positions, separated by transparent soundproof screens. The total area required for such a three-person cabin will be approximately 15 m^2.

Other fittings and finishes will be determined by expert advice, but in all cases there must be a 'quiet' floor (carpet or rubberized finish to eliminate impact noise), acoustically absorbent walls and ceilings, and sound-resistant doors with acoustic sealing round the edges. Partitions between cabins must be sound-resistant.

Services to each individual commentator's position will include microphone, electrical and telephone/fax outlets plus ducting for future services.

Scales of provision are suggested in Table 14.5, but these figures should be checked with the relevant radio stations.

14.5 Television broadcast facilities

14.5.1 Commentators' cabins

These will be similar to those for radio commentators, and scales of provision may be as suggested in Table 14.6 – all subject to advice from the television companies involved.

Table 14.5 Recommended provision of radio commentators' cabins

Stadium and event type	Number of cabins
Football stadia	
National events: Premier Division	3 to 6 cabins
International events: World Cup	24 cabins for the early rounds
	40 cabins for the final rounds
Olympic stadia	60 cabins or more

Table 14.6 Recommended provision of television commentators' cabins

Stadium and event type	Number of cabins
Football stadia	
National events: Premier Division	3 to 5 cabins
International events: World Cup	10 to 30 cabins for the early rounds, some of them temporary
	40 to 50 cabins for the final rounds, some of them temporary
Olympic stadia	75 cabins, some of them temporary

14.5.2 Camera platforms

Provision must be made for camera platforms of at least 2 m by 2 m surface area, in positions agreed with the relevant television companies. Even in small sports grounds television camera positions will be a consideration as these platforms can also be used by the clubs for internal video recording for training or for historic records, or to cater for the increasing sale of video recordings of matches to supporters (the Arsenal football club in London sells about 30 000 of its match videos). There is also the possibility of local television broadcasting, including closed circuit broadcasts to local hospitals and other community outlets.

14.6 Reception, conference and interview rooms

14.6.1 Media reception desk

This is the focus of inquiries and the control point where all media visitors report on arrival before proceeding to the various facilities described below. This area should therefore give access to all other media facilities, and ensure that such access is completely secure.

The media reception desk should be equipped with all facilities needed for dealing with information-seekers, including telephone/fax points, monitoring screens and electrical power outlets.

14.6.2 Toilets and washrooms

These will probably be provided immediately after the reception desk, before the routes to the various media facilities split apart, so that they are passed by all incoming or outgoing visitors. They should be to superior standard, and be hygienic with easily cleaned wall and floor surfaces. Facilities for cleaning and washing down should be provided, with a trapped waste outlet in the floor. Ample natural ventilation through openable windows should be provided in preference to mechanical ventilation systems, which are prone to malfunction or even breakdown, leading to unpleasant conditions which do the image of the venue no good. For some occasions additional temporary toilets may be required outside: see Section 14.2.2.

14.6.3 Canteen, bar and refreshments

Refreshment facilities should preferably also be located in the common entrance area, where all visitors will pass them before the various routes divide up. A good quality eating and drinking area is required, pleasant and attractive but also robust. The room can be fitted out with a variety of dining tables and stackable chairs, standing wall shelves and free-standing units.

In case the above facilities are not adequate for certain occasions, provision may have to be made in the parking area close to the media entrance for mobile catering: see Section 14.2.2.

14.6.4 Press working area

This is the area where media representatives are briefed, gather information packs and press hand-outs, relax and exchange gossip, and carry out their work (such as writing and transmitting reports). It will comprise a cluster of rooms leading directly off the common media entrance zone. All of the following functions must be catered for in the design, almost certainly as separate rooms in the case of larger stadia, but perhaps with some combination of functions into a smaller number of rooms in more modestly sized stadia.

Table 14.4 gives FIFA/UEFA recommendations for the capacities of Press Working Areas overall, and their servicing. These recommendations apply specifically to football events, but suitable provision for sporting events generally can be deduced from them.

Information room
Not far beyond the reception desk, in a location which will be passed by all incoming visitors, should be a room provided with pinboards for press notices and the like, and a mounted work-bench where information packs and brochures can be laid out. The bench-top should be at a height suitable for comfortable writing in a standing position. No windows are needed to the information room, but in that case good artificial ventilation must be provided.

Press lounge
This must be a comfortable room in the same general area as the facilities listed above, fitted with movable comfortable chairs and low tables. The decoration and lighting should be attractive and conducive to relaxation, the floor should be carpeted, and the room should have acoustically absorbent materials fitted to walls and ceiling.

Press conference room
This is a multi-purpose room, probably the last of the sequence of rooms clustered around the media entrance area, intended primarily for press conferences but suitable also for meetings of other kinds when not needed for press functions (very few are used only by the Press). A movable dais should be provided where those addressing the meeting can be seen clearly by all who are in the room. The decoration scheme should be pleasant but not distracting, and allow space on the wall behind the dais, and on the dais front, for information panels.

Table 14.7 suggests conference room capacities required for football events. Capacities for other sporting types may be deduced from these.

Central press work room
For the most efficient use of space this may be a temporary rather than dedicated area, used at other times for meetings and exhibitions. Extensive tables and chairs must be provided, and the latter must be stackable (with adjacent storage rooms, see below, to accommodate them when not needed). There should be a movable dais, also stored elsewhere when not needed, and extensive pinboards on the walls for notices, instructions and general information for the press. A raised floor which will allow services to be run underneath is ideal. There must be generous provision of telephone, fax and video terminals.

Table 14.8 suggests central press workroom capacities required for football events. Capacities for other sporting types may be deduced from these.

Table 14.7 Recommended conference room capacities for World Cup football events

Event	Capacity	Area (m^2)
Preliminary round	200 people	110
Quarter finals	250 people	200
Semi finals	300 people	250
Final round	400 people	350

14.6.6 Administrative facilities

This is the working area of the public relations personnel who are responsible for briefing, meeting and cultivating the Press and other media representatives. It must therefore be adjacent to, and have direct access to, the above group of facilities.

Stadium press officers' room

The press officers' room will be a standard office of about 150 m^2 with desks and chairs, space for filing cabinets, office equipment and cupboards, and preferably with a large wall pinboard. Telephone/fax points must be provided, and services for word processing and computing facilities will need to be considered.

Secretariat

A standard secretarial office of about 100 m^2 should be provided close to the press officer's room. It will need to accommodate one or more desks for typing, word processing and perhaps computing; filing cabinets and cupboards; and must be provided with generous electrical and telephone/fax points.

14.6.7 Interview facilities

Beyond the reception and conference facilities described above, and closer to the playing field, will be a room or group of rooms used by newspapers, radio or television commentators and photographers for interviewing players and others. The reason for locating this section near the playing field is to make it possible to give a view of the pitch, and to allow for easy access to players before they go on to the pitch, or after

Table 14.8 Recommended central press workroom capacities for football events

Event	Capacity	Area (m^2)
National events		
Premier Division	20 press	30 to 40
Major match	50 press	75 to 100
International events		
Preliminary round	100 press	150 to 200
Quarter final	150 press	125 to 300
Semi final	250 press	375 to 500
Final round	350 press	525 to 700

they have come off. This is a desirable but not essential feature.

Table 14.2 summarizes radio and television studio requirements for football events, and provision for other sporting types can be deduced from these. But all of the advice given below is general, and room requirements must be checked more specifically with the relevant radio and television companies to ensure that interviews can be staged and recorded to their satisfaction.

Interview studio(s)

This room (or rooms) should be pleasant, fitted with comfortable movable chairs and low tables. The decoration scheme should rely on simple wall surfaces, possibly covered with plain curtains as a backdrop to televised interviews. While windows are not essential it is an advantage to have good views over the playing fields. The rooms must be artificially ventilated or conditioned so that windows can be kept shut to exclude outside noise, and all such mechanical systems must be silent in operation.

Television control area

The television companies will want a control room adjacent to the interview studio. Requirements should be checked directly with them.

Photographers' working area

Press photographers will need one or more darkrooms, and Table 14.4 suggests room numbers. Dark rooms should be planned without windows, with light-sealed doors and effective artificial ventilation or air conditioning (the latter also light sealed) to get rid of chemical fumes. Sinks and bench tops must be provided, and an illuminated 'room occupied' sign to prevent interruption.

14.6.8 Telecommunications area

Somewhere between, or adjacent to, the press working area and the interview facilities will be the following group of service rooms:

Telephone exchange

This room must have excellent ventilation, which may be either natural or artificial; must be acoustically quiet; and must be fitted with a number of separate telephone positions, each with an acoustic hood for privacy, and a shelf for writing. Windows are not necessary.

Teleprinters, fax and telex facilities

This room must have bright, even lighting; excellent ventilation (which may be either natural or artificial); must be acoustically quiet; and must be fitted with a hard wearing and easily cleanable carpet. It will contain a number of teleprinters, fax and telex machines for use by the media.

Toilets

If the facilities described above are very far from the toilets and washrooms itemized in Section 14.6.2 it may be necessary to provide an additional toilet in this area.

15

Administrative operations

15.1 Basic planning

15.1.1 User types

The majority of administrative personnel to be accommodated will be those employees responsible for the day-to-day running of the stadium, and for administration of the resident sports club (if there is one). Their numbers will be augmented from time to time by an influx of temporary personnel to help manage certain individual events on a one-off basis. A suite of offices and associated accommodation must be provided for both these groups as described in Sections 15.2 and 15.3 below. All of these officials will need hospitality facilities to entertain players and distinguished visitors, and these are described in Section 15.4.

A third group of people to be catered for are the stewards who will be brought in on match days for crowd control. Their requirements are set out in Section 15.5.

Finally, provision must be made for the police and security staff; their needs are described in Section 15.6. All user groups need good access (Figure 15.1).

15.1.2 Locations

Administrative facilities (except for police and security offices) should generally be close to the following areas, with reasonably easy access to them:

- VIP facilities, especially the Directors' and VIP hospitality rooms and viewing boxes (see Chapter 9);

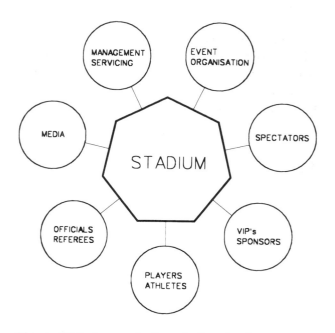

Figure 15.1 Access to the stadium by the seven main user groups.

- media facilities, especially the Press working area and the stadium Press Officer's room (see Section 14.6);
- team managers', officials' and referees' facilities (see Chapter 16).

The administration entrance will normally be in the centre of the main side of the stadium and an area of car parking for officials and their guests must be provided nearby.

15.1.3 Scales of provision

General guidance is given in the sections below, but specific accommodation requirements can

181

only be determined by direct discussion with the client and police authorities. Figures given here are therefore provisional and must be carefully checked as the brief is compiled.

15.2 Facilities for permanent management

Offices and ancillary accommodation should be provided for:

- Staff responsible for marketing, promotion, advertising and ticketing of events.
- Staff reponsible for administration and finance. Their needs will include secure facilities for cash receipts and credit card checking.
- Staff responsible for building services, energy control, lighting, mechanical and electrical equipment and sound equipment.
- Staff responsible for maintenance and security, and for emergency operations.

Subject to detailed discussion with the client, the rooms discussed in the following seven sections will be needed in most cases.

15.2.1 Offices

In a large stadium there should be offices for the Director ($20\,m^2$), secretariat ($12\,m^2$), other staff members ($12\,m^2$ per person), public relations and marketing ($12\,m^2$) and event organization ($12\,m^2$). In smaller stadia some of the above could be combined for economy. These rooms should be designed with finishes, equipment and lighting to good office standards.

15.2.2 Board room

Fittings and furnishings should be of a standard befitting this VIP space. They should include a suitable boardroom table and comfortable chairs, drinks and refreshment cupboard, refrigerator, and perhaps a small bar if the room is to be used for hospitality at events (which is often the case). A display of photographs and a secure cupboard for trophies and mementoes should be considered, the latter to be extremely secure in view of the value of the contents.

The area of this room would typically be between $30\,m^2$ and $50\,m^2$. Depending on the size of the stadium and its operation the board room may be used for hospitality or other purposes.

15.2.3 Appeals room

A room should be available for hearing appeals, but this is usually not a dedicated room.

15.2.4 Stadium control room

This room will normally be between $15\,m^2$ and $20\,m^2$ in area, depending on the size of the stadium, and it must:

- Overlook the pitch and have a clear view of the video and electronic screens described below;
- Ideally be adjacent to the police control room, and possibly combined with it, so that an integrated response to an emergency is possible.

The room must be equipped with TV monitors, telephone links both inside and outside the stadium, microphones for internal sound broadcasting and public address purposes, control panels for stadium lighting, and other technical features. All room finishes must be acoustically absorbent and the door must be soundproof.

Though the windows overlooking the pitch can be openable they will usually be kept shut for noise exclusion, therefore artificial ventilation will be vital.

A benchtop placed against this window will be the main working surface. Personnel should be provided with comfortable chairs, and should be able to see the pitch and central area and the electronic screens from a seated position at this bench. The consequences of lack of good management and design are shown in Figure 15.2.

Figure 15.2 Safe management and design of facilities is vital.

15.2.5 Video and electronic screen control room

This room must be linked with the stadium control room above and similarly designed and furnished, with space for two or three seats. These must have excellent views of the screens described below and of the spectator area.

Video and electronic screens

Any major stadium today must be equipped with one or even two electronic or video screens which may be used for announcements, advertisements, safety instructions, etc. They may sometimes be used for replays, either to entertain the spectators or (more rarely) to assist officials and judges.

Screen size and characteristics will depend on the type of stadium, the kinds of events staged, and the distance to spectators. Increasingly large screens are available and the technology is changing and improving rapidly.

Screens should be at the ends of the pitch where they can be seen by the maximum number of spectators; in some cases it may be desirable to have two screens, one at each end of the playing area. Orientation should be such that the sun does not fall directly on the screen face, as this can severely detract from the quality of the image.

All these matters, especially the position of the screens, should be carefully checked with the sports bodies concerned. Screens must on no account distract participants, particularly in the case of athletics.

15.2.6 Computer equipment room

Computer equipment rooms should be designed with good acoustics in line with the best current practice. Lighting should be even and to a high standard, and ventilation excellent. The floor can be raised with underfloor services and easily cleaned finishes. Vibration and noise from other parts of the building must be minimized. There should be generous provision of electrical outlets.

As computers become smaller and less dependent on special environments the above requirements are becoming less stringent, and the need for special accommodation of this kind may be gradually disappearing. Requirements should be checked at briefing stage.

15.2.7 Building maintenance and services rooms

Accommodation will be needed for building maintenance staff and equipment, the number of facilities depending on the management policy being followed.

Some stadia are operated by hiring the services of specialist contractors, who bring in not only their own staff but much of their own equipment too. In these cases only basic accommodation need be provided, comprising at least the following:

- groundsmen's rooms;
- an equipment room;
- an emergency generator room to cope with incidents when the public supply breaks down, consisting of a 1-hour fire enclosure plus a separate fuel store.

In other cases, stadia are operated by their own permanent staff and equipment; in these cases additional accommodation will be needed.

All equipment rooms must be finished with hard-wearing, low-maintenance surfaces. Floors may be smooth concrete or some other impervious, hard finish. The maintenance of service connections and equipment should be easily carried out.

15.3 Facilities for temporary events management

As stated in Section 15.1.1 additional personnel will be brought in from time to time to manage particular events such as circuses, pop concerts or religious gatherings. These requirements will depend so much on the particular case that no advice can be given here except to stress that the matter must be discussed with the client and appropriate provision made.

15.4 Facilities for visitors

These should include:

- VIP hospitality rooms;
- players' bar;
- facilities for match day stewards.

15.5 Provision for stewards

15.5.1 The functions of stewards

Accommodation is needed for the stewards and security staff who are employed on match days as a vital part of the customer service. Their roles include helping spectators to find their seats, generally assisting with information, and keeping order in a low-key way (more difficult situations being the responsibility of security personnel and/or the police).

The duties performed by stewards and the manner in which they are performed vary not only from country to country but also between sports, and even within a single national sport.

In Britain stewards often used to be voluntary and unpaid, with older men taken on out of loyalty to the club, or so that they may see the game. Frequently they were responsible not only for normal customer service duties but also for crowd control, a task for which they had usually not been properly trained. This pattern is changing and younger men and women are increasingly being recruited on a paid basis. This move is partly a matter of stadium economics, aimed at reducing the very expensive police presence demanded at many matches by local authorities, and partly a move towards better customer care. Training in safety control is therefore essential.

A very different pattern is seen in the USA where stewards tend to be more professional and are supported by 'peer security' in their task of keeping order. The term 'peer security' refers to young people drawn from the same socio-economic group as those attending the event. They are sometimes also referred to as 'tee-shirt security' because of the brightly coloured shirts they wear.

Stewarding in the future is likely to be encouraged to be more interactive, with stewards going out of their way to chat to spectators and make them feel welcome.

15.5.2 Numbers of stewards

Because patterns of stewarding vary so much it is impossible to give simple accommodation advice. Every management will have its own methods, and these should be clarified at briefing stage. The following notes offer a starting point for such investigation.

Based on normal British practice, a stadium with an attendance of 10 000 to 20 000 spectators may require 20 to 60 stewards, while one with an attendance of 20 000 to 40 000 spectators may require 60 to 100 stewards. In situations where peer security is included the acceptable ratios may range from roughly one steward to 75 spectators in small stadia, up to one steward per 200 spectators in larger stadia. This number will be made up of the following broad categories:

- turnstile stewards;
- door stewards;
- security stewards (these include peer security) who may comprise about half of the total number;
- sector supervisor stewards;
- crowd assessors;
- crowd safety stewards;
- fire-fighting stewards.

Ideally the following spaces should be provided to accommodate the above people, but it may be possible for some of these areas to be shared with other staff accommodation:

- Briefing room (based on $1.5\,m^2$ per steward) for issuing instructions to stewards on the day.
- Steward's cloakroom where stewards can change and leave their clothing in lockers.
- Storage room provided by the stadium management for official clothing.
- Small kitchen facility for making hot drinks and refreshments.
- Stewards' refreshment area to encourage their early arrival at the grounds.

15.6 Facilities for police and security officials

Police and related security systems are vital considerations in modern stadia but it is not possible to generalize about the number of police who will attend an event. On any typical winter weekend in the UK when football is being played around 5000 police will be on duty around the country. Individual events can have as few as 10 to 50 in attendance at the grounds while major football matches can have as many as 300 to 400 on site. This will be a decision taken by the police themselves in consultation with the stadium management and the club concerned. The decision will have to take into account the following factors.

- expected attendance;
- club's past record of crowd behaviour;
- number and type of visiting supporters;
- nature and location of the ground;
- experience of stewards.

As a guide to the number of police inside a ground for football matches in the UK we have listed the numbers suggested in *Policing Football Hooliganism* (Home Office, 1990).

Category 1: Smaller clubs (e.g. lower divisions of the Football League), policing may require as few as 30 to 40 officers.

Category 2: Larger clubs (e.g. premier division), some 300 officers may be required on a normal matchday.

Policing was once provided free of charge but now it is usually charged to the stadium management and is a major item in the cost of staging a particular event. In Europe there is a tendency to minimize the police presence required, perhaps because the numbers used in the USA and Canada tend to be less. As an example, the number of police used at events in the Toronto Skydome are as set out in Table 15.1.

In comparing this level of policing it must be remembered that most stadia in the USA and Canada also employ their own security staff. They are generally well trained and in the case of the Skydome are taught at their own Skydome University in Toronto. The selection process is quite stringent with only 1 in 6 applicants being accepted and then they receive between 15 to 40 hours of training before they are deployed.

Table 15.1 Police presence at the Skydome in Toronto, Canada

Family events	0.5 per 1000 spectators
Sporting events	1.0 per 1000 spectators
Concerts	1.6 per 1000 spectators
High-risk events	3.0 per 1000 spectators

Table 15.2 Security personnel at the Skydome in Toronto, Canada

Security managers	2
Full-time security officers	18
Peer security	110
Event security	80

Numbers of security staff employed at the Skydome are given in Table 15.2.

To be able to operate the various aspects of this law and order activity we have suggested the following schedule of accommodation which should be considered at the design stage of a large stadium.

- control room with glass screen overlooking the sports pitch, with video screen consoles in the room;
- detention rooms of say two cells with toilets;
- refreshment and rest room facilities for police;
- waiting and information room;
- mass arrest facilities – requiring two compounds each to take a group of say 30 spectators, if this is required.

These different types of accommodation are described in later paragraphs. In a major venue where there are separate parts of the grounds dividing the spectators into groups of say 20 000 or more, it may be necessary to provide these security facilities in each sector. Video coverage and monitoring will be needed for stadia over 30 000 capacity. For small stadia, say 20 000 or less spectators, there will only be a need for a single police control room. In Holland, court rooms have been provided on the stadium site to enable justice to be swiftly administered. This needs to be discussed with local police authorities as this is quite a rare practice. All the accommodation should be planned as linked accommodation with controlled, secure access.

Police control room

This area should be fitted with a bench in front of the window, with television and video monitors, service connections and telephone links to both inside and outside the stadium. It should be located adjacent to, or integrated with

the stadium control facilities mentioned earlier. There should be movable, comfortable chairs for the police in attendance whilst the actual announcer should be to one side, preferably in a corner to reduce background noise during microphone use. An auxiliary audio control panel could be located in this room which copies the main panel in the management control room.

The control room

All CCTV screens should be grouped together in an organized way and monitored by police and other security officials, as well as officials of the stadium, in the police control room. It is from this police control room that all security operations should be monitored, decisions should be taken and instructions given through telephone, wireless and public radio broadcasts. It is also important that camera orientation can be controlled from this room. Whilst many of the cameras used in a full surveillance can be static it is useful, when covering the area of spectator viewing around the pitch, if the camera is able to move. It should be able to traverse sideways and elevate up and down as well as zooming in to specific areas of the crowd, perhaps identifying individual spectators. Along with this monitoring exercise, a method of taking hard copy printouts of particular images should be available, as well as recording on video tape any image from any of the cameras being used in surveillance.

15.7 Toilets

All the administrative facilities described in the above sections must have access to toilets for both sexes. Some groups will be able to share toilets, but when distances become too great separate provision must be made. In all cases hot

Administrative operations

and cold running water, soap, and towels or other means of drying must be provided; space must also be allowed for vending machines, incinerators and waste bins.

For preliminary overall space estimation, the planning consultants DEGN suggest the following floor areas:

- For men allow $1\,m^2$ per three people for WC, urinal and handwashing space combined. For women allow $1\,m^2$ per three people for combined WC and handwashing space. 1.83 m by 0.9 m is the recommended size of a WC cubicle.
- For overall space planning allow $1.68\,m^2$ per WC, $0.93\,m^2$ per urinal, and $0.75\,m^2$ per washbasin. These areas do not include the outer walls forming the toilet area, nor the entrance lobbies, but they do include cubicle partitions and the standing space at urinals and basins.

15.8 First aid facilities for staff and spectators

15.8.1 Introduction

In addition to the medical and first aid facilities for players mentioned in Chapter 16, provision must also be made for staff and spectators. This is a legal requirement in most European and North American localities, and the specific requirements must be discussed with the local health authority.

Relevant UK regulations include the Health and Safety (First Aid) 1981 Regulations and the Fire Safety and Safety of Places of Sport Act 1987. In the European Community, European Economic Community Directive 89/654 covers health requirements in the workplace and directs in Clause 19 that 'one or more first aid rooms must be provided where the size of premises, type of activity being carried out and frequency of accidents so dictates'. This may lead to a more precise definition of the requirements for a first aid room than those embodied in the UK regulations.

15.8.2 FIFA and UEFA requirements

In the case of football stadia FIFA and UEFA's recommendations for new stadia state that 'every stadium should be equipped with a first aid room or rooms to care for spectators in need of medical assistance. The number, size and location of these rooms should be agreed in consultation with the local health authority.'

Where FIFA and UEFA rules apply, first aid rooms should in general:

- Be so positioned as to allow easy access to spectators and emergency vehicles from both inside and outside the stadium.
- Have doors and passageways wide enough to allow a stretcher or wheelchair.
- Have bright lighting, good ventilation, heating, electrical outlets, hot and cold water (suitable for drinking), and toilets for males and females.
- Have walls and non-slip floors finished in smooth, easily cleanable materials.
- Have storage space for stretchers, blankets, pillows and first aid materials.
- Have a telephone(s) allowing internal and external communication.
- Be clearly signposted throughout the inside and outside the stadium.

15.8.3 The Taylor Report

The Taylor Report (which arose from the Hillsborough Stadium disaster of 15 April 1989 in Sheffield, UK) recommended that in British stadia 'there should be at each designated sports ground one or more first aid rooms, which should be in addition to the club's own medical rooms for players'.

Following this a Medical Working Party of England's Football League made a number of specific recommendations. These are in no sense obligatory but are quoted here as useful guidelines. They state that first aid posts should be sited around the stadium, so that no spectator is too far from one, that they should be very clearly signposted and preferably shown in the match programme, and that room(s) should:

- Be at least $28\,m^2$ and of regular shape. (The *UK Guide to Safety at Sports Grounds* (or Green Guide)), as an interesting comparison, recommends at least $15\,m^2$, or $25\,m^2$ if stadium capacity is above $15\,000$ spectators).
- Be readily available at all times during an event and be used only for purposes of first aid.
- Be easily accessible from all parts of the stadium and be located near to a point of access for transport to hospital.
- Be near to a WC (which should be accessible to wheelchair users) and to a private waiting room with chairs, where patients and relatives can wait.
- Have doorways of sufficient width to allow easy passage of a stretcher plus attendants.
- Have good ventilation, heating and lighting, and be designated a no-smoking area.
- Have sufficient storage space for equipment.

Room facilities should include:

- Provision to treat three patients simultaneously, with reasonable privacy.

- Stainless steel sink, work surface, wash hand basin, drainage, hot and cold water supply (including drinking water), soap and hand drying facilities.
- All surfaces hard, impervious and easy to clean. (We would add the need for a floor drain, as blood cannot easily be wiped from the floor without risk of infection).
- At least six 13-amp electrical outlets.
- Adequate waste disposal facilities, with provision for clinical and 'sharp' waste.
- Effective means of communication to and from a central control point and the emergency services. A telephone link with an exclusive external line would be the best such means.

15.8.4 Dimensions

Recommended room dimensions have been given above. Stretchers are commonly $1.9\,m$ by $0.56\,m$, and minimum dimensions to accommodate stretchers and wheelchairs are $0.9\,m$ for doorsets and $1.2\,m$ for corridor widths. An ambulance access road should be at least $6\,m$ wide.

16

Facilities for players and officials

16.1 Basic planning

16.1.1 General

Every stadium, however small, must provide facilities for the participants in the events held at the venue, but the amount and type of accommodation that is needed varies enormously: a football or rugby match may need facilities for only two teams (including reserves) plus officials, whereas a major international athletics event may attract up to a thousand participants.

It will probably be impossible to provide accommodation on this scale on a permanent basis, and the decision may be to rely partly on temporary accommodation for large-scale events. The guidance below is therefore intended to suggest a 'reasonable' provision of facilities.

If there is a 'home team' then most of the accommodation will concentrate on their requirements as they will be using the facilities on a regular basis for training. If the stadium offers a home to more than one team then it must be decided whether the teams can share facilities or whether a completely separate set must be provided for each. This is usually the case where major sports clubs are involved, although some sharing of training equipment may be possible.

Team changing facilities for the resident team is a very special area. It is their 'home', a place to which few people can gain entry. We recommend that, as with a house, the resident organization be very closely consulted on design, layout and character. If the stadium is also to be used for concerts and other purposes this must be taken into account.

16.1.2 Location of facilities in the stadium layout

Access to outside
There must be direct access between players' changing facilities and the service road outside. This road will be used by coaches conveying teams to and from the stadium, and also by ambulances. The service road should give access to the team entrance, and also to the playing area so that injured players can be reached quickly and easily by ambulances, etc.

Access to the pitch
There must also be direct, protected access between players' changing rooms and the pitch. At events where players and referees may be subject to attack (such as the hurling of missiles) by the crowd, safety requirements are stringent. Football matches in countries with strong traditions of team loyalty fall into this category, and recommendations are outlined below.

In the case of new stadia for World Cup and European Championship finals, FIFA/UEFA recommend that:

Ideally, each of the teams' dressing rooms and the referees' dressing room should have its own corridor for access to the pitch. These corridors may join up near the exit to the playing area.

The point where the players and the referees enter the playing area, which ideally should be at the centreline and on the same side as the VIP box, press stand and administrative offices, must be protected by means of a fireproof telescopic tunnel extending into the playing area far enough to prevent the risk of injury to the match participants caused by missiles thrown by spectators.

Such telescopic tunnels should be capable of being extended or closed quickly so that they may be used during the match when a player is leaving or entering the field, without causing unduly lengthy viewing obstruction.

Alternatively, the entrance to the playing area may be by means of an underground tunnel, the mouth of which is situated a similarly safe distance away from spectators.

There should be no possibility of public or media interference at any point within these corridors or security tunnels.

In the case of European Club competitions, the UEFA recommendations simply state:

In order to guarantee the safety of players and match officials, participating clubs shall provide for an access to the field ensuring safe entry and exit.

Location
Whenever possible players' and officials' accommodation should be situated at pitch level to allow easy and direct access to the playing area.

16.1.3 Scales of provision

Table 16.1 (players' accommodation) and Table 16.2 (officials' accommodation) summarize the requirements of various football authorities

Table 16.1   Recommended provision of dressing room facilities for players in new football stadia in the UK

Competition	Minimum size of dressing room (m^2)	Washing facilities	Toilet facilities	Massage tables	Medical and other requirements
FIFA/UEFA recommendations for new stadia	60	10 showers 5 wash basins 1 foot basin 1 sink for boot cleaning	3 urinals 3 WCs	2	Dressing room must provide seating, lockers, etc. for 20 persons. Also, 1 refrigerator, 2 shaving points, 2 hair driers, 2 wall mirrors.
Football League	18	1 bath (min. $8\,m^2$) or 4 showers 1 wash basin	1 urinal 1 WC	1	separate medical room in vicinity
Scottish League	30	1 bath (min. $8\,m^2$) or 8 showers 2 wash basins	1 urinal 1 WC	1	separate medical room
GM Vauxhall Conference	18	1 bath (min. $6\,m^2$) or 4 showers 1 wash basin	1 urinal 1 WC	1	separate medical room in vicinity
Beazer Homes League	18	1 bath (min. $6\,m^2$) or 3 showers 1 wash basin	1 urinal 1 WC	1	Grade C and D need have separate medical room adjacent to home dressing room only
Diadora League	12	1 bath (min. $6\,m^2$) or 4 showers 1 wash basin	Grade A: 1 urinal 1 WC Grade B and C: 1 WC	1 (unless exclusive use in separate treatment room)	Grade A only need have separate medical room in vicinity
HFS Loans League	15	1 bath (min. $4.5\,m^2$) or 4 showers 1 wash basin	1 urinal 1 WC	1 (unless exclusive use in separate treatment room)	separate medical room in vicinity

* FIFA/UEFA actually state that it is preferable for new stadia to have 4 separate team dressing rooms
All figures quoted are per dressing room

Table 16.2 Recommended provision of dressing room facilities for match officials in new football stadia in the UK

Competition	Minimum size of dressing room (m^2)	Washing facilities	Toilet facilities	Other requirements
FIFA/UEFA recommendations for new stadia	min 25	2 showers 1 wash basin	1 urinal 1 WC	Dressing room must provide seating, lockers, etc. for 4 persons. Also, 1 shaving point, 1 hair drier, 2 wall mirrors, 1 massage table, 1 table
Football League	6	1 bath or 1 shower 1 wash basin	1 WC	Regulations require a reserve official to change and be on-hand. New stadia should therefore ideally provide seating, lockers, etc. for 4 persons.
Scottish League	15	1 bath or 3 showers 1 wash basin	1 WC	Practice at major games is for a reserve official to change and be on-hand. New stadia should therefore ideally provide seating, lockers, etc. for 4 persons.
GM Vauxhall Conference	6	1 bath or 1 shower 1 wash basin	1 WC	
Beazer Homes League	4	1 bath or 1 shower 1 wash basin	1 WC	
Diadora League	4	1 bath or 1 shower (preferably 2 showers) 1 wash basin	1 WC	Match officials should not have to share a dressing room with other persons, including match officials at other games being played in the vicinity
HFS Loans League	6	1 bath or 1 shower (preferably 2 showers) 1 wash basin	1 WC	

from FIFA and UEFA (in the case of major international championship matches) down to the various English non-league bodies for local ones (GM Vauxhall, Beazer Homes, etc.).

Requirements for other sports are not officially laid down in such specific detail as for football, and must be determined by discussions with clients. In such cases these tables form a useful starting point.

16.2 Players' facilities

16.2.1 Introduction

The facilities described below should be directly linked with the media area (see Section 14.1) and the team administrative offices (see Section 16.1), and if possible also with the team directors' suite or chairman's box (see Section 9.1). If these facilities cannot be at ground level,

as recommended above, they should be served by an elevator.

Corridor and door widths should be generous, because these are busy areas on a match day: 1.2 m is a minimum width, and 1.5 m preferable. Good ventilation is essential to prevent condensation, as well as a heating and/or cooling system in the changing areas depending on local climate and seasons of play.

The whole area should be secure against unauthorized entry, inaccessible to the public and the media, and have direct, protected access to the pitch as outlined in Section 16.1.2.

Finishes must be robust and easily cleanable, and recent forms of non-slip plastic matting and hard-wearing carpets are ideal for the changing rooms themselves.

16.2.2 Changing rooms for sports

A changing room or locker room (Figure 16.1) should be provided for each home team and at

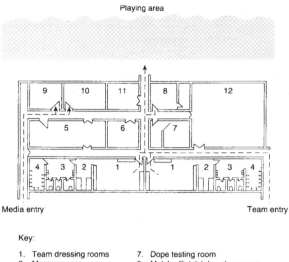

Playing area

Media entry   Team entry

Key:
1. Team dressing rooms   7. Dope testing room
2. Massage area   8. Match officials' dressing rooms
3. Toilets   9. Press interview room
4. Showers   10. Media room
5. Equipment area   11. Match delegates' room
6. Medical examination room   12. Warm-up area and gymnasium

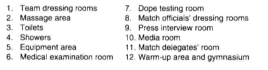

Figure 16.1 Sample layout of dressing rooms and related facilities, as recommended by FIFA/UEFA for new stadia.

least one visiting team. Two such rooms should be provided for visiting teams if a match is to be held between two visiting teams – unless of course the home team is prepared to allow use of its facilities (which is unusual) or the visiting teams are willing to share (which is more usual). Some stadia start the day's events with a 'curtain-raiser', which is often a match between teams in a lower league or junior teams, or even an event from a different sport, and these teams also require changing facilities.

Each changing room should contain a locker, bench seat and hanging space for each individual player (including reserves), each such space being between 600 mm and 900 mm wide and at least 1200 mm deep. In the case of football FIFA requires twenty of these positions, and the requirements for rugby will be very similar. The benches should be designed so that clothes can be kept dry and in good order. American football teams often prefer individual cabinets or open hanging units with side panels, to the open benching that is common for football and rugby.

In the case of new football stadia catering for major matches FIFA/UEFA recommend four

separate team dressing rooms, and Table 16.2 gives minimum sizes.

16.2.3 Massage rooms

At least one massage table or bench is required in each changing area, and two are needed for major stadia (see Table 16.2 and Figure 16.1).

16.2.4 Washing and toilet facilities

Washing facilities should be directly accessible from the changing area, without going through the toilets. As a general guide there should be one shower per 1.5 or 2 players, allowing 1.5 m^2 per player; more specific recommendations for football stadia are given in Table 16.2. Outside the showers there should be drying areas fitted with benches and towel rails.

Toilets fitted with both WCs and urinals (if it is a male team) should be provided in the ratio of one position per three players, or as in Table 16.1 when FIFA/UEFA rules apply. Both washing and toilet areas should be very well served by natural ventilation, and designed to allow thorough washing down of all surfaces, which should be durable and impervious.

16.2.5 Ancillary accommodation

The following accommodation (Figure 16.2) should be provided as part of the changing areas described above:

- a large training room which can be used for preliminary warm-up exercises;
- a players' first aid room near the pitch, *en route* to the changing areas.

Additional facilities which may be included or shared between teams, depending on the teams' importance, are:

- a general meeting room for use by the team, with projector and screen (this room could also be used for other purposes such as press interviews);
- a players' bar and games area where players can relax after a game or training session (it

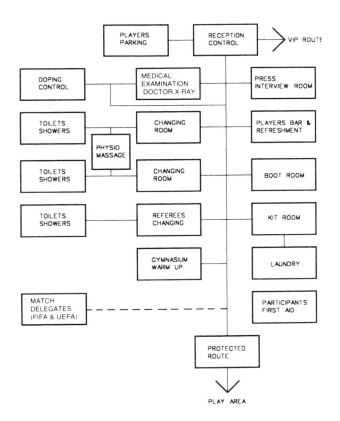

Figure 16.2 Circulation route for players/competitors/performers.

should be equipped with a light refreshment kitchen);
- a gymnasium, weights and exercise area;
- a sauna and hydrotherapy area;
- a waiting room with its own toilet for players' relatives;
- an equipment storage area with shelves and cupboards;
- a laundry and clothes drying area;
- a boot cleaning and storage room.

16.3 Team management facilities

This area is not to be confused with the stadium management facilities described in Chapter 15 – unless of course it has been established that stadium managers and team managers will be one and the same body for a particular stadium.

16.3.1 Location

There is no specific requirement, but these facilities are usually on the main side of the stadium, in the same general area as the administration area (see Chapter 15) but probably at a lower level.

16.3.2 Facilities

The rooms to be provided will depend largely on the size of the sports club involved, but will probably comprise the following:

- reception area of approximately $12\,m^2$ to $15\,m^2$;
- general office and secretarial area;
- executive offices with private entrance;
- board or meeting room of approximately $25\,m^2$ to $30\,m^2$, with bar facilities;
- team manager's office of approximately $18\,m^2$;
- assistant team manager's office of approximately $12\,m^2$;
- team coach's office of $12\,m^2$ to $18\,m^2$;
- possibly an office for an assistant team coach;
- a chairman's suite connected to the executive offices.

16.4 Officials' facilities

For every event which takes place on the field there will be officials, judges, umpires, linesmen and referees who require separate changing and toilet accommodation. They will also need some administrative space, which may be shared space in the case of smaller stadia. Provision will depend on the sport being played as well as the number of games being staged in one day.

16.4.1 Location

The rooms described below should be close to the players' dressing rooms, but without direct access. They must be inaccessible to the public and the media, but have direct protected access to the playing area as described in Section 16.1.2.

16.4.2 Facilities and scales of provision

Changing rooms

As a general guide, referee and linesmen's changing accommodation should comprise four spaces, allowing $2.5\,m^2$ per official, with associated lockers, toilets and showers.

A slightly separate area within the room should be provided with a table and chair for report-writing.

The most precise guidance that is available on scales of provision are the FIFA/UEFA recommendations for new football stadia for major matches, and while these cannot be directly applied to all stadia, they give a useful starting point for compiling the brief (see Table 16.2).

Appeals room

Every sport is based on a firm set of rules and players who transgress those rules will have action taken against them by the officials of the sport. To allow this judicial process to take place an appeals room or 'court' must be provided. The room must accommodate a jury of five or six people, plus two or three others. It need not be a dedicated space but can use one of the other areas in the stadium if suitably located and planned (see Section 15.2.3).

Match delegates' room

FIFA and UEFA's recommendations for new stadia for major football matches require a special room for the competition officials who sit on the centre bench of the pitch. This room should be close to the general dressing room area and be at least $16\,m^2$ in size. Equipment should include:

- one desk;
- three chairs;
- one clothes locker;
- one telephone.

16.5 Medical examination facilities

16.5.1 Location

The accommodation described below should be close to the players' dressing rooms, whilst also having easy access to the outside entrance and to the playing area as described in Section 16.1.2.

16.5.2 Facilities and scales of provision

The specific requirements of local safety authorities and the relevant medical teams will take priority, and must be established as part of the brief. Subject to that, the following advice is given by FIFA and UEFA for new football stadia for major events.

Medical examination room

There should be a room of at least $25\,m^2$, equipped with:

- one examination table 600 mm wide, accessible from three sides;
- two portable stretchers, kept alongside the pitch during games;
- one wash basin;
- one glass cabin for medications;
- one treatment table;
- one oxygen bottle with mask;
- one blood-pressure gauge;
- one heating apparatus, such as a hotplate, for instruments;
- possibly some physiotherapy equipment.

See also Section 15.8 dealing with medical facilities for spectators.

Resident doctor's room

In larger stadia the team doctor should have his own room of $100\,m^2$ adjacent to the medical examination room and linked to it internally.

X-ray room

Where justified, an X-ray room of about $20\,m^2$ may be provided close to the medical examination room for examination of injuries.

Dope testing facilities

Stadia to be used for major competitions will probably require a room of at least $16\,\text{m}^2$, equipped with the following:

- one desk;
- two chairs;
- one basin;
- one telephone.

Adjacent to this room, with direct private access to it, should be a toilet comprising WC, wash basin and shower. Near the dope testing room there should be a waiting area with seating for eight people, clothes hanging facilities or lockers for four people, and a refrigerator.

16.6 Ancillary facilities

Depending on the size of the stadium other facilities can be included which will assist in its operation. These additional spaces must be judged on their merits for each particular occasion.

Figure 16.3 Changing benches for American football (Dolphins Stadium). Architects: HOK.

- Media interview room: this should be adjacent to the team room, and be supplied with electrical and lighting equipment suitable for television broadcasting.
- Players' warm-up area and gymnasium for use before the game.
- A field toilet and drinking fountain close to the access route to the pitch.
- Enclosures or 'dug-outs' which are covered and have direct access to the appropriate team's changing areas.

17

Services

17.1 Lighting systems

17.1.1 Introduction

If a stadium is to achieve its full potential use and be operated at night or late afternoon a comprehensive lighting system is essential. Two main types of illumination are needed:

- Lighting of passageways and escape routes so that spectators can enter and leave the stadium safely.
- Lighting the pitch so that players and spectators can see the action clearly and without strain. It may be necessary also to illuminate the pitch for television cameras, in which case the requirements become more stringent.

Both safety and pitch lighting are required together, since one without the other would be redundant; the only exceptions being:

- night-time concerts using their own stage lighting systems fed from a power supply on the grounds (which is common practice); or
- sporting events which finish while there is daylight, but darkness falls before all the spectators have left the grounds (this is most unlikely for major stadia).

In these cases the stadium would need only to supply safety lighting for spectators.

17.1.2 Safety lighting for spectators

Requirements
Safety lighting must fulfil two functions.

- Illuminate escape routes and exits clearly, so that spectators are in no doubt about the correct direction of movement in an emergency, and can move along safely without risk of stumbling and falling even when hurrying and in a panic.
- Illuminate alarm call points and fire-fighting equipment.

Luminaires should be provided along each passageway and escape route so that there are no dark areas, especially on stairs and landings and at emergency doors; and an illumination level of at least one lux should be aimed for. All such emergency lighting must continue to operate even if the main power system fails, coming on within five seconds of mains failure.

Installation design
It is difficult to give recommendations for the spacing of luminaires along the general runs of routes, and an inspection of existing buildings may be the most practical guide. For illumination at critical locations we suggest that luminaires be situated within 2 m of all exits and at all points where it is necessary to emphasize the location of potential hazards and safety equipment. Such locations include:

- along each stair flight to illuminate the nosings;
- at all stair intersections, to illuminate the nosings;
- near each change of level;
- in front of each exit door;
- in front of each fire door;

- at each exit or safety sign required for safe egress from the stadium;
- near each fire alarm call-point and each item of fire-fighting equipment.

It may sometimes be difficult to achieve the recommended illumination level of 1 lux in the large spaces found under stadium structures. Wall-mounted luminaires help overcome this problem, and illuminated signs can make an excellent contribution. Until now such signs (particularly neon signs) have been infrequently used in sports stadia owing to their cost. However the Skydome in Toronto, Canada, is a striking example of the exploitation of neon advertising signs to create a bright and cheerful atmosphere under an otherwise dark grey structure, and to highlight certain locations.

Stand-by power
There must always be a stand-by generator system in case of failure – a requirement enforced by law in many countries including the UK. Emergency lighting may be provided in one of two ways:

- As a minimum there might be a separate circuit, usually designed to operate for a specific period of time when there is a mains power failure, and providing only enough illumination to allow for the safe movement of people out of the affected area – at least 1 lux, as suggested above. The length of time it is required to operate will depend on the circumstances and on the local regulations, but is usually not less than two hours.
- More ambitiously the entire lighting system including pitch illumination (see below) may be switched to the stand-by system, maintaining full illuminance levels if the mains system fails, thus enabling the event to continue.

With both methods automatic restart time in case of failure should not be more than five seconds.

17.1.3 Pitch lighting for players and viewers

Illuminance requirements
If play is to take place at night the playing area should be illuminated to allow those playing and those watching both at the grounds and at home on television to see the action clearly. This means that the level of brightness, contrast and glare must be correctly designed over the entire playing area. The most demanding of these requirements is that of television, particularly colour transmission, and this specialist area will be discussed later.

The reason we can see any object is because it contrasts with what is behind it in colour or brightness or perhaps both. Colour contrast of a ball and a pitch or an athlete and a running track is largely controlled by the sports governing bodies and therefore is usually out of the control of the designer. An interesting exception to this was the yellow balls and bright clothing introduced by Kerry Packer in Australia some years ago for his night-time cricket World Series. This was a deliberate attempt to make the traditionally white attire and dark red ball more visible to the spectator and hopefully more popular to the public since they would be able to follow the game more easily. It was also essential for the players to see the ball when it was hit high into the night sky. Cricket is traditionally played during the day when the dark ball contrasts against a blue, or at least grey, sky but it would be impossible to see at night. Brightness and glare are therefore the only real controls we have over the visibility of a sport.

Levels of illumination for sport at night are often lower than those for indoor events or daylight events but the careful design of lighting can compensate and good visibility can be achieved. Illumination levels will depend on the sport because of the different speeds, distances and colour contrasts involved; the faster the object moves the higher the illumination required; the higher the standards of play the higher the level of illumination required. Lighting levels will also depend on the size of the venue since those sitting furthest from the action require the greatest level of illumination for them to see to the same standard. The last consideration which may be relevant to a stadium is that our standard of vision deteriorates with age and we require more light to achieve the same level of visibility when we are older. This deterioration can be quite significant, with the illumination levels required by a 60-year old possibly six times that of a 20-year old, simply to achieve the same standard of visibility.

Table 17.1 summarizes typical lighting levels, and degree of uniformity, for a variety of sporting types. The table takes into account the deterioration of illumination level relative to the age of the fitting. It is meant only as a general guide: specific up-to-date requirements should always be obtained from the particular sporting associations concerned before commencing design.

Glare control requirements
One of the major factors to be considered in designing the lighting system is glare, not only does it affect the players and the spectators but it is often perceived as environmental pollution

Table 17.1 Minimum maintained lighting requirements for outdoor sports facilities[1]

Facility	Recreational/training use		Club/county use		National/international use	
	Lux	Uniformity	Lux	Uniformity	Lux	Uniformity
Archery (Target)	750	0.8	750	0.8	750	0.8
(shooting zone)	200	0.5	200	0.5	200	0.5
Athletics	100	0.5	200	0.5	500	0.7
Basketball	75	0.5	200	0.6	500	0.7
Bowls: lawn	100	0.5	200	0.7	300	0.7
Crown green bowls	100	0.5	200	0.7	300	0.7
Cycle racing	100	0.5	300	0.7	500	0.7
Cycle speedway	100	0.3	200	0.5	500	0.7
American football	75	0.5	200	0.6	500	0.7
Association football[2]	75	0.5	200	0.6	500	0.7
Rugby league football	75	0.5	200	0.6	500	0.7
Rugby union football	75	0.5	200	0.6	500	0.7
Hockey[3]	300	0.7	300	0.7	500	0.7
Mini hockey	200	0.5	300	0.6		
Lawn tennis[4]						
Over court	300	0.7	300	0.7	500	0.7
Over playing area	250	0.6	250	0.6	400	0.6
Netball	75	0.5	200	0.6	500	0.7
Roller hockey	200	0.7	300	0.7	500	0.7
Golf driving range	50	0.25				
Artificial ski slope	100	0.3				

Source: *Handbook of Sports and Recreation Building Design (Vol. I Outdoor Sports)*, The Sports Council
Notes:
1 The recommended levels do not include lighting for television broadcasting and for these requirements refer to Vol. 2, ch. II, *Facilities for the Media*, CIBSE Lighting Guide: *LG4 – Sports*, and CIE Guides 67 and 83.
2 There are specific requirements by FIFA and UEFA for international matches and competitions and many domestic leagues and competitions have specific requirements (such as the FA Cup, FA Trophy, Football League, GMCV, etc.). Refer to the *Guide to the Artificial Lighting of Football Pitches*, FIFA/Philips Lighting BV and *Digest of Stadium Criteria*, FSADC.
3 The FIH recommend 250 lux for ball training and club competition. Refer to the *Guide to the Artificial Lighting of Hockey Pitches*, FIH/Philips Lighting BV.
4 The ITF have produced recommendations. Refer to the *Guide to the Artificial Lighting of Tennis Courts*, ITF/Philips Lighting BV.

by neighbours. Some glare may be impossible to eliminate, but the control of the levels of brightness of the light source and the adjacent background will help to reduce its effect. Other devices such as screening the light source by the use of louvres or using deep reflectors can be used to control its effect. Another approach is to position the fitting outside the observers' line of sight: players and spectators are likely to be affected by glare when the light reaches them at angles near the horizontal. This is sometimes difficult to avoid in stadia where the flood-lighting is mounted on the front edge of the roof.

Daylight can also present glare problems but has a positive psychological effect on both the participants and the spectators. On a bright day the contrast between areas on the pitch which are in light and those which are in shadow can present a glare problem particularly for television coverage. This contrast can often be minimized by the use of translucent roofing materials which allow some light through the overhanging roof and balances the contrast on the pitch. Translucent roofing materials are discussed in Section 4.8.5.

Installation design

The correct design sequence is to decide the performance levels that are required (see above) together with cost and other limits, then to get competitive quotations for meeting these requirements, and only at that stage to decide the number and type of lamps, their mounting heights and their spacings. It is a mistake to approach the matter the other way round (as is sometimes done) and to decide at an early design stage the number and the heights of lighting towers, and perhaps even the number and placement of individual lamps, and then to seek quotations. Alternative lamp types and fittings will require different spacings and locations to give the same result, and until the fittings are known the spacings cannot be decided. Subject to that proviso the following general notes may be helpful.

Small stadia are usually lit by a side-lighting system consisting of three or four fittings located on one side of the pitch mounted at a height of not less than 12 m. The angle between the fitting and the pitch centre should be between 20 degrees and 30 degrees; and the angle between the fitting and the side line between 45 degrees and 75 degrees.

Larger stadia may use corner columns or masts, with perhaps a number of fittings along the side(s) so that an optimum illumination can be chosen for any particular type of event. Corner masts are probably the most common system in use. They are expensive but have the advantage of not obstructing any views to the pitch. They should be offset at least 5 degrees from the side, and 15 degrees from the end of the field of play, taken from the centre of the respective side or end. Mast height should be at least 0.4 times the distance on plan between the mast and the centre of the field and mounting angles should be as in the previous paragraph.

In very large stadia the lighting system will be governed partly by the design of the stadium structure:

- Open stadia will probably use the system described above of four corner masts, about 40 m high, possibly supplemented by additional masts around the perimeter if justified by the stadium size. It must be noted that these tall masts can present a major structural and aesthetic design problem.
- Roofed stadia may have side lighting in the form of continuous strips mounted along the leading edges of the roofs. These fittings should be mounted at least 30 m above the playing surface to reduce the risk of glare, which may be an insurmountable problem because light reaches the spectators at angles near to the horizontal. On the positive side, the increased illumination of the vertical plane associated with roof-edge lighting may be beneficial to television broadcasting.

For larger schemes two or three switching levels may be provided to allow different illumination levels for different kinds of event, ranging from training to a full-scale televised match. It may also be necessary for the floodlights to be rotatable by remote control to illuminate different areas of the arena for different types of events. These matters must be clarified with the client at an early stage.

With regard to the structural design of towers, lattice towers are now rarely used. Masts and columns are cheaper, easier to maintain, and visually less intrusive. Hinged columns or 'raise and lower' masts facilitate regular cleaning relamping and maintenance, all of which are vital if lamp performance is to be maintained.

17.1.4 Pitch lighting for television

Requirements
Because the camera lens cannot adapt as quickly as the human eye to the variations in lighting on a playing surface, lighting for professional television coverage must satisfy more stringent requirements than even the best spectator standards. If the stadium is to allow for television coverage its lighting design must therefore be based on television standards rather than visual ones. Such standards must take into account the distance at which the action is being filmed, the type of lens being used, the type of camera being used as well as the speed of play. It is essential that these criteria be developed with expert help, but broadly they are the following.

- First, a certain minimum illuminance on the playing field. British football clubs require a minimum figure of 250 lux to enter the football league, and FIFA require a minimum of 1500 lux for World Cup venues. For other sports, approximate values may be deduced from Table 17.2.
- Second, the distribution of light must be uniform, without contrasting dark and light patches on the field.

- Third, the lighting must be shadow-free.

Up-to-date guidance on all the above requirements must be obtained from the relevant governing bodies of the individual sports (such as the International Olympic Committee for athletics, or FIFA for international football competitions) and from the professional lighting institutions in various countries. In the UK the *CIBSE Lighting Guide: Sport LG4* (Chartered Institution of Building Services Engineers, 1990) is the essential reference.

Turning from professional to private coverage, many clubs have their own video camera systems for recording games, and the lighting levels required for this are much lower than for professional coverage. A domestic video camera may pick up details at levels as low as 50 lux on the vertical plane, which equates to roughly 100 lux on the playing surface.

Installation design
Designing a system that will achieve the above standards requires a great deal of expert calculation, and lighting companies such as Philips, Thorn and others have developed sophisticated computer programs which can calculate the exact range of illumination across the entire playing area. It is essential to make use of this expertise.

Positioning of the lighting system should take into account the fact that television coverage of directional sports will be from one side of the stadium only, otherwise cutting backwards and forwards between camera positions will confuse the viewers.

The lighting fittings themselves are now much more efficient than even a few years ago, and it has become cheaper and easier to provide the

Table 17.2 Television lighting requirements

	Illuminance in lux at maximum filming distances		
Speed of Action	25 m	75 m	150 m
Slow	500	700	1000
Medium	700	1000	1400
Fast	1000	1400	

quantity and quality of light required by colour television cameras. It is common to see old lighting towers with spaces for 20 or 24 lights using only 10 or 12 new fittings. Strike-up times have similarly improved, and instead of taking 10 to 15 minutes to achieve full illumination there are now instant re-strike lights. The latter greatly ease the problem of efficiently illuminating events which start in daylight but continue into darkness. Table 17.3 summarizes the main properties of the commonly available light fittings, but these are constantly improving and specific data must be obtained from manufacturers before design.

Stand-by power

Pitch lighting is sometimes supported by an emergency generator, but the latter would have to be far more substantial than that for emergency escape lighting and could only be justified if the potential financial loss from an aborted sports event were very large. Stand-by generation for pitch lighting is at present limited to major venues.

17.2 Closed-circuit television systems

Closed-circuit television systems (CCTV) may be used for two purposes in a stadium – for security and crowd control (where its use is becoming ubiquitous), and for informing and entertaining spectators, where its huge potential is not yet fully exploited.

17.2.1 CCTV for security

The need for better control of crowd movement has led to virtually all major stadia now having CCTV installations allowing management to monitor crowd densities, movement patterns and potential trouble spots before, during and after events.

Cameras have become smaller and less obtrusive, so that it is possible to monitor spectators without the latter being aware of the fact and feeling intimidated; picture quality has improved to the point where individual spectators can later be identified from a video recording, particularly if computerized enhancement techniques are applied. A striking example

Table 17.3 Sports stadium light fittings

Type	Name	Wattage (W)	Life (Hours)	Initial cost	Running cost
Incandescent	Tungsten Halogen	up to 2000	2000	low	high
Tubular Fluorescent	White Colours	up to 125	7500	medium	low
High Intensity Discharge	Mercury Fluorescent	up to 2000	6000	medium	medium
	Metal Halide (single cap)	100–2000	4000	high	low
	Metal Halide (double cap)	35–2000	4000	high	low
	Metal Halide (compact)	50–2500	1000	high	low
	High Pressure Sodium (single cap)	50–100	8000	high	low
	High Pressure Sodium (double cap)	25–1000	8000	high	low

Average life expectancy is the time an average of 20% of a batch of lamps fail.

of the degree of miniaturization already available is a 150 mm by 25 mm camera fitting into a hollow wicket for close-up action shots of cricket matches – and no doubt even smaller cameras will be available by the time this is published.

Returning to the security aspect: it would be too expensive to place a camera in every corner of the stadium, but a general overview of all areas, plus targeted coverage of all potential trouble-spots must now be regarded as an essential feature of any new stadium design.

In the first instance control personnel should be given a clear view of all spectator approaches to the stadium so that they can identify a potentially troublesome build-up well in advance. As an example the control room of London's Wembley Stadium is linked to cameras at a traffic junction some five miles away where many cars heading for the stadium turn off a major motorway. The police are thus able to identify supporters' coaches and take early precautionary measures if necessary.

Subsequently, they should be able to monitor crowd build-up and behaviour at all areas of dense congregation as spectators move to their seats – for instance entrances to turnstiles and vomitories, staircases and the like.

Systems integration

The monitoring facilities described above should not be seen in isolation, but in the context of an entire electronic communication system embracing the telephone, public address, crowd surveillance and recording, perimeter access control, general security, fire monitoring and fire alarm, and emergency evacuation systems. Additional aspects such as time and attendance records, parking control, elevator control and the like can also be integrated into the system.

As an example of how such integration may currently operate, an attempted illicit entry into a secure area can be detected by an electronic surveillance system which then activates a recording camera, auto-dials a message to stadium security officers and suggests what steps must be taken, issues a pre-recorded warning to the intruder, sets off an alarm, and makes a video record and computer printout of the entire sequence of events for future reference. All the

correct actions can be taken and a reliable record kept with minimal risk of human error.

Ideally all the services described above should come from a single interconnected source, and it is essential to take expert advice to avoid incompatibilities between sub-systems which ought to be working together to give maximum benefit to the stadium management. For the same reason the information given here should be read in conjunction with other sections of this book such as sound systems (Section 17.3), fire alarm systems (Section 17.4) and so forth.

Stand-by power

A stand-by power system is essential for security services.

17.2.2 CCTV for information and entertainment

CCTV offers spectators the possibility of a running commentary on the game, replays and information about the players on the field, highlights from other games, and other possibilities as yet unthought of – all 'narrowcasted' on small personal TV receivers or on huge screens mounted above the pitch.

These are not just gimmicks but an essential element in managements' array of techniques to win back spectators from the comfortable alternative of watching sports events free of charge, with close-up shots, action replays and the like in the comfort of their living rooms. The proportion of events being televised increases all the time, enhanced by the spread of cable and satellite television, and stadia must struggle hard to retain their markets.

One can foresee the day when spectators will collect a small closed-circuit television receiver plus earphones, receiving only the stadium channel, as part of the ticket price. Perhaps these devices will be plugged into 'stadium television' or 'stadium radio' sockets in the seat armrest, rather as in an aeroplane, and they will offer a range of services which might include expert commentary, replays and information on the game; the ordering of purchases to be delivered to the seat at half-time; or an interactive facility allowing spectators to dial up information or statistics on a player or team, highlights from past matches, etc.

First signs of this developing process are to be seen at the Hong Kong Jockey Club, where spectators may use a key pad to find out the current odds and place bets from their seats. It can only be matter of time before a miniature screen is added to the device, allowing the spectator to see the race from viewing angles and close-ups not available from his seat.

Turning from speculation about the future to present-day design, there are basically two technologies in current use.

Scoreboards

The provision of simple numerical or text displays above the pitch is now commonplace. They display scores, the real time, the elapsed and remaining time for games, the names and data of players and teams and the like; and even small stadia or sports halls will have scoreboards of this type. Guidance must be obtained from the governing body for the sporting type concerned, from manufacturing and installation companies, and possibly from independent consultants, to ensure correct location, positioning, size and specification. If this aspect is not considered at a sufficiently early stage it may prove impossible to install a completely satisfactory system.

Colour video displays

These are a completely different technology from the above, much more expensive but also much more dramatic. Colour video displays are like giant television sets which can screen action replays, highlights from past games or from simultaneous events at other venues, and of course commercials which are a useful source of stadium revenue.

In addition to attracting and pleasing audiences, thus increasing gate revenue, pre-programmed entertainment sequences on big video screens can also usefully slow down the rate at which people enter and leave the stadium. Keeping a proportion of the audience in their seats after the final whistle, instead of rushing for the exits, makes for a safer stadium. It can also make for a more profitable one if people

are persuaded by entertaining video programmes to arrive earlier than they otherwise would do, and to stay longer, using stadium restaurants and other facilities before and after the game.

Video screens may either be permanent fixtures, or temporary ones erected in as little as six hours for a particular occasion. As these screens are very expensive to install, maintain and operate (with a capital cost of several millions for the largest sizes) the 'rent by event' approach may be the only feasible one for most stadia.

Very large screens are particularly apt for rock concerts and festivals; and at the time of writing the largest available size for mobile daylight screens is $48\,m^2$. Permanently installed screens may be up to $70\,m^2$ in area, consisting of 120 smaller high-resolution screens – 10 vertically and 12 horizontally. These are controlled from a console which allows the screen area to be used for one giant single image, or a mosaic of smaller images, giving great scope for exciting and entertaining effects.

Choice, positioning and operation of these very expensive facilities are critical matters which must be got right. Some requirements are obvious – for example:

- screens must be easily visible to all members of the audience;
- screens must not obstruct a direct view of the pitch or play in any way;
- sunlight should never fall directly on to video screen surfaces.

However, other aspects are too technical, and too fast-changing, to describe here. Designers must get the best expert advice both from independent consultants and from companies in the field before taking decisions.

17.3 Sound systems

Badly designed or inappropriate sound systems can harm the performance of the stadium, therefore audio design must be taken seriously. There are well-documented cases in the USA where participants had to wear earplugs to allow them to concentrate on the game, and there are many instances of spectators being irritated by announcement systems which are too loud for comfort, too quiet to be heard above the background noise, or hard to decipher.

17.3.1 Requirements

The first step in designing such a system is to define as clearly as possible the results the system must achieve when in use. Matters to be considered include the following.

Specific functions

Managements require sound systems in sports stadia for as many as four different functions:

- to communicate with the spectators in the stands (general announcements, commentary on the events being staged, etc.);
- to give information and instructions in emergencies;
- to provide entertainment (music, light amusement, etc.);
- advertising.

At times some of the above functions may be in conflict with each other, and to prepare for this eventuality a clear set of priorities must be decided at briefing stage and built into the system. A typical sequence of priorities, with the first item overriding all others, and so on down the line, might be as follows:

1 police announcements from the police control room (see Section 15.6.2);
2 management announcements from the events control room (see Section 17.3.3);
3 general announcements and match commentary;
4 pre-match events information;
5 musical and other entertainment;
6 advertising.

Audibility

To be effective a sound system must be heard over the background noise of the crowd by a significant margin. The designers must therefore establish what the level of background noise actually is, either by measurement (in the case of an existing stdium) or by calculation (in the case of a new stadium).

Crowd noise is generally specified as an L value, which is the sound level that is exceeded for only 10 per cent of the time, and it is important to take into account the peak levels (for example, when goals are scored) when determining this value. As a guide, the sound system should be in the order of 6 dB louder than the crowd noise level as specified above.

The next step is to determine the evenness of the sound distribution in the stadium, since it would be of no use for spectators in one area to hear clearly while others could not hear at all. The degree of evenness should, as a rough guide, be in the order of $+6$ dB and -3 dB for at least 95 per cent of the spectator area, but perhaps for only 75 per cent or 80 per cent of less important areas such as entrance concourses and turnstiles.

The amplifier must be of suitable design and power capacity to maintain the above performance regardless of varying levels of background noise level, and modern systems are able to do this, adjusting automatically to the background noise level.

Intelligibility

Having enough sound volume does not necessarily ensure intelligibility (as anyone who has neighbours with a powerful hi-fi will know) and it is necessary to measure, specify and calculate sound levels in the 4 kHz octave band. Emergency messages often need to be complex and must not be misunderstood, therefore any testing of a sound system should replicate real use and not be confined to a simple reading out of 'one, two, three, testing ...'.

Reproduction of music

If a stadium is intended for multi-purpose use (which is now common) it must be suitable for hosting musical events, and music sets the most demanding criteria for sound quality. Designing the permanent sound installation to these criteria will be expensive – probably too expensive if the stadium is not often used for musical events. In that case temporary systems may have to be brought in for such events, but then very careful thought must be given as to how these temporary systems will be installed, how the stadium will perform acoustically when they are in use, and what the relationship between the permanent and temporary systems will be. Many acoustic problems arise from lack of forethought about these matters.

Provision for people who are blind or hard of hearing

A 'loop' system can be installed for certain areas so that blind and deaf people can listen to the commentary.

17.3.2 Design

Stadium shape and materials

Acoustic design begins not with the audio system, but with the shape and materials of the stadium itself. In completely open stadia the influence of shape and materials will be small, but in fully or extensively roofed stadia, to which the following notes are principally addressed, the effects of sound reflection and of noise build-up could be severe. As an obvious example, hard surfaces that are parallel to each other (such as an acoustically reflective roof over a hard floor; or two parallel walls facing each other) may generate echoes and/or excessive reverberation which reduce or destroy intelligibility.

This is not to suggest that reflected sounds from the crowd must be totally eliminated. In Wimbledon's Centre Court the buzz of crowd excitement that is reflected back at key moments by the metal roof above contributes greatly to the sensation of a closely shared experience; and in roofed football stadia the reflected aural ambience may add similarly to the excitement.

But these aspects must be kept under control. Particularly problematic acoustic areas are the corners of the stadium 'bowl', the seats below overhanging upper tiers (where sound intensities can build up even in open stadia) and the area under the roof of a fully covered stadium. If such a roof is domed the problem may be even worse because of the focusing effect of the curved surface. Generally, the underside of enclosed stadium roofs must always have acoustically absorbent surfaces, perhaps (if the roof is solid) as panels fixed to the soffit or suspended some distance below it, or (if it is a double-layer fabric

roof) by inserting an absorptive material between the two layers.

When planning fully enclosed stadia it is helpful to note that irregularly shaped plans may create fewer acoustic problems than rectangular or curved ones; that surfaces which are broken up by mouldings or irregularity probably create fewer problems than smooth flat ones; and that the careful location of acoustically absorbent materials is essential for reverberation control and the avoidance of echoes.

The above notes are of course only generalizations, and expert help should be sought.

Placement of speakers

Designing a system that will meet the performance criteria noted in Section 17.3.1 above is a matter for specialists and detailed advice would be out of place in this book. In the UK the Sports Council has published an excellent guide by the Football Stadia Advisory Design Council, which should be studied. But one aspect with which stadium designers will get directly involved is the pattern of sound distribution. There are three layouts: centralized speakers, partial distribution of speakers, and a completely distributed system of speakers.

A centralized system collects all the speakers together in one location, which makes it the cheapest of the three options. The disadvantage of this configuration is that there is less control over sound distribution if all the sound comes from one point, so that the sound may be too loud for those close to the speakers or too soft for those far away. A usual location in open stadia is at the end of the bowl, often adjoining or as part of a video display. In covered stadia a usual location is centrally above the pitch, suspended under the roof, and this may well be the most appropriate use of the centralized system – though such a central placement may exacerbate problems of reverberation time.

A partially distributed system has several clusters of speakers placed around the bowl at regularly spaced intervals – for instance, mounted on floodlighting masts. It is also called a 'satellite system' and is popular in covered stadia in the USA.

The fully distributed system, which is more popular in Europe, has an even distribution of speakers dispersed throughout the spectator areas. It is the most expensive of the three options because of the extensive cabling that is required. It may not provide good sound projection on to the playing area, so that an additional temporary system may be needed if this zone is used by the public, for example during concerts. But those disadvantages apart, this system does provide the best general sound quality of the three options and the best control. Speakers can be located on each tier of the bowl, and can separately serve each section of seating area. Good synchronization with video displays can be achieved, by fractional time delay, if necessary.

17.3.3 Control room

Whichever approach is adopted the public address system must be controlled from the stadium control room, which should overlook the pitch and have a secondary control from the police control room not far away. Other announcers using the system might be located in various parts of the ground and provision should be made for a microphone to be plugged in at pitch level for player interviews and crowd entertainment by a professional 'showman', although a radio microphone could be used for this purpose. Other control considerations are generally based around who should get what messages and what type of musical input is used, CD players now being in common use. Advertising would generally break through background music unless the advertising is co-ordinated with the video board which may make this a little difficult.

Stand-by power

As already mentioned in Section 17.1.2, a stand-by power system should be considered for major stadia so that safety announcements can be made in the event of a power failure. It is unlikely that batteries alone would be enough for a major system and therefore the emergency generator is often used for this purpose in conjunction with an immediate battery back-up system. As well as the stand-by generator and

battery room, an equipment room to accommodate the sound system must be included. This can be surprisingly large and should be as close to the control room as possible. Generally the system will be housed in racks about 800 mm by 600 mm in plan and standing up to 2 m high. In addition approximately 1.5 m should be allowed on all sides of the equipment to give easy access for servicing. A network of cable trays and trunking will commence at the equipment room and spread to all parts of the stadium. Their route through the stadium and its protection should be taken into account at an early stage.

17.3.4 Typical design criteria for a sound system

A sound system for a sports stadium may typically contain the following criteria.

1 The statement should set down the basis upon which the design is undertaken and on which its performance will be judged when installed.
2 It should state the standards and codes of practice upon which the design should be undertaken.
3 The systems function should be stated as:
   a to communicate emergency messages
   b to provide public address messages
   c to be used for other specific messages.
4 The frequency response should be stated. The following is an example.
   General public areas
   a Frequency response pre-equalization. Total system 100 Hz–6 kHz +6–3 dB (essentially smooth).
   b Frequency response post-equalization. Total system 100 Hz–6 kHz ±3 dB. Concourses, turnstiles and entrances.
   c Frequency response pre-equalization. Total system speech only 200 Hz–6 kHz +6–3 dB (essentially smooth).
   d Frequency response post-equalization. Total system speech only 200 Hz–6 kHz ±3 dB.
5 The intelligibility rating should be stated with a given occupancy noise.
6 Sound pressure levels and coverage should be quantified, such as the following example.

a Sound pressure level 6 dBA > L10 for 95 per cent of public

b Coverage to be within ± 2 dB for 95 per cent of public areas where L10 is sound pressure level which is exceeded 10 per cent of the time.

7 Different zones should be identified and the system should allow access to the different areas identified independently or as a group of areas. A typical range of zones is given below for guidance:

- north side stand
- north concourses
- north turnstiles
- south side stand
- south concourses
- south turnstiles
- east side stand
- east concourses
- east turnstiles
- west side stand
- west concourses
- west turnstiles
- executive suites
- car parks
- restaurants

8 A priority system should be indicated, with the police and security services given the highest priority. A typical order of priority might be as follows:

- police announcer in police control room
- management announcer in event control room
- general announcer and commentator
- pre-match events commentator
- musical entertainment and 'Disc-Jockey'
- advertising

9 Any additional requirements should be stated.

17.4 Fire-fighting systems

17.4.1 Stadium layout and construction

Designing for fire safety begins not with the installed systems, which are a second line of defence, but with the physical layout and method of construction of the stadium. Un-fortunately, building codes and regulations seldom give specific requirements for stadia, and applying those which apply to apparently similar building types will often be inappropriate, therefore we recommend early discussion with local fire and safety authorities.

Subject to the above it may be said that the method of fire compartmentation is a key issue when the stadium layout is being evolved. Appropriate methods of compartmentation will vary depending on the location, size and layout of the stadium, but it has become accepted practice to separate high-risk spaces (for example concessions where cooking is done) from other areas by means of fusible-link fire-shutter doors. This allows public concourses and stairs to avoid the multitude of fire doors which would otherwise be necessary, inhibiting the flow of spectators and thereby causing an escape risk.

17.4.2 Installed systems

Fire detection devices, fire alarms, and fire-fighting services will be necessary in high-risk zones such as cooking areas, and in the case of roofed stadia possibly throughout the building. The latter will certainly be true of a totally enclosed stadium where the arena may be used for trade exhibitions, or other events using combustible materials.

The detection and alarm systems will probably be linked in with other electronic services as described in Section 16.2 above, and the water-borne fire-fighting systems might include:

- automatic sprinkler systems;
- stand-pipes and fire-hose cabinets;
- fire protection water mains with connection points.

A thorough analysis of the stadium, its possible functions and patterns of use, its means of escape (see Chapter 12), and its materials of construction must be undertaken and discussed with the relevant authorities and with expert consultants as part of the briefing process.

17.5 Water supply and drainage services

17.5.1 Requirements

When thousands of people collect in one place for most of a day, particularly in summer, an enormous amount of liquid will be consumed and eventually recycled. We have already set out the requirements for toilet facilities but those appliances must have sufficient water to operate. Depending on the duration and type of the event water consumption in the order of 5 to 10 litres per person must be planned for if the taps are not to run dry. Equally important is the speed of distribution around the stadium to ensure an even pressure to all levels of the facility. If the stadium is planned as an integral part of the urban or rural infrastructure then it is likely that the established water mains will be sufficient to provide for this demand. It is important to be sure of this at an early stage however since water authorities are often not aware of the quantity of water required in a stadium. If the water mains is not large enough to provide sufficient pressure water storage must therefore be accommodated on site and pumped to its destination.

17.5.2 Installation design

There are a number of ways in which this water storage can be planned. Large underground storage tanks with a fully pumped circulation system or smaller storage tanks in each of the individual areas they service or a combination of both. The extent of water storage which can be accommodated in the building and therefore allow gravity feed to the outlets will be influenced by the building's design. Most local authorities require a minimum water storage to be on site and a percentage of that total to be sufficiently high to allow the outlets to be gravity fed. Another common requirement by local health authorities is that the outlets which are providing drinking water must be served directly off the mains to avoid the possibility of contamination while the water is in the storage tank. This can sometimes be a problem when the top level of the stadium is 20 to 30 m above the ground and the local water pressure is not sufficient to reach. This can be a problem when the rest of the facility is drawing off water from the same mains at its peak rate. Some South American stadia, for example Curitiba, have incorporated water towers into the general stadium and lighting installation design.

Whatever the methods used to provide sufficient water during an event the system will remain unused for much of the time. Depending on how long this is systems may require draining down between events. Drain down outlets must be provided to each storage tank and to each run of pipework if it does not drain directly to a storage tank. This requirement can usually be accommodated by the use of one drain down point per section of stadium provided it is placed at the lowest point of the system and free draining can take place. As well as being drained down between events, during the winter months in cold climates the storage tanks and pipes holding water must be protected from frost damage. This is usually done by the use of 'trace' heating to the pipework and tanks combined with the use of insulation to all exposed surfaces. If the system is inside a heated space trace heating will not be needed as long as the heating is operating on at least a minimum background setting which will stop temperatures dropping below freezing. After all this water has been allowed for and distributed to the correct areas of the stadium – including the pitch itself – a drainage system is required to take most of it away again. If the stadium is sited in an area where it can form part of a large urban infrastructure this is not likely to be a problem.

18

Maintenance

18.1 Introduction

18.1.1 A maintenance policy

Just as a motor car has a planned maintenance regime which requires certain procedures to be carried out at frequent intervals, and others less frequently, so stadium planners should develop a clear 'maintenance cycle' for their building and pitch which can be passed on to the owners in the form of a *Maintenance Manual*.

To apply such a policy successfully, the stadium management will require:

- well-trained personnel;
- suitable equipment for these people to operate;
- supplies of the correct quantity and quality of materials to be used;
- adequate space allocation in the stadium grounds for storage and workshops.

18.2 Pitch maintenance

18.2.1 Maintenance of natural grass

In theory, and given proper maintenance, a natural grass pitch will last almost indefinitely in contrast to synthetic surfaces which usually must be replaced every 5 to 10 years. But in practice grass pitches can suffer irreparable damage if maltreated. The actual lifetime will depend on factors such as:

- Intensity of wear. This varies enormously: in northern Europe play is limited to a couple of months in summer, giving around 50 hours of use per annum, whilst in southern Europe play is possible all year round giving 500 or more hours of play per annum.
- Type of usage. The harder the pitch, the more use it can take.

It is essential to follow the procedures briefly outlined below. More detailed guidance will be given by the consultant and specialist suppliers who specified the pitch in the first instance, as discussed in Section 5.1.3.

Mowing
This is an important activity and should take place at the correct growth period for the particular sport involved. At the latest grass should be cut when it reaches a height of 40 mm for hockey, and 60 mm for football. It should then be mown back to a length of 20 mm for hockey, 40 mm for football, and somewhat more for rugby.

Fertilization
The adding of nutrients is required periodically and is subject to an analysis of the residual substances which will be in the grass. It is important to get the timing and quantity of application right and these factors will be influenced by the sport concerned. A fertilizer and seed spreader should be used to ensure an accurate rate and distribution of seed.

Irrigation
Depending on how much natural precipitation occurs in the region, natural rainfall should be supplemented by a centrally controlled automatic

sprinkler system. Irrigation usually takes place at night as this is when the least amount of water will be lost to evaporation and the risk of 'burning' the grass is eliminated. An alternative and preferable irrigation method, if it can be afforded, is to install a network of porous pipes beneath the surface which feed water and a mixture of nutrients and pesticides to the roots from below as described in Section 5.1.3.

Many stadia are now recycling irrigation water from rainfall, using artificial pumping systems. Eighty per cent of the irrigation water used at Manchester United Football Club's Old Trafford stadium is recycled.

Drainage
A drainage system of either the 'passive' or 'active' type must be installed to ensure that excess water is rapidly removed from the pitch during irrigation and also during rain or other forms of precipitation. Systems are described in Section 5.1.3.

Repair and maintenance
Bald patches must be sown with new seed or repaired by the laying of pre-grown grass to make good damage from play. Thatch needs to be removed by aeration, perforation or slotting and sanding; and hard areas must be softened by the use of slots and holes to loosen the earth. Lawn aerators, perforators and sweepers should be used particularly where a spectator invasion of the pitch has occurred. The problem with this practice is that spectators' feet compact the earth and prevent good grass growth in the area affected.

Cleaning
Grass pitches should be cleaned on a regular routine basis just as for synthetic surfaces. See the section on cleaning below, much of which applies equally to natural grass.

Protection
Grass damage from frost and other sources of harm must be avoided. Underground heating is a useful method of protection against frost and an aid to faster snow removal, and is gaining popularity in colder climates. In Scandinavian countries metal foil sheeting is often used to protect pitches against frost.

18.3.2 Maintenance of artifical surfaces

While synthetic surfaces require less maintenance than natural grass it is wrong to assume that they can be laid and then forgotten about.

First, it may be necessary to enforce certain limitations on their use in accordance with manufacturers' recommendations. One of the most critical is a limitation on shoe spike length for athletic events. Second, regular repair, maintenance and cleaning is essential as described below.

Repair
When maintenance is carried out the original properties of the surface must not be changed. For example, if the surface is meant to be porous then the repair material must also be porous.

Markings will have to be replaced approximately every four years. Damaged sections – whether this is due to sports use, cuts and cracks, or ageing and flaking – must be repaired by removing the damaged portion and the area around it and replacing it with new material.

Cleaning
Dirt and harmful materials are produced in surprisingly large quantities. They include oil and fuel dropped by vehicles, chewing gum and paper from the participants, and sand, mown grass, leaves and air pollution from the environment. All of these must be cleaned from the surface regularly by either manual or mechanical means. Manual cleaning can include rinsing with water jets, sweeping, applying cleaning agents, and pulling up weeds. Sponge rollers, freezing agents for chewing gum, and high pressure water equipment are more specialized techniques.

General cleaning should be carried out to a regular routine either daily or weekly; and these operations should be supplemented with a major clean twice a year using a high pressure suction method for in-depth cleaning.

Artificial turf surfaces require a different cleaning approach using sweep-suction machines for both sanded and non-sanded turfs. Although almost unlimited use can be derived from these surfaces the markings need to be replaced regularly and there is also a need for watering or at least moistening of these surfaces, preferably with an automatic sprinkler system, so that the exact time of watering and quantity of water can be controlled. In the case of sanded surfaces the sand must be replaced from time to time, using sand of exactly the same quality.

Protection

It is advisable to protect the surface when it is used for activities other than sport, particularly when heavy vehicles are required in the setting-up process.

18.3 Stand maintenance

18.3.1 Design factors

The stand should be designed to have unobstructed floor surfaces without fixings and nooks and crannies in which rubbish can collect, and where cleaning machines cannot easily reach. For this reason riser-fixed seats (which leave the floor surface unobstructed) are far preferable to seats with tread or nose fixings (see Section 8.6.2). And bearing in mind that the seats themselves will also need periodic cleaning, and perhaps snow-removal, it is best to specify the tip-up variety.

Passageways should be wide enough for cleaning machines to move about easily and quickly. Expert advice should be obtained at an early design stage about the minimum widths needed for rubbish-collecting vehicles.

Finally, there should be a generous provision of service points such as compressed air outlets, water supply outlets, drainage outlets, rubbish disposal chutes and the like. Expert advice from cleaning specialists must be obtained at an early design stage to ensure that cleaning contractors can work efficiently in the completed stadium.

The following short checklist lists the most important points to be considered from the outset of design:

1 fixing of seats to steppings;

2 width of seatway to allow easy access;
3 width of seatway in front of first row to allow vehicular collection of rubbish;
4 rubbish disposal chutes near gangways;
5 water points at convenient points on each tier;
6 integral compressed air system with outlets on each tier;
7 rubbish compactors at ground level with access for heavy vehicles;
8 rubbish containers on each level of the stadium;
9 drains for the water used to clean the stands;
10 openable panels in balustrades to allow rubbish to be pushed through.

18.3.2 Cleaning methods

In addition to the work required to the pitch, the stands also need to be maintained and the most important part of this process is the cleaning of the stands after every event. There is sometimes a tendency to leave the cleaning of the stands until the period immediately before the next event rather than immediately after the event just finished. This is because if the events are some time apart the stands and particularly the seats will need cleaning again. This practice should be resisted for a number of reasons, the first of which is that during the time between events the stadium will appear very dirty and untidy which is bad for the image of the venue. Second, it is usually much easier to clean a stand immediately the event is over when spilt drinks and food have not yet stained the steppings. This is not a consideration when the stadium is holding events regularly but for the majority of venues there can be a number of weeks between events and at least the seats will need to be wiped down before the next occasion.

The process of cleaning can be very demanding in both personnel and equipment and it is wise to have thought about this at the early planning stage. The careful design of steps and details at the front of the tier are important if the cleaning process is to be made as easy as possible. The inclusion of openable panels in the front balustrade of a tier are very useful particularly if a rubbish container can be positioned in front or below this opening. The use of riser fixed seats rather than tread or nose fixings are also preferred for ease of cleaning. Bearing in mind that individual seats will also need to be cleaned and sometimes snow removed it is better that these are of the tip-up variety.

The amount of time it takes to clean a stadium will depend on its design but an approximate guide is 30 to 40 man hours to clean every 10 000 seats. Methods used for cleaning will depend on the equipment available and to some extent the type of rubbish to be removed. Stadia in the far east require more use of water since less paper is used for packaging and the fast food eaten at the grounds is usually more fluid. Sweeping the rubbish together along rows and then down the tier into a single pile can be done by manual brooms and also mechanical blowers which are faster. It is then transferred to sacks and taken down the stand by hand, perhaps using a service lift if one is available. More sophisticated methods are also available, such as the building in of a compressed air suction system which allows large diameter hoses to be connected at key points on each tier and the rubbish is sucked into the hose and down into the system where it collects in large compactors, loaded on to trucks and removed. At the Utrecht Stadium in Holland rubbish is blown and swept into the moat between the seating and the pitch, where it is then gathered and cleared.

19

Operation and funding

19.1 Stadium finances

19.1.1 Introduction

As stated at the beginning of this book stadium economics are such that it is difficult – though not impossible – for a stadium to earn a profit for its owners. The essential starting point for a viable development is therefore a comprehensive feasibility study comprising not only constructional matters but also an in-depth examination of how the stadium will operate financially.

The findings of the feasibility study will influence the design, form and content of the final project, and the study will need to address the following factors:

- initial *capital cost* of the project;
- anticipated *operating costs* of the stadium;
- expected *income generation*.

The notes below deal with each of these in turn, and the advice given is necessarily 'broad-brush'. There is so much difference between countries, between various types and sizes of stadia, and costs of all kinds change so much in the space of a few years, that specific data in a book such as this would be misleading. We therefore concentrate on principles rather than specifics. In a real project, cost consultants and other specialists would be retained to give precise guidance.

19.2 Capital costs

19.2.1 Cost per element

The pie chart in Figure 19.1 sets out in elemental form the construction costs of a new open-roof stadium in the UK. It is important to note that the 'external works' element does not include parking and similar landscaping works. These are likely to be significant elements in the total project cost of a new development, but not in a stadium refurbishment project.

Such elemental costs will vary from project to project depending on many factors, from site conditions to standards of finish in the private boxes. But several significant points do emerge. The first is that for an open-roofed stadium (which is the case here) the size of the 'services' element is less than for other types of buildings. This is a reflection of the fact that most of the stadium's large concourses and viewing terraces would have no form of heating or cooling.

Another item which has been identified as a separate element is the cost of the seats themselves. Fixed seating in a building would normally be included in the overall cost of 'fixings', but since seats are such an important cost item in the case of stadia we have identified them separately.

To blindly apply elemental cost factors from one project to another can be misleading and sometimes grossly inaccurate; but if sensibly handled, a comparative study could be very useful to a design team at the early stages of a new scheme.

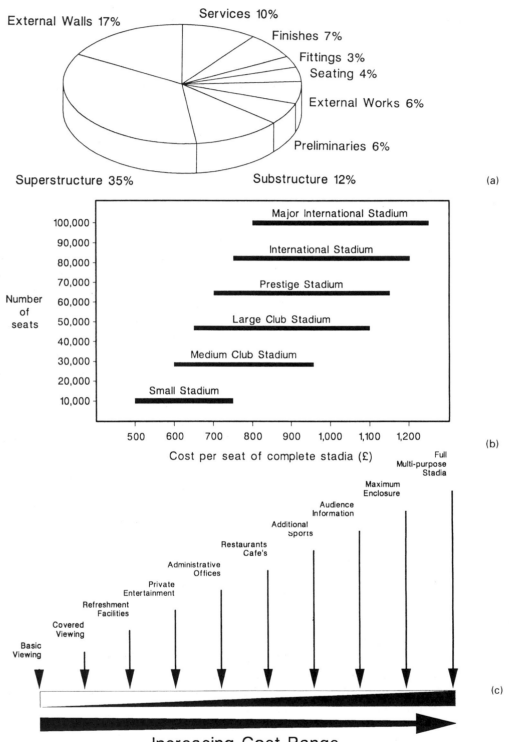

Figure 19.1 (a) Capital cost of a new open-roof stadium in the UK analysed by element. This chart illustrates only the principle involved: specific figures or ratios will not necessarily apply to other projects. (b) Capital costs for a range of UK stadia analysed in terms of 'cost per seat' rather than 'cost per element'. (c) Capital costs for new stadia in the UK related to quality of construction

19.2.2 Significant design factors

The following checklist identifies those factors which have a significant impact on stadium costs, and must be discussed fully with cost consultants at an early design stage:

1 Type of structure: see Table 7.2.
2 Number of seats and tiers in development: see Table 7.2.
3 Phasing of construction programme.
4 Quality of finish externally and internally.
5 Extent of roof coverage.
6 Quality and extent of car parking.
7 Quality and extent of external works.
8 Method of construction to be used.

19.2.3 Stadium conversion costs

Although not often a consideration in the USA, the conversion of standing terraces to seating is a major factor in the UK and to a lesser extent in the rest of Europe. The interest in this change from standing to seating is due not only to a sudden desire to provide comfortable viewing but a result of the Taylor Report into the Sheffield Hillsborough disaster in the UK, published in 1990 which recommended that within a set period of time most football grounds should become all-seated – a policy which is consistent with FIFA recommendations. But this move to all-seater stadia through all the divisions of the football league has since been modified.

A major problem in estimating the cost of this type of conversion is the extent of construction required to provide a base for the seat, as mentioned in Section 8.4.7. At one extreme, if an existing standing terrace is sound and profiled to the correct angle to provide a good standard of view, the conversion can be as simple as fixing the new seats directly on to the existing risers or treads. The other extreme can be when the existing concrete steppings are so poor that they have to be removed, or when ground conditions are poor and have to be reinforced and a new roof must be constructed to protect the installed seats from the elements. It is therefore impos-sible to give a reliable range of costs for this type of refurbishment.

In new stadia it is possible to design risers and treads in a way that allows for subsequent adaptation to either standing or seating.

19.2.4 Costings for a prototype stadium

Perhaps the most effective way of conveying an appreciation of new stadium costs is to examine a particular project. All real projects have a range of specific criteria which the planners must solve, and which combine to make it unique. For this exercise we have therefore chosen a prototype stadium project evolved in 1990 by LOBB Partnership and the Technical Unit for Sport at the Sports Council, headed by Geraint John. The object was to develop an idealized stadium design suitable for both the short-term needs of phased construction and the long-term needs of flex-ibility and expandability. The concept, for which YRM Anthony Hunt Associates were the struc-tural engineers, included the latest ideas in technology and construction techniques. A ca-pacity of 20 000 all-seated spectators was chosen, although the design would allow additional seating if needed. It included a full complement of modern catering and retail facilities below the stands and most importantly it can be developed in phases over a period of time. The ability to phase a development is crucial to a club wishing to 'remain open for business' during the period of redevelopment.

It must be emphasized that this project was not designed to be the cheapest solution. The aim was to combine:

- the best current practice in safety, comfort and viewing for all spectators;
- the best current practice in construction technology;
- the highest achievable aesthetic quality.

Phase 1
Construction of the first tier of the main stand possibly with a temporary roof. Administration offices and catering facilities are located at the rear.

Phase 2
The construction of the main stand opposite the first phase and the installation of floodlighting.
Phase 3
Completion of the first phase main grandstand and construction of the external concourse.
Phase 4
Construction of the first end stand.
Phase 5
Completion of the second end stand which completes the stadium 'bowl' internally.
Phase 6
Finally the roof is completed with a fixed or opening roof over the pitch.

19.3 Operating costs

18.3.1 Running costs versus first costs

In the enthusiasm of building a new stadium the capital costs of the project are usually investigated and planned in great detail while the running costs get much less attention. This is probably because the latter are less easy to quantify at the planning stage than capital costs, and also because running costs are felt to be a problem for tomorrow rather than today.

This is a counter-productive approach because the running costs over the lifetime of any building usually far exceed first construction cost – a trend that is likely to intensify as the costs of energy and labour continue to rise in most countries. The aim should be a stadium proposal that gives value for money not only in terms of first costs, but also in terms of:

- maintaining the playing surface and the fabric of the stadium in a safe and functionally satisfactory condition year after year;
- keeping the stadium, playing field and grounds clean;
- the actual operation of the stadium (staffing, lighting and heating, security, etc.) – the building should be designed in a way that will encourage efficiency in these matters.

In all these cases 'value for money' does not simply mean the least cost, but the least cost to maintain a pleasing, efficient and attractive stadium – because it is only by attracting paying customers that the owners can get a return on their investment.

Maintenance and cleaning have been covered in Chapter 18 and lighting, security and other services in Chapter 17. Some notes on staffing follow below. Of necessity these can only be very general: each case must be analysed individually.

19.3.2 Staffing costs

Staffing is a significant factor in the operating policy and will consist of a number of different categories of staff from well-trained specialists to general untrained operatives. A typical list of staff categories would include:

- administration;
- stadium maintenance and groundsmen;
- tradesmen including electricians, carpenters, gardeners, cleaners and general workmen;
- auxiliary unqualified workers;
- additional staff for event days;
- stewards;
- security personnel.

Adequate accommodation must be provided for all these people and the equipment they will need (see Chapter 15).

19.4 Income generation

19.4.1 Sources of funds

The stadium which is fully funded by the community is probably the most common around the world, but the significance of private finance is growing, with more and more money being generated by the top sports clubs and individuals. In the USA private financing has usually been limited to the smaller indoor venues, accommodating up to 200 events a year, to ensure their viability. Large stadia can generally attract only around 20 to perhaps 75 event days a year and therefore are hard pressed to justify the significant financing necessary. This limitation on event days is largely due to the fact that most stadia have an open roof making them vulnerable to the elements and also that there are a limited number of events which can attract an audience of 50 000 to 100 000 spectators. Pop groups these days prefer to book a venue for three nights at an arena of 20 000 than one night of 60 000 because if all three nights are not sold out they can always cancel the last night rather than go on stage to a half full stadium lacking atmosphere. Completely covered or domed stadia are able to achieve in the order of 200 event days a year and there have been studies done which show that up to 250 or even 300 is possible with the increased multi-purpose use the enclosure provides.

Stadium funding nowadays is usually a combination of both private and public money using a number of different methods to get on the balance sheet. We set out below several of these methods and explain the usual form they take, though in practice many variations will be encountered.

Sponsorship

Private companies justify the injection of capital into a stadium development for a whole range of reasons from loving the sport with no need for a return on the money invested, to a planned commercial investment in return for some form of franchise. A major drinks company may inject millions in return for their drink being sold exclusively in the stadium. This can also be true for other fast-food products.

Advertising

The greater the number of event days a year at the venue the more spectators will attend and the greater the value of the advertising rights. If the events are televised this will also significantly increase the revenue generated. A combination of advertising positions is available around any stadium from fixed display boards on the perimeter of the ground to fixed or movable strip boards around the outside of the pitch. Front edges of roofs and upper balconies can also be utilized but the aesthetic balance of the stadium can be ruined if this is not carefully judged. Video display boards and colour matrix score boards can also be used to show advertising before and after play.

Seating

The most obvious area of revenue generation is selling the seats themselves and a range of standards and positions is important to maximize the return. Private hospitality areas and club enclosures are all part of providing this range of seats to everyone wanting to attend the event and have the advantage of usually being paid for in advance. These more private facilities can be a deciding factor in the viability of a new development. In Europe seat sales tend to account for the major proportion of stadia income but in the USA income from seating ranks lower than income from concessions.

Named stadia

There have been a significant number of stadia around the world which have been largely funded by a company in return for naming the stadium after that company. This can be another form of advertising but not necessarily. The Carrier Corporation in the USA contributed several million dollars to the construction of the domed stadium at Syracuse University now known as the Carrier Dome.

Concessions

Selling concessions in a stadium is effectively letting space to the food and beverage industry to sell their goods and merchandise at the grounds. It can be the source of significant revenue but the concession areas must be well planned at an early stage to ensure they are attractive to the prospective competing concession holders. A percentage of the sales made is often part of the deal but this will vary with the venue.

Parking

Car, bus and bike parking is often limited at a stadium and therefore the demand can be exploited by charging for this facility. Depending on the number of vehicles accommodated the revenue generated can be substantial as parking charges are often a quarter to a half of the actual ticket price for the event.

Club funding

If a stadium is not actually owned by a club but by an independent organization then the club which uses the facilities can support the venue by injecting initial capital. In return the club will usually expect some part of the equity of the grounds or a return of the income generated.

Land deals

An increasing number of football clubs in the UK are finding this method to be suitable to their situation where they lack the funding to improve their grounds but own the land on which it sits. Provided their land is of sufficient value they can often pay for a new facility on less valuable land by the sale of their existing site. Land swap can also include the local authority where an area of land surplus to the local authority's requirements can be sold to the club so that they move from their original location.

Syndication

This is simply where a group of companies or individuals come together to fund the development. Their motives can vary and are not important provided certain similarities exist in their expectations of the new facility.

Land donation

A public authority may feel that there is sufficient benefit to the community in retaining a facility in its area to justify providing land for its use. Often this method of donation is done because it is the only asset the city owns and the least difficult to administer.

Tax reductions

In countries where the control of local taxes is within the jurisdiction of the authority it can reduce these taxes to benefit certain developments. This method is not possible in the UK but in the USA a city authority which would like to assist in the development of a stadium can reduce or defer its local taxes on the development.

Tax increase

The converse of the above approach and one which can also only operate under similar conditions is where a city uses revenue from a tax or introduces a new tax in order to pay for a stadium development. A popular method in the USA is the tourist tax where a percentage is added to hotel and motel bills so that people coming into the city help pay for the facility.

Government bonds

A range of different types of bonds are used in countries where local authorities, as well as central government, are allowed to raise them. These bonds can vary from General Obligation Bonds where the city sells bonds to finance the construction of a facility and these are paid back from the general city revenue funds, to the Revenue Bond which is sold and then paid back from the revenue generated at the facility when it is operational.

Club debentures and bonds

A quite different type of bond is often used in the UK to fund new development and that is where members of the public are offered the right to buy a seat for a fixed period of time. The period can be from a few years to 125 years which is a period used recently by a number of football clubs. This method of funding allows the club to finance new development and still maintain their future income from seat sales.

Grants

By far the most attractive method of funding as far as the developer is concerned is the direct grant from a city or local authority. A grant may be offered for a number of reasons and can be very substantial. Florida in the USA for example is reported to be offering $30 million for a professional team to move into the state. Grants can also take the form of specific financial assistance with such things as road systems, drainage and general infrastructure which can be significant at the early stages of development.

Betting revenue

Sometimes this is a politically sensitive subject, but the betting revenue which accrues from sport is enormous. Although largely generated from horse-racing, all sports promote some degree of betting. In countries where it is possible to reinvest a proportion of the profits the sports facilities will benefit. In the USA betting on American football and baseball is illegal but it is not in the UK and a number of other countries, and it is not uncommon to find a betting outlet at a sports ground.

Outside income

Income can be generated to help finance a project from outside the main operating area of the development. This usually involves the joint development of the stadium with other, perhaps more financially viable activities. Other developments can range from those directly related such as sports and health clubs to completely unrelated activities such as offices and workshops.

19.5 Controlling costs and revenues

19.5.1 Typical headings

If the feasibility study indicates that all the above factors can be balanced to give a viable project, the next step is to ensure effective financial control in all parts of the facility. This includes the careful recording and checking of all transactions for both income and expenditure. It is important that the individual sources of income and expenditure are identified to allow their assessment at a later date.

We list below typical headings for these individual categories. They should be read subject to the proviso that some carry very much more weight than others. The outgoing cost of financing the capital can account for as much as 70 per cent of the total.

Income
1 Spectator attendance
2 Visitors to the ground
3 Club income from membership
4 Advertising revenue
5 Television revenue
6 Ground rental for events

Expenditure
1 Staff costs

2 Administration costs
3 Maintenance expenses
4 Public relations
5 Operation costs
6 Fuel and energy
7 Machinery and repairs
8 Events costs
9 Taxation (if applicable)
10 Financing and depreciation

19.5.2 Club participation policy

An important aspect of operational policy relates to the players who use a stadium owned and run by a club. The skill of the players, managers and trainers largely dictates the success of the team, and the success of the team in turn determines the financial strength of the club. A signficant factor in this equation is the cost of 'buying' players in professional sport and the cost of training them. The league system is ideal for training as it gives all clubs a chance to find new and promising players who they can train to their financial benefit, but the North American college system is probably even better as it effectively pushes the cost of training on to the educational system. The cost of training players in American football and baseball is therefore relatively low.

It also benefits the financial stability of a sport to limit the number of teams who can take part, although this is against the principles of most amateur sports since they believe in as wide an involvement as possible. Rugby Union in the UK for example has something in the order of 2000 registered clubs whilst at the same time the Football League in the UK is having a hard time preventing their league reducing from approximately 60 clubs. The theory is that if the number of top clubs is reduced and the number of spectators at least stays the same there will be more spectators at the clubs who do survive. Eliminate your competitors and so increase your market share, obviously it is inevitable that sport becomes a market place when the financial risks and profits are so high.

One of the reasons for the perceived success of American sport is because the governing bodies of American football and baseball limit the number of clubs they allow to play in their competition by not granting playing franchises to new clubs. This has increased demand for the clubs who do have a playing franchise among the cities of the USA since they value the recognition and financial advantages a major league club brings to their community. The asset they believe they acquire from a team being based in their city can vary from the extra cultural perspective to the community to the secondary spending from out of town fans on restaurants and hotels in the city. This situation puts the sports club in a very strong position to negotiate the terms of their moving to a city or their continued presence in a city. It is not uncommon for a club to have a new stadium built for it by the city authorities and even a cash payment for the move.

19.6 Conclusion

Stadia must be designed to an exacting set of financial controls in terms of both their initial capital cost and their ongoing operating costs by building into the design the maximum potential for generating revenue. This is the beginning and the end of all developments but for stadia the sums are often more difficult to 'make work' than other forms of development and therefore there is less room to make mistakes in their financial planning as many organizations have found to their cost in the past. Modern, safe, efficient and beautiful new stadia are possible, but if they are to survive anywhere near as long as those our ancestors have handed down to us they must also prove themselves on the balance sheet.

20

Environmentally Sustainable Development (ESD)

20.1 Environmental considerations

20.1.1 Visual aspect

Environmentally sustainable development, or ESD for short, is becoming an increasingly important consideration for buildings of the future. Care and respect for the environment should be an integral part of the design and development process, and should cover not only the practical aspects, such as materials, energy and waste, but also the visual impact of the building and hence its effect on the quality of life.

It is the responsibility of designers to create buildings which protect and potentially enhance the environment and community in general, and ensure that the visual environment is not polluted with ugly buildings. This chapter takes these areas into consideration but deals more specifically with the material aspects of environmental pollution.

20.1.2 Energy efficiency

One of the most important aspects an architect must consider is the amount of energy a building will use, since the less energy a building uses, the less fuel will be required to create that energy. Consideration should be given to the possibility of utilizing Combined Heat and Power (CHP) and/or the energy potential of the building structure or site. Power from natural, renewable sources of energy such as the wind, the sea, hydroelectricity and the sun could also be

investigated, and this would result in a reduction of the use of finite energy resources and the associated energy usage in the manufacturing and building processes. Of course, decisions related to the use of energy efficient buildings have to take capital and recurrent costs into account.

Approximately fifty per cent of the UK's annual carbon dioxide emission is generated from buildings, and this is typical for most other industrialized nations. Better application of cost-effective current technology and management of building services and materials could reduce and minimize the related environmental impacts. Good design and management would also improve the quality of the indoor environment and subsequently the health and wellbeing of its occupants. Discharges to land and water need to be monitored to negate or minimize contamination and protect wildlife habitats. Noise and traffic are further identified as major pollutants which need to be addressed in the construction and servicing of developments.

20.1.3 Waste

Strategic waste management is the key to reducing costs, not only in the use of materials but in their disposal and the related environmental impact. Waste should be evaluated from the raw material source rather than just the demolition process, and purchasing and recycling strategies are therefore important components to incorporate into waste management.

An example of this, in practical terms, would be the use of wood products from managed forests, thereby avoiding hardwood from non-renewable sources such as the rain-forests. This practice means the use of recycled and recyclable materials whenever possible, both in the design and operation of the building.

Because of the function of stadia, designers also need to take into account problems such as the packaging and type of consumer goods which are likely to be brought into the building, bearing in mind whether they are produced from recycled materials and designed to be recycled. The quantity of waste produced by spectators is enormous and although this is largely a management problem, it is not without its implications at the design stage. Athletes and spectators should be provided with food and drink, but in a way which minimizes the effect on the environment.

20.1.4 Use of materials

The selection and assessment of the source of materials used in the construction of buildings should be carried out on the basis of life cycle costs and the environmental impact. Practically this may suggest where possible the use of natural materials, e.g. wood from renewable sources instead of steel and concrete, and/or recycled materials. In addition, consideration should be given to factors such as energy used and pollution generated during extraction, processing, manufacture, transport, treatment and disposal of these materials. It is a good idea to consider the life of the materials to be used in construction in order to extend the period before replacement is needed.

Materials which are produced using toxic substances should be avoided, whilst those performing a similar function should be selected on the basis of least toxicity, e.g. boron-treated wood as opposed to lindane-treated wood and water-based rather than solvent-based paints. Components containing CFCs and HCFCs such as extruded polystyrene, should be avoided along with materials that emit volatile organic substances such as formaldehyde, tuolene etc. Even the use of PVCs is under re-examination

and future research may help to give further guidance on this.

20.1.5 Water conservation

Water is a valued resource and methods for conservation should play an integral part in service design. Consideration should be given to water saving initiatives such as rainwater collection which can then be stored around the stadium and used for cleaning and toilet flushing. More importantly, it can be used for watering the grass pitch, as at the Manchester United Ground. Grey water recycling is another method of conserving water, whilst economies can also be made by using water restrictors, cistern control, vacuum toilets and leak detectors.

20.1.6 Power and energy

There is a great potential for effective energy management in stadia. Stadium roofs are enormous and therefore the opportunity exists for the utilization of both passive and active solar power, encompassing solar panels and photovoltaic cells. This is a good illustration of the use of the energy potential of the site and structure, another example of which is CHP.

20.2 The Olympic Movement and the environment

20.2.1 Introduction

The International Olympic Committee (IOC) has added care for the environment to its objectives of Sport and Culture. The following notes, taken from the *IAKS Journal S & B*, April 1995, explain the IOC position and objectives, following the first World Conference on Sport and the Environment.

> The idea that 'future generations should not inherit an environmental capital inferior to that bequeathed to the present generation' has progressively been accepted as an element of sustainable development.

Olympism

Olympism is a philosophy of life, exalting and combining in a balanced whole the qualities of body, will and mind. Blending sport with culture and education, Olympism seeks to create a way of life based on the joy found in effort, the educational values of good example and respect for universal fundamental ethical principles.

The goal of Olympism is to place everywhere sport at the service of the harmonious development of man, with a view to encouraging the establishment of a peaceful society concerned with the preservation of human dignity.

The goal of the Olympic Movement is to contribute to building a peaceful and better world by educating youth through sport practised without discrimination of any kind and in the Olympic spirit, which requires mutual understanding with a spirit of friendship, solidarity and fair-play.

The role of the IOC is to lead the promotion of Olympism in accordance with the Olympic Charter. For that purpose, the IOC seeks that the Olympic Games are held in conditions which demonstrate a responsible concern for environmental issues, and collaborates with the competent public or private organizations and authorities in the endeavour to place sport at the service of humanity.

The Olympic Movement and the environment

As an integral part of society, the Olympic Movement is also concerned with the environment. The history of sports practice amply shows how it has developed, become more sophisticated, and modernized over time. Large stadiums with a communications network and extensive car parks are now necessary. Every large-scale sports event implies the gathering of a crowd of spectators who must be welcomed, seated, fed, entertained, informed and looked after. The result is often an impact on the environment that should not be ignored.

Sport and the environment are factors in the well-being of humanity, and both are linked in the sense that one influences the other and vice-versa. The Olympic Movement is a universal one, almost all of whose members are young athletes and voluntary officials. As an integral part of society, they aspire to live in peace in a non-polluted world where the fauna and forests, rivers and lakes, plants and animals are protected for the well-being of mankind.

The Olympic Movement has become a real social force of global significance that reaches people at all levels in all cultures . . . Aware of its responsibility and in accordance with the fundamental principles set out in the Olympic Charter, the IOC, in its capacity as coordinator of the Olympic Movement, has resolved to broaden its field of action in environmental matters.

The Olympic Games and the environment

The IOC wants the Games to be an exemplary event in this respect. One of the first initiatives has been to include in the list of specifications of the cities bidding a file relating to new requirements in terms of the environment. These requirements are as follows:

- Supply an official guarantee from the competent authorities stating that all the work necessary for the organization of the Games will comply with local, regional and national legislation and regulations regarding town and country planning and the protection of the environment.
- Indicate whether impact studies have been carried out with a view to the harmonious and natural integration of the Olympic Games into the environment and whether they have been established by official bodies or bodies recognized as authoritative and scientifically competent.
- State whether the ecological organizations in the city, region or country have been informed or consulted. If this is the case, state their opinions and attitudes regarding the candidature. Indicate the size of these organizations and their representivity.
- Describe the plans for waste treatment and energy management, particularly for the Olympic Village, competition venues and media sites.

- Indicate whether the staging of the Games will give rise to advanced technology being developed in the area of environmental protection and if so, describe this.
- Indicate the efforts to be undertaken regarding transport, particularly with a view to minimizing atmospheric pollution.

It is vital that all studies relating to infrastructure take environmental parameters into account from the outset, and be geared towards avoiding, or at least minimizing, any damage to the environment. These criteria are merely minimum standards which the cities are called upon to develop and expand. The current trend is actually in this direction, as environmental measures are occupying an increasingly large place in the candidature file and are of particular importance in the choice of the host city. The IOC commission responsible for evaluating the candidatures now includes an environmental expert.

20.2.2 Olympic facilities

The facilities for the Winter Olympics in Lillehammer were the first live demonstration in built form, of energy and environmentally conscious buildings. The successful Sydney bid for the Olympics in the year 2000 featured a major case for environmental issues and this was one of the main reasons for the success of their bid. (See Fig. 20.1 and Appendix 3).

So what does all this mean for stadium design?

20.3 The environment friendly stadium

Unfortunately environmentally responsible stadia are few and far between, if they exist at all. This part of the chapter is therefore aimed at heightening awareness of what can be done in designing environmentally responsible stadia.

20.3.1 Energy use

There are three main aims for the use of energy in stadia: firstly to minimize the demand for energy; secondly to supply as much of the reduced demand for energy as possible from energy resources which are renewable; and thirdly to meet the remaining energy demand with efficient use of the cleanest possible nonrenewable fuel.

In order to achieve the aim of minimizing the amount of energy used, energy efficient appliances are needed in the stadium, including good control and information systems as well as educational policies to help raise user awareness.

The second issue of using renewable energy sources has become a stated aim of the International Olympic Committee and is applicable for all Olympic stadia (see 20.2.1). The IOC uses the phrase 'widest possible use of renewable sources of energy' in its documentation to bidding cities for the Olympic Games. Energy usage should be based on a detailed 'load profile of the venue' to match its needs with available renewable resources of the area. The designer needs to develop a clear understanding between the relationship of base energy loads and peak energy loads, particularly where the value is to be multipurpose. There will also be considerable differences in energy usage between event days and non-event days when only the ancillary facilities will be in use with relatively low energy demands.

The third aim recognizes that different fuels have different levels of environmental impacts. Cost cannot be the only factor that influences a decision when choosing an energy source for a stadium because the market does not currently reflect the true environmental impact of conventional energy sources. One criterion must be to reduce CO_2 emissions which will call for new standards of energy production. This has already taken place in some parts of the world where all new developments, including stadia, require the use of improved energy sources such as solar water heating.

Energy standards must therefore respond to the needs of the whole community for improving performance and cannot be judged on cost alone, in the same way that fire safety issues would not be assessed solely on capital cost criteria. The single greatest impact of energy use in the latter part of the twentieth century is the greenhouse effect, which is largely the result of the growth in CO_2 emissions since the Industrial Revolution. A number of countries around the world are committed to a programme of reducing CO_2 emissions and this should, therefore, be a clear aim in stadia design. It is imperative to aim to minimize the CO_2 emissions throughout the complete life cycle of the building, from construction through use and eventually to its demolition. A large part of this third objective is to attempt to reduce the dependence on mains electricity supplied from the national grid.

20.3.2 Saving energy

To many people electricity appears to be a 'clean' fuel in use but it has a significant environmental impact at its point of production. It is interesting to note that electricity generated in coal-fired power stations, which emit high levels of CO_2, allows only 35 per cent of the energy generated in many cases to be distributed to the actual socket as usable power. The remaining 65 per cent of energy is lost through the heat from the cooling towers or through the transmission in the grid. Heating water by gas can produce around 70 per cent less CO_2 emissions than by electricity, and solar water heating, supplemented by a gas back-up, can achieve a 90 per cent reduction or more in certain parts of the world. Certainly self-generation of energy in stadia using photovoltaic cells, which is the conversion of sunlight into electricity, is becoming more viable. Cladding panels are now being manufactured with built-in photo cells which not only clad the building but also generate its electricity. As a guide, a photovoltaic array in a stadium of around 2500 square metres could produce up to 40 per cent of the venue's energy requirements. The roof of a stadium is a very large area which can be used for such a purpose.

Energy can also be recovered from waste water by heat exchange, with the possibility that where there is a suitable nearby river or water area, heat can be recovered. Wind fans are another possibility which could be considered, along with recycling waste energy from plant systems and the use of CHP, which should be examined.

20.3.3 Energy load profile

In order to develop a true load profile for a stadium it is necessary to look at each of the energy consuming components of the venue.

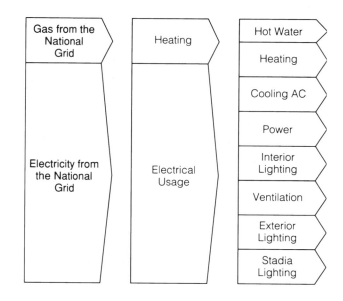

Figure 20.1 A typical energy load profile.

The illustration shows a typical load profile for a stadium which represents a starting point against which future stadia projects may be compared. The exact values of each of the energy components will vary between vanues but by starting to set down this type of data we can build up a stock of knowledge on the subject for future comparison and analysis.

20.4 Lighting

20.4.1 Use of daylight

An overriding aspect of stadia design should be to allow us much daylight as possible into the building, thus avoiding the use of artificial lighting as much as possible. Translucent roofs can provide daylight to the spectator areas and this is not only beneficial from an energy point of view but is also preferred by spectators, providing a more pleasant outdoor 'ambience' for the user. The stadium is, after all, a building which has its origins in outdoor sports.

Moreover, more natural lighting also improves the quality of growing conditions for the central pitch area. Indeed some existing stadia have replaced solid roof areas over spectator areas with translucent roofing for this reason.

20.4.2 Artificial lighting

Flood lighting

The first and perhaps the most obvious energy using component is the flood lighting for the event area. The lighting of this space requires a huge amount of energy, perhaps to the order of 100 to 150 Mwh/y, which means that there are considerable savings to be made in this area through more efficient light fittings, rationalized lighting levels, improved distribution, maintenance and control systems. Light fittings for pitch lighting are gradually improving in their efficiency but really major leaps forward in technology could be just around the corner. Microwave sulphur lamps which produce light by the microwaving of argon and sulphur gases achieve a greatly extended life. Microwaves convert the gas into a plasma which produces a pure white light with a continuous spectrum very similar to natural daylight, which is ideal for arena lighting. There are a number of current prototypes which indicate that they will be ten per cent more efficient than metal halide lamps. This technology is developing and improving rapidly.

Indoor lighting

In addition to the lighting of the actual event area, indoor lighting is also a significant factor in stadia design because of the large public areas involved. There are, of course, minimum lighting levels, laid down by local authorities, required for all buildings, but a stadium which is designed to achieve ESD should take into account a number of factors which can minimize the amount of artificial indoor lighting necessary. Natural daylight should be used as much as possible and taken into account when designing the building structure. This can be achieved either by using light 'shelves' at the perimeter of the building to reflect natural light into internal spaces, or perhaps through the use of light wells to bring daylight into the building.

The support areas of accommodation in a stadium are often buried deep under the spectator areas and those who work in and operate the building will benefit from more naturally lit spaces. Similarly, restaurants and social spaces will also benefit. Light wells and atria are two devices for achieving this.

Light control

Artificial light fittings should be low-energy fittings with an efficient control method, perhaps using photocells to control when lights need to be used and movement sensors to switch lights on and off in infreuquently used spaces.

The illumination of external spaces is another major user of energy and is required for both security and public safety. Significant improvements are also evolving in this area in lamp and control technology and when combined with careful distribution of fittings around the exterior of the stadium can minimize the amount of energy required in this zone of the complex.

20.5 Water heating

20.5.1 Energy efficiency

In order to minimize the energy demands for water heating, the distribution of hot water through a stadium should be carefully considered at the design stage, particularly where hot water is required to all public toilet outlets. Experience shows that hot water taps in public toilets in stadia are rarely used and their installation can be minimized where possible. The energy and water efficient design of appliances should also be considered, using mixer spray taps and water efficient shower heads in the players' changing areas. Solar energy can be a significant contributor to water heating in some parts of the world. However, a major problem in stadia is the intermittent use of hot water and the consequential inefficiency due to its loss in storage. An instantaneous gas water heating system could provide overall efficiencies and may be considered for peak loads.

20.6 Ventilation and cooling

20.6.1 Natural ventilation

Although the primary focus of any stadium is the event area, the off-field activities also play a significant role on both event days and non-event days. If a stadium is to be used for a range of functions it must be commercially successful and therefore these spaces must provide an acceptable level of comfort in terms of temperature, air quality and humidity. The energy used in cooling and air-conditioning can be significant and, therefore, areas that require this type of environmental control must be carefully considered. Comfortable conditions can be achieved in many parts of the stadium, including public concourses, through the use of natural ventilation using 'stack' effect ventilators and venturi effect extract supplemented by extract fans without resorting to artificial cooling. This type of approach must be considered at a very early design stage as its use will fundamentally influence the stadium's planning and sectional layout. This is the case even in the more tropical areas of the world where good air movement and the removal of hot air can be facilitated by the use of thermal chimneys throughout the structure. A good example of this approach is the Royal Selangor Turf Club grandstand in Kuala Lumpur, Malaysia, where the central atrium acted as a large 'chimney' to the warmed air and induced a through ventilation in the spaces leading off this central core (see Fig. 4.25).

20.6.2 Temperature

The position of glazing on a stadium should also be controlled to ensure minimum solar radiation build-up within internal spaces and perhaps protected at certain times of the day using sun awnings. Insulation from both heat and cold is also an important element in ensuring the minimum possible energy usage, although it must be borne in mind that conditions for watching sport and many other events don't need to be the same as for sitting quietly in an office or at home. Because of this a more flexible approach to the environment parameters to which stadia are being designed must also be taken into account. A typical temperature range for an office building may be from 20 to 22 degrees, whereas an acceptable temperature range for sitting in a stadium to watch an event may be between 18 and 26 degrees. This decision on its own may signficantly reduce the energy demands on a venue. It is also important to remember that air movement itself can reduce perceived temperature to quite a large degree. For instance, it can be shown that ventilation rates of around five air changes per hour, with a typical speed of say 0.23 metres per second, can in fact reduce the temperature by around 1 to 1.5°C.

20.7 Heating

In temperature climates some form of heating will be required in many of the ancillary areas of a stadium, but in calculating the heating needed with an aim to reducing the energy necessary to achieve those heat levels, the thermal mass of the structure itself must be taken into account. This thermal mass, together with the secondary heat gain from spectators and the appliances in the venue, must be calculated as these will have quite an effect on the extent of energy consuming heating required in the stadium. In the same way as the extent of external fenestration and its orientation is a major factor in cooling, so it is with heating. Heat radiation build-up from the sun's energy can be a significant contributor to reducing the extent of artificial energy required to achieve comfortable temperatures. Carefully positioned insulation to avoid cold bridges in the external fabric of the structure can improve the perceived comfort levels within the space.

From studies we have conducted on recently designed stadia, it is interesting to note that although the large spectator events create considerable peaks in the overall base load of energy consumption, the energy demand from general administration and operational functions, together with that required for security lighting through the year may have a total energy demand of half of the stadium's total annual energy use. A total annual energy usage for a major multi-purpose stadium could be in the order of 4000 to 4250 Mwh/y (megawatt hours per year). The total energy usage for the Melbourne Cricket Ground in Australia, for example, is 4200 Mwh/y and it has an annual attendance of around 2.93 million spectators. Some interesting comparisons can be derived from this type of information as regards the energy usage per spectator.

20.8 Life cycle cost analysis

20.8.1 Long-term costs

Some technologies will not only reduce running costs but are likely to reduce capital costs as well. Others may be initially more expensive in terms of capital cost but because they reduce the running costs of a stadium, they will prove to be cheaper in the long term. Natural ventilation and daylighting options may well lead to cheaper stadia than conventional equivalents so it is

important to analyse the energy usage of any stadium, not just in terms of its initial capital cost but also its long-term life cycle costing. This life cycle assessment (LCA) takes into account not only capital cost but also the running cost, the maintenance cost and replacement costs over its life cycle. Life cycle assessment has been described in the past as 'from cradle to the grave' accounting of the inputs and outputs of the energy usage of a building.

20.8.2 Aspects to consider

LCA examines all the energy and raw materials used, as well as the emissions to air, water and solid waste over the entire life cycle of a product or material. This takes into account the extraction of the raw material through its production, distribution, use and disposal. We suggest that the full life cycle assessment of a stadium should be taken into account at an initial design stage. Unfortunately there is very little historical information available to be able to establish rules of thumb or good practice, or even best practice examples. It is only by applying our minds to new developments, quantifying these factors and publishing the results, that we will start to achieve truly environmentally sustainable stadia.

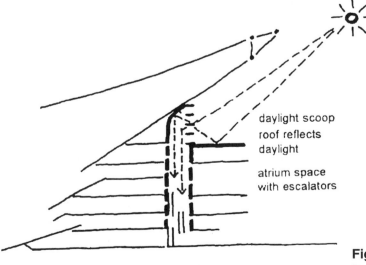

DAYLIGHT SCOOP

Figure 20.2 Australia Stadium 2000, Sydney. Daylight scoop feature of successful bid (see p.224 and Appendix 3). Architect: HOK + LOBB.

21

Stadia and tourism

21.1 Introduction

Stadia have a role in helping to create a vibrant image for a town or city, and at their best can be used as part of the tourism infrastructure and appeal of a city. The actual events in the stadium attract tourists but also these landmark buildings themselves can act as magnets and draw visitors to them. In addition the emergence of the sports visitor attractions, museums and halls of fame in the stadium are increasing its market appeal. A good example is Barcelona's Nou-camp Stadium which attracts a huge number of visitors each year. The success of the new Huddersfield Stadium with its blue roof and exciting shapes has had a major impact on the city itself and the Toronto Skydome has clearly become part of the image of that city. Images of these venues appear in tourist brochures as an attraction of the city or town. Television coverage of major events such as the World Cup in football or rugby and the Olympic Games have brought images of dramatic and often aesthetically memorable stadia into the living rooms of millions of people. The tourism impact of such coverage for a city is immense.

A considerable amount of research has been carried out on these stadia tourism concepts, with some of this work in North America reviewing the interdependency between the stadia and city redevelopment. The impact of the Olympic Games and the legacy of the facility provision and the implications for urban areas is a favourite subject for discussion. It has been suggested that many cities are 'clamouring' for new stadia and arenas because of their potential as 'flagships' in urban regeneration and in the development of entertainment districts. It has been asserted that the mass popularity of sports and the close relationship between civic identity and local teams makes the construction of sports facilities an important tool for promoting public and private spending aimed at solving the problems of civic development.

21.2 Stadia and tourism

The concept of multi-purpose utilization can help to stimulate wide economic regional regeneration as has been the case in the USA, and proposals for many new stadia are particularly notable as regenerative projects, in which there is an important potential for tourism. Sports stadia are becoming more readily integrated and accepted as a fundamental component of the leisure industry in general. As well as the benefits that accrue to the owners from successful operations, local authorities, regional and national governments are increasingly realizing that stadia and arenas can play a vital role in creating a vibrant image and contributing to the economic and social wealth of the community in which they are located.

An essential feature of a city's ability to host a major league sports team, or indeed a primary sporting event or festival, is the provision of modern, high capacity stadia and arenas. The economic rewards inherent in major sporting activities have stimulated considerable development in facilities, particularly throughout the USA. The public sector has recognized the added value of investment in stadia and accepts that they can rarely be expected to make a profit and that the political risk involved is outweighed by wider economic gains for their community.

A good example of a new stadium being integrated into the wider urban planning of a city is in Baltimore, USA, where Oriole Park, designed by HOK, was sited to anchor the south side of the city's waterfront regeneration scheme. This effectively turned the derelict Camden Yards docklands into an extension of a thriving entertainment and tourist centre, creating a landmark in destination marketing. The high-rise buildings of downtown Baltimore can be seen towering over the stadium creating a view for its 46 000 visitors of the city's commercial and economic centre. The economic impact of this development clearly shows the potential of stadia to generate tourist visits with 1.6 million fans (that is 46% of all fans) coming from out of town, with 24% of those coming from outside of the Washington DC area, with many staying overnight in the Baltimore area. This ability to generate secondary spend in and around the stadium is a critical factor. Spending on merchandise inside the facility, together with spending on hotels, restaurants, petrol stations and in the local shops outside the facility will not only have a marked effect on operating profits, but will reverberate around the local economy with a multiplier effect typically five or six times the original level of spend (Table 21.1). The potential to generate additional spending outside the stadium largely depends on being able to develop synergy between the stadium or arena and the central business district, or commercial centre. In the case of Baltimore, for example, more than 40% of all fans going to the ballgame combine their trip with other downtown activities such as 'pleasure travel', 'work downtown', a 'business trip' or 'attending a convention'. Consequently, spending exceeded expectations by as much as 300% with increases in hotel, restaurant and other trade. Moreover, when compared with the previous Memorial Stadium, 80% of fans indicated that they were more likely to spend time in the stadium area before and after games. As the Baltimore example suggests, stadia are also potent landscape features contributing to positive destination imagery, considered so essential in tourism destination marketing.

21.3 The stadium as an attraction

Their potential has also been likened to a sleeping giant – capable of realizing its potential through its development as an all year-round visitor attraction. For example, in 1993 the Cardiff Arms Park in Wales hosted three International World Cup Soccer matches, three 50 000 capacity pop concerts (including U2, the Rolling Stones and Phil Collins) and the Bruno–Lewis heavyweight world title fight, and it is estimated that this range of activity contributed in excess of £52 million to the local economy. At a more fundamental level, stadia attract large numbers of people to the regular sporting events that they are host to. For example, in Britain at 3.00 pm on Saturday 15 June 1997 over 800 000 were accommodated in stadia during a full soccer and international rugby programme in England, Scotland and Wales. Thus, even when allowance is made for visitors that come from local areas, it is likely that the number of day visitors and those from further afield could exceed the most popular of other forms of visitor attraction.

The potential for sports stadia to be developed as all-year-round visitor attractions is closely linked to the growth in the day visitor market and in special interest tourism, as well as urban tourism marketing, which includes travelling to watch sport. In the UK, recent strategic documents from the English Tourist Board, the West Country Tourist Board of England and the Wales Tourist Board establish the policy link

Table 21.1 Increase in trade resulting from Oriole Park at Camden Yards, Baltimore

Venue	Percentage increase
Sheraton Inner Hotel	21
Tremont Plaza Hotel	20
National Aquarium	8
Maryland Science Centre	3.2
Baja Beach Club	15
Babe Ruth Museum	110
Ball Sports Bar	50 (on game days)

between tourism and sport. In the US, the remarkable transformation achieved by the Indiana Sports Movement translating 'Indiana-no-place' to 'the star of the snowbelt' is testimony to an integrated tourism and leisure strategy featuring world-class sports facilities.

The emergence of successful tourism programmes centred upon stadia and arena developments are also evidenced in St Louis and Chicago in the USA, Calgary in Canada and Melbourne in Australia. Cities such as Sheffield (World Student Games), Barcelona (Olympic Games) and Vancouver (Commonwealth Games) have also restructured their tourism product based upon their stadia infrastructure. New dome facilities for example in Atlanta (Georgia Dome), in Toronto (Skydome) and in Japan (Fukuoka Dome) extend this concept by providing real multiple-use options, especially for convention and conference markets. Consequently, there should be a much closer relationship between sport, the stadium and tourism. Rarely, however, has the potential of the stadium location been exploited as it has, for example, in the case of FC Barcelona (Spain), where the museum attracts 500 000 visitors each year, mostly on day trips from the resorts on the Costa Brava.

The introduction of commercial activities is now essential as stadium owners search for innovative ways to secure new sources of revenue. Perhaps the most significant potential exists in the development of stadia as sports-based visitor attractions, especially since the attractions industry is dynamic and anxious to find new applications and settings in which to create exciting visitor experiences. The inherent appeal of stadia as special places where heroes played and legends are made, captured so vividly in Alden Robinson's 1989 film *A Field of Dreams*, gives them the type of attributes upon which more recognized visitor attractions are based; atmosphere, sense of occasion, evocation and emotion. It is therefore surprising that, since sport makes a significant contribution to cultural identity and heritage, there are very few sports-based visitor attractions outside the US. In the UK, for example, these are limited to museums at Manchester United, Liverpool,

Aston Villa, and Arsenal football clubs: the Wimbledon Tennis Museum, the Newmarket Horse Racing Museum and the British Golf Museum that opened at St Andrews in 1990. Elsewhere, many stadia now operate 'guided tours' but few have the same level of sophistication expected from other forms of visitor attraction.

Examples from North America illustrate the most advanced application of the visitor attraction concept i.e. 'the sports hall of fame', which uses sport as the dominant theme. Even here the attractions are often very staid, with traditional museum style presentations. There is considerable scope to develop and apply techniques, designs and technologies from the wider leisure industry (especially theme parks) to create a new generation of sports attractions offering exciting visitor experiences. Few sports 'Halls of Fame' have been located to optimize market potential and generating significant and commercially viable levels of attendance. This does not appear to have been an important consideration; the genesis for their location tend to be non-market related criteria, such as location of administrative offices or the owners desire to convert a lobby into a public display. Most are located outside the main metropolitan areas, and when compared to the geography of major league franchises, and hence major stadium developments, it is apparent that the opportunity to physically link sports stadia with sports visitor attractions has largely been missed. Consequently, only a handful of the sports halls of fame have visitor attendance figures in excess of 150 000 per annum.

A new generation of sporting visitor attractions are now emerging. For example, at Turner Field (Atlanta) 'Home of the Braves' a new interactive plaza entertains fans before games and at other times. A similar concept has been deployed to a lesser extent in the designs for the new Chelsea Village and in the master plan concept for a number of other stadia. The potential for modern visitor attractions offering broad market appeal to an obvious development for stadia. A 'World of Rugby' at Cardiff Millennium Stadium, Newcastle's Helix Centre, the Dallas Cowboys Experience and the Olympic

Figure 21.1 Toronto Skydome is a multipurpose stadium with a closeable roof. Its down-town location with an integral hotel makes it a tourist destination.

Figure 21.2 Homebush Bay, Sydney: the grouping of facilities for the Olympics in an area regenerated from a previous rubbish disposal site. The whole site will now become a leisure and tourist destination.

Spirit in Munich are forerunners of a new and exciting trend in stadia's role in city development.

The stadium as a potential host venue is a logical proposition to meet the criteria for a new sports visitor attraction and should be reviewed positively as a potential venue for development. The infrastructure is generally in place; space, facilities and services are available, the site is an appropriate setting, often steeped in history, given the desire amongst owners to achieve optimum use, the current momentum to build and rejuvenate stadia could embrace the potential to include wider, year-round visitor attrac-

tions. It does not automatically follow however, that the location is capable of optimizing visitor markets and the emphasis must be on identifying locations likely to achieve high levels of attendance (150 000 per annum) and where the public's awareness of the attraction is underpinned by exposure to large numbers. At the same time, schemes must build upon the physical and psychological sense of place essential to creating the right environment to enhance the visitor experience.

The 'real' potential of a stadium or arena depends much more on the inter-relationship between other factors such as: location; catch-

Figure 21.3 Oriole Park at Camden Yards, Baltimore, USA, is an example of successful down-town regeneration, encouraging visits, shopping and tourism.

ment; the nature, structure and organization of the sports that are played in them; the characteristics and demands of spectator and market trends, and the stage of stadium development. In Britain, stadium development is still in an embryonic stage; owners have been forced to spend heavily on their stadia to meet new safety standards and it is unlikely that the majority of developments will aspire to the new 'fourth generation' facility given that few have the funds or are located in areas with a critical mass to support such a venue. For stadia owners in this position the basic objectives will be to secure good core attendance at regular sporting fixtures, efficient operational and commercial management in relation to the facility's primary use, and maximizing secondary spend and alternative revenue streams by involving the local community and businesses in activities such as corporate entertaining, product launches, and meetings and conference business.

21.4 The wider potential

The potential of a facility is generally determined by the interaction of market and socio-economic variables. Most facilities constructed before 1940 in the UK, having the same attributes as the 'classic stadium', i.e. neighbourhood focus, are dedicated to a single sporting activity having basic and limited amenities for spectators. In the USA however the 'real' potential is usually much greater. Assisted by the fact that the USA population has a narrower range of sporting interest than the UK and Europe and with a wide cross-section following and participating in fewer sports, the economic rewards inherent in major sporting activities have stimulated considerable development of new facilities over the past 20 years. The public sector has recognized the added value of investment in stadia and accept that they can rarely be expected to make a profit. Moreover, there is increasingly recognition amongst municipal and state governments that new facility development, or refurbishment to upgrade an existing facility, is essential in attracting and retaining major league sport and that the political risk involved in not investing in facilities is outweighed by wide economic gains to the community.

As markets mature, new technology being developed for the leisure industry in general, and for theme parks in particular, is likely to provide the main vehicle that will allow stadia to be fully exploited as venues for a wide range of leisure activities and as significant entertainment venues. In the USA the phenomenon of pre-match entertainment and the associated 'Fan-Fests' have been a prominent feature of pro-football and major-league baseball games. The 1991 Walt Disney production of the pre-match and half-time show at the Florida Superbowl, however, gave this concept a new dimension and created the benchmark for others to follow. Disney's inventive multimedia show combined the best of theme park technology with live entertainment, pyrotechnics and lasers turning the stadia into theatre, stage and film set at the same time.

Of particular relevance to the realization of this potential are associated technologies: stimulators, photography, interactive exhibits, participation equipment, laser and pyrotechnics, sound systems, video and information panels. If contemporary and new stadia are to realize their potential, management becomes as critical as the original design. The economic survival imperative requires stadia designers and operators to understand user demands, and to optimize and create revenue opportunities. This is reflected in a shift towards the privatization of the management of facilities. Management interests are now involved in the conceptual and design process. This is an essential prerequisite if the enormous capital and real estate asset of the facility is to be realized. Stadia and arenas must be regarded as a microcosm of the hospitality industry, reflecting trends in the socio-cultural leisure environment and rapidly becoming multi-faceted complexes hosting a diversity of events that involve a wide range of hospitality services and management skills.

Stadia, whether locations for great sporting events, host venues for visitor attractions, or 'cathedrals' with inherent architectural appeal, are a fundamental part of a destination's tourism infrastructure. Just as great heritage properties have become icons of place promotion, so stadia will join them. These are the 'sleeping giants' of tourism.

Appendix 1

Stadia briefing guide

General design information

Status of commission	Feasibility study Full design	Previous studies Board requirements Local authority needs
Finances	Financial constraints Maximum costs Revenue potential	Present income Projected income
Programme	Planning timetable Building start date Target completion date Close season consideration	Determine phasing Determine financing

Project objectives

Compactness	Provide good visibility Minimum view distances	Running track included Additional sports
Catering	Participants Spectators Administrators	
Convenience	Accessible to transport Location in city	
Comfort	Inviting environment Easily understood	
Flexibility	Arrangement of spaces Juxtaposition of spaces Relationship of spaces	
Economics	Initial capital expenditure Annual maintenance costs	

Project parameters

Clients requirements	Accommodation schedule	Participants Spectators Administrators
Traffic movement	Car, bus, pedestrian, rail	Public and private vehicles Inside and outside stadia
Ground capacity	Seated and standing	Consider trends Design to be convertible
Site services	Present and future	Service phasing
Phased development	Options with flexibility	Pattern of use Phased financing
Safety and control	Police and stewarding	

Site considerations

Investigation and survey	Old or new stadium site	Previous land use
		Mining surveys
Accessibility	Access and egress	Convenience
	Crowd safety	Safe segregation zones
Constraints	Boundaries	Property deeds
	Buildings	Planning restrictions
	Roads and rights of way	
Orientation	Sun aspect	Pitch maintenance
	Prevailing winds	Player comfort
	Micro climate consideration	Spectator preference
Unusual difficulties	Identify special problems	Sub-soil stability
		Water table
Unusual advantages	Shared use of site	Sports and leisure
	Unique location	Commercial considerations
Vehicle parking	On the site	Planning requirements
	Near the site	
	Remote from the site	
Neighbours	Visual implications	Consult local authority
	Construction implications	Local services

Spectators

Capacity of ground	Proportion of types	Flexible arrangement
	Number of standing	Range of quality
Entry and exit of stadia	Fill time for events	Legislation requirements
	Timed exit analysis	Follow good practice
Seating areas	Gangway location and size	Legislation requirements
	Radial or longitudinal	Minimum travel distance
	Vomitory arrangement	Sized for convenience
Toilet facilities	Proximity to spectators	Male female ratios
	Near catering outlets	Numbers required
Catering outlets	Good range of quality	Food distribution policy
	Convenient to spectators	Satellite kitchens and stores
First aid centre	Central or dispersed	Alcohol or no alcohol
	Operation methods	Ambulance park nearby
Concourses	Adequate width	Unrestricted to full length
	Access to toilets	Adequate signposting
	Access to catering	Act as reservoir space
Provision for disabled	Wheelchair access	Legislation requirements
	Ramps or lifts not stairs	Numbers to be provided
		Dispersed location to be considered.

Participants

Size and type of play area	Warm up facilities	
Protective measures	Club requirements	
Practice area, equipment	Weather protection	
Trainers and reserves	Seats at edge or in dug-out	Protection from spectators
	Not restricting view	Access to team rooms
Team rooms	Changing and wash rooms	Manager requirements
	Treatment areas	Trainer requirements
	Kit storage and lounges	Comfortable temperature
Access to field	Tunnel access	Separate routes for teams
	Protected route to field	Join before exit to field
Referee, umpires, linesmen	Changing and wash rooms	Adjacent to team rooms
	Lounge area and store	Access to management

Media

Press	Location and number	Local requirements
	Seats for reporters	National requirements
	Positions for photographers	International requirements
Radio	Location and number	Local requirements
	Cabin for announcers	National requirements
	Cable servicing	International requirements
Television	Location and number	Local requirements
	Cabin for announcers	National requirements
	Interview studios	International requirements
Media support facilities	Catering and rest areas	Servicing requirements
	Interview and briefing room	Access from administration

Management

Administration	Scale and location	Team managers
		Accounts section
		Secretarial facilities
Directors	Lounge and entertainment	Board and guest rooms
	Box for viewing	Access to viewing box
Sponsors and club area	Lounge area	Access to directors' area
	Box for viewing	Good quality areas
Ground staff	Changing and toilets	Vehicle access for loading
	Equipment stores	Safe store of chemicals
Private viewing areas	Number, location and type	Well catered and serviced
	Range of quality	Well located in tier
Restaurants	Size to suit regular usage	Catering strategy
	Close to main kitchen	Vehicle access for loading
Private vehicle parking	Television van parking	Size dependent on stadium
	Directors and team park	Close to management areas

General services

Type of system	Central or local units	Short distribution runs
	Emergency back-up plant	Plant near load centres
Plant location	Basement, ground or roof	Access for venting
	Individual plant areas	Duct access
Fuel type	Gas, oil, coal, electricity	More than one system
	Alternative solar use	Running costs
Space requirements	Fuel storage and equipment	Vehicle access
	Workshop areas	
Thermal considerations	Building insulation	Zone control for efficiency
	Zoning energy control	Non-event day control
Fire requirements	Sprinklers, alarms, hoses	Stand-by generator
	Emergency lighting	Start-up time
Cleaning	Water and power supply	Cleaning policy
	Materials storage	Man power requirements
General installation	Power and lighting	Location and servicing
	Telephones and facsimiles	Visible video board
	Public address and CCTV	

Ancillary areas

General	Any special areas	
	Time and duration of use	
Floodlighting	Standards for play	Colour television demands
	Standards for viewing	Discuss with TV company
	Television standards	
Video or indicator board	Viewing location	One end or both ends
	Adequate sizing	
Pitch heating	Electric cabling	Alternative economics
	Hot water or hot air	
Stand heating	Under seat radiation	Seat price economics
	Slab warming	
Concourses	Lighting and ventilation	Often unheated or cooled
	Environmental control	
Telephones	Management requirements	Depends on standards
	Media requirements	
Communications	Crowd control by police	Discuss with police
	Management and police	

Appendix 2

Video screens and electronic scoreboards

Since the publication of the first edition, there have been huge developments in giant screens and electronic scoreboards. Indeed, they have become a necessary feature in modern stadia and technology in this area is rapidly developing.

Larger stadia will often use the Large Screen Colour Video Display (LSVD) but there are options for stadia with more modest budgets to use limited video capability, providing text information and high quality graphics. For those stadia considering investing in this type of technology, early dialogue with manufacturers and suppliers is advisable. The following notes offer brief guidance:

The **Large Screen Colour Video Display** (LSVD) can represent a major capital outlay and should be carefully selected to suit the needs and light conditions of the stadium as well as the budget the client has available for such a purchase. Considerations also need to be given to the integration of the scoreboards, the video production room and the LSVD, as the specification and performance of one of these elements can have an effect on the others.

The expertise of the simple scoreboard companies is usually not applicable to the LSVD companies and vice versa. In order to secure the best value for each particular stadium, consideration will need to be given to whether or not high definition (or even very high definition) is required. For example, scoreboards need relatively low-tech lightbulb solutions whereas to use the same technology to replay action from a cricket match would be inappropriate.

Figure A.2.1 Screen at Tottenham Hotspur Ground, London.

Technology

There are generally four main types of technology presently used in screens which are as follows:

Cathode ray tube (CRT)
This technology is generally regarded by many as the best available at present (time of writing).

Fluorescent discharge tube
This produces a similar quality to the CRT technology.

Base matrix
This is the simplest of technologies being used currently. It is also probably the cheapest in capital cost and is widely used.

Light emitting diode (LED)
This is still in its early stages of development but is generally seen to be the future of large screen technology.

All of the above technologies achieve the images required of them by the use of the three base colours, red, blue and green. These three colours when combined in various ways can produce the theoretical 16.7 million colours possible.

Life cycle

While the life cycle costing of screens is important, their longevity is less important in a stadium situation. Most stadia will only use their screen for around 250 hours per year and since most screens will have a life span of around 20 000 hours this is not a major consideration. The cost of maintenance, refurbishment and operation is, however, a key component in the life cycle analysis; a decision has also to be made about how long the screen will remain at the 'cutting edge' and how long it will be before it needs renewal, not because it is worn out but because it is out of date.

Quality

The quality of the screen image is mainly determined by the brightness of the pixels and the pixel pitch of the screen. Generally the smaller the pitch the better the image, i.e. the closer together the pixels are to each other. For example, the Sony JumboTron Screen JTS35 has a pitch of 35mm while the JTS17 has a pitch of 17mm, providing a better image. A typical matrix screen will have a pitch of around 50mm or more in some cases.

Screen size and position

The size of a screen for any given location is determined in the ideal circumstances by its height, which should be three per cent to five per cent of the maximum viewing distance from the screen. The screen itself should have a proportion of four wide by three high or preferably sixteen wide by nine high. Therefore in a stadium where the maximum viewing distance is 200 metres, the screen should be 6 metres high and 8 or 10 metres wide. This would produce a screen of 48 square metres or 60 square metres and would weigh around 5 tonnes. It should be noted that screens also have minimum viewing distances, with a viewing distance of around 8 metres being a good minimum. It is obviously necessary for the screen(s) to be visible to all spectators.

Cost

After all considerations have been taken into account, it is the budget available which will be the main determinant in the selection of a screen. A Sony JumboTron JTS35 screen, for example, will cost around £30 000 per square metre, while the sharper JTS17 will be around £60 000 per square metre. This is based on an electricity supply of 100 KVA being provided within five metres of the site of the screen. The running costs of these screens are around £30 000 to £50 000 per annum for CRT screen, not including the production of the actual signal.

Screen companies

It seems that there are over 4000 screen companies currently in existence but probably only twenty to thirty who could be considered to be major players.

Programme

The procurement strategy may consider a hire arrangement which can be very attractive if the utilization is low, perhaps as a single package or split into two or three packages. Lead times are of the order of one month for the development of an invitation to tender, a month for tenderers to respond, with a further four to five months for manufacturing and a final month for installation.

Appendix 3

Case studies of recent stadia developments

Atlanta: 1996 Stadium

The 85 000 seat Olympic Stadium was built to hold the opening and closing ceremonies and the track and field events of the 1996 Olympics. Following the games it has been converted into a 50 000 seat baseball park for the Atlanta Braves. The total cost of the project is reported to be US $209 million.

The Stadium has been built in an older downtown neighbourhood so its height and mass have been scaled to blend in with its location. The challenge for the designers – Heery International; Rosser International; Williams, Russell, Johnson; and Ellerbe-Beckett – was to incorporate the usual oval track configuration, providing for the later removal of some 40 000 temporary seats. The stadium has been equipped with high quality heating, ventilating and air conditioning systems whilst the brick masonry used will provide a long-life exterior.

Dublin: Croke Park Stadium

Croke Park in Dublin is the National Stadium for Gaelic Sports, and incorporates a significantly larger pitch than most soccer and rugby venues. A new three-tier stand was completed in 1996 as the first stage of a complete redevelopment of the grounds which will see its capacity climb to 95 000 seats. The design was developed with the aim of keeping spectators as close as possible to the large pitch and avoiding long

Figure A.3.1a Atlanta, 1996 Olympic Stadium. Photo: Heery International.

Figure A.3.1b Exterior of the 1996 Atlanta Olympic Stadium. Photo: Heery International.

viewing distances. This ambitious plan was drawn up by LOBB Sports Architecture and HOK, with the executive team of Gilroy McMahon as architects and Horgan & Lynch as engineers. The new stand accommodates 25 000, all seated, and there are 46 executive boxes at the mid-level, with bars, restaurants and other facilities. Ramps are provided for spectators and allow vehicle access.

Figure A.3.2b Exterior of new stand at Croke Park showing ramps and glazed restaurant. Photo: Geraint John.

Figure A.3.2a New stand at Croke Park showing 3 tier design of spectator area. Photo: Geraint John.

positioning of the seating around three sides of the ball field at various different levels means that, with the roof open, an unobstructed view of downtown Phoenix is provided.

Other amenities include a stadium club with a VIP parking structure, a picnic area, teams offices, a team store, beer gardens and restaurants. The extensive use of fabric tents and other shading devices will give a unique image to this traditional ballpark in a desert environment.

Phoenix, Arizona: Phoenix Major League Baseball Stadium

The conceptual design – by the Architects Ellerbe-Becket – for this 45 000-48 000 seat baseball facility is based on a ballpark featuring: 77 suites; a 149 200 square foot playing field area 24 feet below ground level; a 16 310 square foot restaurant; a 9 600 square foot lounge with bar; 1380 linear feet of concession counters; air-conditioned stairs and ramps; and seven passenger elevators and six escalators. It was completed in 1998.

The design incorporates a retractable fabric roof, allowing a maximum opening over the field of play for evening games, or a closed, air-conditioned environment for summer afternoon games. The retractable roof makes the use of a natural grass playing field possible and the

Figure A.3.3 Phoenix Major League Baseball Stadium, Phoenix, Arizona. Architects: Ellerbe Beckett.

Figure A.3.4a Australia Stadium 2000, Sydney. A view of the post Olympics configuration of the stadium with openable tiers.
Photo: HOK + LOBB Partnership.

Figure A.3.4b Australia Stadium 2000, Sydney. Exterior view of the entrance to the stadium. Photo: HOK + LOBB Partnership.

Sydney: Sydney Stadium

The Olympic Games are to be held in Sydney in the year 2000 and the centrepiece of a coordinated suite of venues built for the event will be the 'spectacular' multi-use stadium, which will provide 1 100 000 seats during the Olympics and reduce to 80 000 after the Games. The design has been described as environmentally excellent and includes a substantial number of state-of-the-art environmental features which maximize the use of environmentally responsible materials.

Financing for the Australia Stadium 2000 includes public participation through a fully underwritten listed vehicle, the Australia Stadium 2000 Trust, and long-term debt facilities to both fund construction and ensure the long-term

Figure A.3.5 Johannesburg Athletics Stadium. Exterior view of the stadium in its setting.
Photo: Arup Associates.

viability of the stadium. The stadium's flexible structure will allow multiple sports usage, integrated mass communications systems and environmental innovations which set new standards for stadium development and are proving both practical and affordable.

Johannesburg: The Johannesburg Athletics Stadium

Apart from athletics, the Johannesburg Stadium, designed by Arup Associates, has also been the venue for a number of other events, including soccer, concerts and spectaculars. The stadium holds 38 000 spectators in an area between the circular perimeter and the oval arena, the geometry of which was exploited to create varied scale in the bowl from 9 metres to 36 metres high. The thin elegant roof is supported by a tracery of masts. The stadium's location allows essential ancillary areas to be added around the perimeter and there is a security moat between the arena and spectator area. Other facilities include a warm-up field near the start line with ramped access so that athletes do not have to negotiate steps. Shallow gradient ramps, which also allow vehicle access, are used for the spectator areas.

Figure A.3.6 Amsterdam Arena. Aerial view of project. Photo: Aerophoto Schipol.

Amsterdam: Stadion

1996 saw the completion of the Stadion, Amsterdam, a completely new 'stage of the art', 50 000 seat stadium with a retractable roof, which is the home of the Ajax Football Club, as well as catering for a range of entertainment events. The stadium is located in the south east of Amsterdam and is accessed by an underground station and an underground/railway station. Access by car is from main highways and there is a 'transferium', a large car park for 2600 cars under the stadium, as well as 5000 car park spaces within walking distance.

Food outlets are provided in wide walkways around the stadium, which will be provided with TV monitors showing the event in the stadium.

The stadium also has two giant video screens and supporting facilities include a museum devoted to Ajax; a TV studio; numerous restaurants; conference rooms; and advanced facilities for the players.

London: Lord's Cricket Ground – new stand

Lord's holds a unique place as the headquarters of English cricket and is one of the world's most important cricket grounds. The new Grandstand by Nicholas Grimshaw and Partners has been redesigned to provide maximum seating with uninterrupted views and to increase its capacity from 4000 to 6000 increasing the overall capacity

Figure A.3.7 Lord's Cricket Ground (© Peter Cook).

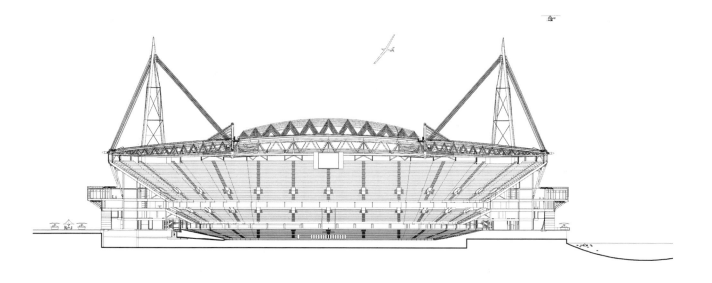

Figure A.3.8 The Millennium Stadium, Cardiff Arms Park. Cross Section. Architects: HOK + LOBB Partnership.

of the ground to 30 500. The stand also incorporates bars, boxes and a dining room with associated catering areas. Telephone, data and television services are provided to each box. The new stand complements the redevelopment of the ground begun by the Mound Stand, designed by Sir Michael Hopkins and Partners. On the same site is the award winning new indoor cricket school designed by David Morley and Partners.

Cardiff: Millennium Stadium at Cardiff Arms Park

This stadium was built for the 1999 Rugby World Cup in the historic Cardiff Arms Park site in the centre of the city, close to bus and rail links and the new light rail system being developed. Intended for all-year, all-weather use, the stadium has a retractable roof which will also incorporate acoustic insulation to reduce noise breakout. The design for the stadium – by the LOBB Sports Architecture – brings spectators close to the central field area, using three overlapping tiers. Those spectators who are disabled have direct access and escalators; lifts and staircases are used to reach the

middle and upper levels. The 75 000 seat stadium, which has also been designed for flexible multiple purpose use, will not only be the home of Welsh rugby, but will also be a venue for football, entertainment, culture, pop concerts and festivals.

Saint-Denis, Paris: Stade de France

The Stade de France has been built in the centre of the town of Saint-Denis, Paris. This impressive project, designed by Architects Macary and Zublena, Regembal and Costantini, is distin-

Figure A.3.9 Stade de France, Saint-Denis, Paris. External view showing the spectacular 'disk' roof.

guished by its spectacular eliptical disc roof, raised 43 metres into the air by 18 steel masts at 45-metre intervals, following the curve of the nearby Saint-Denis canal. The roof disc is constructed from metal and glass and is designed to illuminate the stadium with filtered light. The vision behind the design is to create an atmosphere which discourages aggressive, violent behaviour.

Although the stadium mainly caters for football and rugby, the eliptical design also means that it can be adapted for Olympic standard athletics, by the use of a mobile first ring of spectators' accommodation, supported by Teflon rollers. There are four rings of spectator accommodation, which allows for the capacity to be modulated according to the event, varying from 10 000 to 100 000 spectators. Private boxes around the perimeter accommodate 2500 spectators and there is further accommodation for 2500 press places, with its own bars, restaurant, laboratories and conference rooms.

Jacobs Field Baseball Stadium Cleveland, USA

Jacobs Field stadium is in the heart of downtown Cleveland and its location serves as both a landmark and a focus for regeneration.

Designed by HOK Sport, this is a 42 000 seat facility which includes training rooms, weights and sports injury treatment rooms: spectator amenities include wide concourses, restaurant and food concessions, a pre-game picnic area and 128 private suites. The architectural treatment reflects the traditional masonry architecture of the city.

Figure A.3.11 Jacobs Field has been used to promote city regeneration.

Hong Kong Stadium, China

This stadium was completed in 1994, designed by HOK.

Nestled in the valley of a tropical forest where the topography soars 300 feet above the surface of the pitch, the facility takes on an air of high drama that bespeaks the essence of site-structure unity.

A continuous seating bowl, elliptically shaped about the pitch, gracefully transitions the surrounding hillsides into the structure of the stadium. The new stadium incorporates two levels of seating to accommodate 40 000 spectators and includes 50 private air-conditioned suites on an exclusive club level. In addition, the complex houses a 300-seat café/restaurant,

Figure A.3.10 Jacobs Field is one of the new breed of city edge ball parks in the USA. Architects: HOK + LOBB.

Figure A.3.13 Reebok Stadium for Bolton Wanderers Football Club places great emphasis on external form and visibility. Architects: HOK + LOBB.

Figure A.3.12 Hong Kong Stadium nestles in a valley close to the city centre. Architects: HOK + LOBB.

forming a full bowl. The spectators are located, in the British football ground fashion, as near as possible to the playing field to maintain closeness to the action and to generate an exciting atmosphere.

wide concourses with improved restroom and concession facilities for the general public, large-screen video, sound and public announcement systems and full media facilities. Also included within the complex is 50 000 square feet of office space for the Hong Kong Sports Department Board in a separate office building, complete with its own lecture theatre.

The versatile design allows the stadium to host international concerts, rugby union, gridiron games and mass entertainment.

Reebok Stadium, Bolton, UK

Designed in 1995 by LOBB Sports Architecture, this is a 25 000 seater stadium which reflects the aspirations of Bolton Wanderers Football Club to provide a regional sports and leisure facility for the North West of England. The facility was completed in 1997 at a cost of £25 million.

The Reebok stadium was conceived as a single phase development within a single envelope. Each stand comprises two tiers, the lower

Figure A.3.14 The Reebok Stadium was designed with an extensive range of spectator facilities.

The dramatic superstructure of the stadium creates a landmark structure. The building form focuses visually on a dramatic roof oversailing a simple oval plan, providing constantly changing perspectives from any viewpoint. The roof was conceived as four leaning tapering tubular towers supporting the pitch floodlighting and the main roof trusses which span the full length of each side. The trusses are curved top and bottom to reflect the true viewing nature of the bowl and the natural integrity of the structural elements. The composition achieves a floating scalloped canopy over the bowl, each element fitting neatly to the other and the whole reading as a unified form.

Internally, continuous concourse and corridor links at all levels provide circulation around the entire stadium for staff and spectators allowing easier stadium management and access for building users to a greater number and variety of concessions and attractions once inside the stadium. Spectator facilities include private and club hospitality suites, restaurants, shops, conference suites, exhibition spaces, a crèche/nursery and medical facilities.

Externally, car parking is linked to the stadium by an external concourse surrounding the building, providing space for concessions and pre-event entertainment and acting as a well-defined 'place of safety' in cases of emergency.

The stadium is sited on 'grey field' land which was once a refuse site.

Figure A.3.15 Ericsson Stadium is typical of a North American NFL bowl. Not having to design for a roof simplifies structural and planning options.

light show on games nights, visible for miles around.

The facility is designed as a self-contained headquarters for the NFL franchise and includes: a home team training facility with a weight room, meeting rooms, locker facilities and racquetball courts: and an administrative area for team organization, scouting, marketing and public relations. Adjacent to the stadium and a part of the training facility component are two practice fields, one of natural grass and the other of artificial turf. These practice fields are accessible from the stadium via an underground tunnel.

Ericcson Stadium, Charlotte, USA

With its massive archways, domed towers, and striking black façade, the Ericsson Stadium was designed by HOK Sport. Completed in June 1996, after a 30-month construction schedule, the $184 million, 72 350-seater stadium has an enclosed bowl and three entrances flanked by elevator towers. The stadium presents a fortress-like exterior to approaching spectators, which features a black obsidian granite stone façade and a silver and blue seating bowl. The light domes atop the entry towers create a spectacular

Alfred McAlpine Stadium, Huddersfield, UK

This design by LOBB Sports Architecture followed a limited architectural competition in 1991. The winning scheme for a new stadium was based on the Stadium for the Nineties; a theoretical project referred to earlier in this book. The 50-acre site for the project is on the west, and a wooded bank to the east.

The intention was to design the stadium to act as a social oasis, which would attract future investment into leisure and retail developments

Figure A.3.16 Alfred McAlpine Stadium in Huddersfield where the details have been carried through in the design over three phases of development.

on the site. Initially, the scheme was designed to function, temporarily; with only two stands which had to house all the club facilities as well as maintenance and service facilties. These stands were also required to accommodate commercial facilities that would help fund future developments – including 26 private suites overlooking the pitch, 5 guest lounges and a 500-person conference and banqueting suite.

The roof was designed to allow uninterrupted viewing from all seats as well as the addition of roofs to the end stands. The arch (which became affectionately known as the banana truss) consists of a white tubular-steel prismatic structure, the largest element of which stretches 140 m and weighs 78 tonnes.

Public amenities, including an indoor swimming pool, council offices, health club and a hotel have been designed into the perimeter of the stadium.

The key to this ongoing development was thorough masterplanning. Since its opening in August 1994 the Alfred McAlpine Stadium has won many awards, most significantly the 'Building of the Year' award from the Royal Institute of British Architects in 1995.

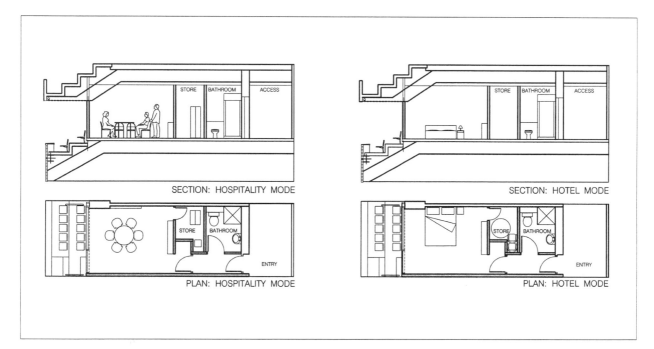

Figure A.3.17 The north stand at the Alfred McAlpine Stadium has been designed so that the hospitality suites can be converted into hotel rooms on non-match days.

Figure A.3.18 Alfred McAlpine Stadium: Huddersfield with its North stand under construction. Architects: HOK + LOBB.

Oita Sports Park Stadium, Japan

The stadium is being built for the Football World Cup in 2002. Designed by Kisho Kurokawa and The Takenaka Corporation, the estimated cost is 2500 million Japanese Yen. The stadium has a flexible seating arrangement allowing 41 957 seats for football and 35 590 seats for athletics. It is financed by the Oita Prefecture (Local Government).

Figure A.3.19 Oita Stadium. The 2002 Football World Cup has prompted some fine sports buildings where invention and originality has been encouraged.

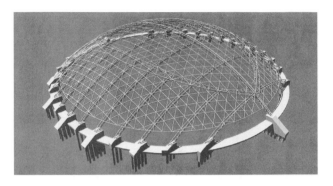

Figure A.3.20 Oita Stadium: Japan is an example of the more adventurous structural solutions evolving around the world.

The stadium has a roof which can be opened or closed. When open some main beams will remain exposed over the central area.

Sapporo Dome Stadium, Japan

This stadium will be built for the 2002 Football World Cup. The owner is the Sapporo City Council, who are financing the project together with private finance. The cost is estimated to be 3600 million Japanese Yen. It is scheduled for completion in May 2001. The designers are Professor Koji Hara and the Takenaka/Taisei Corporations.

A natural turf pitch is used for football: this is moved into the covered dome from the outside by a 'hoover' air-supported system.

Figure A.3.21 Sapporo City Stadium Japan.

The stadium is designed to be used for baseball (42 243 seats) and football (43 000 seats).

Kashima Prefectural Stadium, Japan

The stadium for the 2002 Football World Cup has been designed by Nikken Sekkei and is scheduled to be completed in May 2001. It has a seating capacity of 43 340 and has been designed exclusively for football. It has a cantilever/tension structured roof of fluoric acid resin coated glass fibre over the spectactor areas.

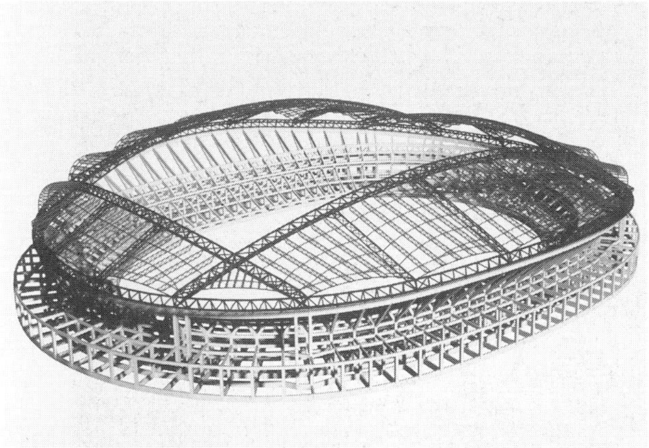

Figure A.3.23 Nigata Stadium Japan.

Figure A3.22 Kashima. Capacity 15,000 seating.

Figure A.3.24 Nigata Stadium Japan.

Stadium in Nigata, Japan

This stadium will be completed for the 2002 Football World Cup in May 2001. Its seating capacity is 41 950. The stadium will be used for athletics after the World Cup.

The designers are Nikken Sikkei. The design features a double crossed arch structure using a welded pipe truss system. The roof membrane is made of fluoric acid resin coated glass fibre covering the spectator seating areas.

Media Centre at Lord's, London

Future Systems won a competition to design this innovative media centre for journalists and broadcasters at Lord's, the UK's primary cricket ground. It was completed in 1999.

The construction is a semi-monocoque structure composed of a stressed skin of welded aluminium plate, curved over aluminium ribs. The accommodation includes tiers of desks for journalists with a row of boxes for radio and TV commentators, all looking down on the pitch through huge sheets of toughened glass. There is also a VIP reception room and a restaurant.

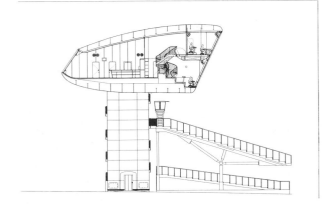

Figure A.3.25 Lord's Cricket Ground Media Centre is a brave new direction for a relatively conservative sport. Architects: Future Systems.

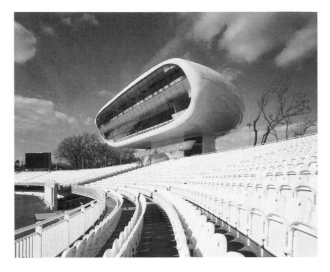

Figure A.3.27 Lord's Cricket Ground Media Centre sets new standards by which these facilities will be judged in the future. (© Richard Davies)

Figure A.3.26 Lord's Cricket Ground Media Centre (© Richard Davies)

The central arena will cater for football, rugby and be adaptable for use as an athletics arena as well as concerts and other assemblies. The design is modern and spectacular in concept with a structural solution based on reflecting the heroic nature of its functions.

The New Wembley Stadium, London

The original Wembley Stadium built in 1926 is one of the most famous stadia in the world. However after several modernizations, it has now come to the end of its useful life. It will be demolished and replaced by a new National Stadium on the same site. Construction is to begin in 2001.

The new stadium will seat approximately 90 000 and will have a range of private boxes and other private and corporate facilities.

Figure A.3.28 Wembley front view (exterior)

Figure A.3.30 Wembley interior view

Figure A.3.29 Wembley side view (exterior)

Bibliography

Association of County Councils, Joint Working Party on Ground Safety and Public Order (1991) *Ground Safety and Public Order, Hillsborough Stadium Disaster*, London, Association of County Councils Publications.

Blackwell, Lewis (1984) Astrodome for Birmingham. *Building Design*, 10 February, 5.

A blueprint for British stadia. (1993) *Sports Industry*, September–October, 3–4.

Centre for Accessible Environments (1992) *Football Stadia: Facilities for People With Disabilities*. Football Stadia Facilities for People with Disabilities Seminar, London, 1 October 1992, London, Centre for Accessible Environments.

Cettour H. (1991) Stapes et Terrains de Sports (French). Paris Editions du Moniteux.

Chartered Institute of Building Service Engineers (CIBSE) (1990) *CIBSE Lighting Guide: Sport LG4*, London, CIBSE.

Colbeck, David (1981) Football clubs into leisure centres? *Leisure Management*, **1**, June/July, 14–15.

Collins, Pippa (1990) Playing safe: Rod Sheard and Geraint John talk about the changing design of stadia. *Atrium*, April.

Comitato Olympico Nazionale Italiano (1990) The stadiums of 1990 FIFA World Cup. *Spaziosport* 9 (2).

Comitato Olympico Nazionale Italiano (1994) The stadiums of 1994 FIFA World Cup. *Spaziosport* 13 (2) 1–128.

Croker, Ted (1979) The Secretary's column: Ted Croker looks at the possibility of covered stadia in England. *FA Today*, **1**, October, 8–9.

Darbourne, J. and Darke, G. (1972) Stamford Bridge Stadium Redevelopment, Chelsea Football Club. Feasibility study and outline proposals.

Department of the Environment (1990) *Planning Policy Guidance: Sport and Recreation*. DOE, London.

Department of the Environment (1991) *Planning Policy Guidance Note: Sport and Recreation*, London, HMSO.

Faulkner-Brown, H. (1972) Standing ovation. *Building*, 26 May, 52–62.

Fédération Internationale de Football Association, Union of European Football Associations (1991) *Technical Recommendations and Requirements for the Construction of New Stadia*. Zurich, Fédération Internationale de Football Association.

Fire Safety and Safety of Sport Act 1987 (HL) (1987) London, HMSO.

Football Association (1991) Crowd safety memorandum: the safety of spectators. *FA Handbook 1990/91*, London, Football Association.

Football Association (1991) The control of crowds at football matches. *FA Handbook 1990/91*, London, Football Association.

Football Stadia Advisory Design Council (1991) *Football Stadia Bibliography 1980–1990*. London, Football Stadia Advisory Design Council.

Football Stadia Advisory Design Council (1992) *Designing for Spectators With Disabilities*. London, Football Stadia Advisory Design Council.

Football Stadia Advisory Design Council (1992) *Digest of Stadia Criteria*. London, Football Stadia Advisory Design Council.

Football Stadia Advisory Design Council (1992) *On The Sidelines, Football and Disabled Spectators*. London, Football Stadia Advisory Design Council.

Football Stadia Advisory Design Council (1991) *Seating: Sightlines, Conversion of Terracing, Seat Types*. London, Football Stadia Advisory Design Council.

Football Stadia Advisory Design Council (1991) *Stadium Public Address Systems*. London, Football Stadia Advisory Design Council.

Football Stadia Advisory Design Council (1992) *Stadium Roofs*. London, Football Stadia Advisory Design Council.

Football Stadia Advisory Design Council (1993) *Terraces, Designing for Safe Standing at Football Stadia*. London, Football Stadia Advisory Design Council.

Football Stadia Development Committee (1994) *Design-Build. A Good Practice Guide Where Design-Build is Used for Stadia Construction*. London, Sports Council.

Football Stadia Development Committee (1994) *Stadium Control Rooms*. London, Sports Council.

Football Stadia Development Committee (1994) *Toilet Facilities at Stadia*. London, Sports Council.

Football Spectators Act 1989 (1989) London, HMSO.

Ford, A. J. (1990) *Guidance notes for the procurement of CCTV for public safety at football grounds*, Home Office Science and Technical Group: Police Science Development Branch Publication no. 4/90. St Albans, Home Office.

Gratton, C. and Taylor, P. (1987) Indoor arenas. The missing market. *Leisure Management*, **7**, October, 32–34.

Greater London Council: Department of Planning and Transportation (1972) The characteristics and impact of travel generated by Chelsea Football Stadium. Research Memorandum – 344, London, Greater London Council.

Ham, S. (1987) Legislation: Fire Precaution Act and new sports grounds regulations. *Architects' Journal*, **13**, April, 61.

Happold, Edmund and Dickson, Michael (1974) The story of Munich. Zodiac 21. *Architectural Design*, 6, 330–344.

HMSO (1975) *Safety at Sports Grounds Act 1975*. London, HMSO, esp. ch. 52.

HMSO (1988) *Safety at Sports Grounds Act 1975* (rev. edn.) London, HMSO.

HMSO (1990) *Safety at Sports Grounds Act 1975* (rev. edn.) London, HMSO.

Home Office (1985) Committee of inquiry into crowd safety and control at sports grounds. Chairman: Mr Justice Popplewell. Interim Report, London, HMSO, CMND 9595.

Home Office (1986) Committee of inquiry into crowd safety and control at sports grounds. Chairman: Mr Justice Popplewell. Final Report, London, HMSO, CMND 9710.

Home Office (1989) The Hillsborough stadium disaster. 15 April 1989. Inquiry by Rt Hon. Lord Justice Taylor. London, HMSO.

Home Office (1990) The Hillsborough stadium disaster, 15 April 1989. Inquiry by the Rt Hon. Lord Justice Taylor. Final Report. London, HMSO

Department of National Heritage/The Scottish Office (1997) Guide to Safety at Sports Grounds: Fourth Edition. The Stationary Office, London.

Home Office/Scottish Office (1986) *Fire Safety and Safety at Sports Venues*. London, HMSO.

Home Office/Scottish Office (1997) *Guide to Safety at Sports Grounds* London, HMSO.

Home Office (1990) *Policing Football Hooliganism*. London, HMSO.

IAKS (1993) *Planning Principles for Sports Grounds/Stadia*. Köln, IAKS.

Inglis, S. (1982) Football Grounds of Great Britain; Football Grounds of Europe; The Ibrox Stadium Redevelopment (GB). *Acier Stahl Steel*, **2**, 59–67.

Inglis, S. (1990) *The Football Grounds of Europe*. London, Willow Books

Inglis, S. (1992) *The Football Grounds of Great Britain*. London, Collins Willow.

John, G. and Spring, M. (1987) Where are our big arenas going? *Baths Service and Recreation Management*, **46**, 128–129.

Kay, P. (1989) Let the games commence. *Chartered Surveyor Weekly* (Leisure Supplement), September, 35–36.

Laventhol and Horwarth (1989) *Convention Centres, Stadium and Arenas*. Washington DC, Urban Land Institute.

Luder, Owen (1990) Sports Stadia After Hillsborough. Papers presented at the Sports Council/Royal Institute of British Architects Seminar, RIBA, 29 March 1990. London, RIBA/Sports Council in association with the Football Trust.

Millbank, Paul (1975) Football clubs: time to open their gates to all sports. *Surveyor*, 16 May, 12–13. Olympic Stadia. Mexico City. Building for the XIXth Olympic Games (1968) *Building*, 6 September, 87–90.

Panstadia International (1992) *Panstadia International – Leading the Field. A Worldwide Guide to Stadium Newbuild and Management*. Harrow, Panstadia International.

Perrin, Gerald (1985) Seating for sport and leisure. *Leisure Management*, **1**, January, 14 and 16.

Ridout, G. (1989) Safe stadiums. Structural ground rules. *Building*, 10 December, 74–75.

Safety at Sports Grounds Act 1975 (1990) Rev edn. London, HMSO.

San Pietro, S. and Vercelloni, M. (1990) *Stadi in Italia*. *Milan*, Edizioni Archivolto.

Schmidt, T. (1987) A Stadium which reflects the Games. Architectural history of the Seoul Olympic Stadium. *Olympic Review*, **239**, September, 441–444.

Schmidt, T. (1988) Building a Stadium. Olympic stadiums from 1948–1988. Part 1. *Olympic Review*, **247**, June, 246–251.

Shepley, C. (1990) Planning and Football League Grounds an RTPI Survey. *The Planner*, **76**, September.

Shields, A. (1989) *Arenas: A Planning, Design and Management Guide*. London, Sports Council.

Setting new limits at Toronto's Skydome. *Athletic Business*, **12**, September, 35–36.

Sports Council, Royal Institute of British Architects, UIA Work Group for Sports, Leisure and Tourism (1990) *Sports Stadia in the 90's*. London.

Sports Council (1992) *Planning and Provision for Sport*. Section on planning for stadia. London, Sports Council.

Sports Council Technical Unit for Sport: Geraint John and Kit Campbell (1993) *Handbook of Sports and Recreational Building Design*. Vol.1. Outdoor Sports, 2nd Edn. Butterworth-Heinemann..

Spring, M. and John, G. (1987) Sporting new arenas. *Building*, 17 April, 42–44.

Spring, M. (1990) World Cup Winner. *Building*, 5 January, CC4 (1), 39–43.

Stadia. The concrete Olympiad. *Consulting Engineer*, October, 36–30, 32.

Stadia development in San Siro and Bari. *Impianti* (2).

Stadia. *Spaziosport*, March 1989.

Thorburn, A. and Van de Lee, K. C. W. (1983) Design and Construction of the New Ibrox Stadium. *The Structural Engineer*, **61A**, February, 55–64.

Wimmer, M. (1976) *Olympic Buildings*. Edition Leipzig (out of print).

Index

Page references in **bold** are those of illustrations and tables. Stadia are mostly entered under the names of towns in which they are situated.